The Conversation on Guns

Critical Conversations

Martin LaMonica, Series Editor

The Conversation U.S. is an independent, nonprofit news organization dedicated to delivering expert knowledge to the public through journalism. Every day The Conversation produces 10–12 stories through a collaboration between scholars and editors, with the scholars writing explanatory journalism and analysis based on their research and the editors helping them translate it into plain language. The articles can be read on TheConversation.com and have been republished by more than a thousand newspapers and websites through a Creative Commons license, meaning that the content is always free to read and republish.

The book series Critical Conversations is published collaboratively by The Conversation U.S. and Johns Hopkins University Press. Each volume in the series features a curated selection of subject-specific articles from The Conversation and is guest-edited by an expert scholar of the subject.

■

The Conversation on Guns is guest-edited by James Densley, a Professor of Criminal Justice and the Department Chair of the School of Law Enforcement and Criminal Justice at Metro State University.

Martin LaMonica is the Executive Editor and Project Manager.
Chris Calimlim is the Editorial Assistant.
Anissa Cooke-Batista is the Marketing and Communications Manager of The Conversation U.S.
Beth Daley is Editor and General Manager of The Conversation U.S.
Bruce Wilson is the Chief Innovation and Development Officer of The Conversation U.S.

We would like to express our gratitude to the editors and scholars who produced the articles collected here and to thank our colleagues and funders who allow us to do this important work in the public interest.

THE CONVERSATION
on Guns

edited by James Densley

Johns Hopkins University Press
BALTIMORE

Johns Hopkins University Press
2715 North Charles Street
Baltimore, Maryland 21218
www.press.jhu.edu

Library of Congress Cataloging-in-Publication Data is available.

ISBN 978-1-4214-4736-0 (paperback)
ISBN 978-1-4214-4737-7 (ebook)

A catalog record for this book is available from the British Library.

Special discounts are available for bulk purchases of this book. For more information, please contact Special Sales at specialsales@jh.edu.

Contents

Part II.
The Many Forms of Gun Violence   75

Part III.
The Trauma of School Shootings   133

Part IV.
The Effects of Gun Violence   169

Part V.
The Politics and Policies of Gun Control   205

Part VI.
Technology and the Future of Gun Ownership 281

Why Read a Book on Guns?

SOMETIME IN THE LAST DECADE, the number of guns in the United States surpassed the number of people. No other country in the world comes close to this ratio. Guns are also deeply rooted in our national narrative, with stories of self-reliant 19th-century settlers and, in recent decades, news reports of mass shootings and gun violence.

Despite the prevalence of guns and gun culture in the United States, most of the discussion around firearms comes during times of crisis—often after yet another shooter takes the lives of innocent people. In the wake of these events, there are many emotions, including shock, sadness, and despair and much talk about how to prevent more gun violence. This book aims to inform those discussions with research from academics who have spent years studying this issue from multiple vantage points—criminal justice, public health, sociology, psychology, and more. This book is for anyone interested in learning more about how the United States became so saturated with guns and how daily life is being shaped by that legacy.

Each chapter in this book was originally published as an article on The Conversation, a news analysis and explanatory journalism website with a powerful editorial model. Academic experts collaborate with editor journalists to cover events in the news and to share their knowledge with a general reader in mind. Since launching in the United States in 2014, we have published more than 16,000 articles from more than 12,000 scholars at more than 1,000 colleges and universities. Our stories are read more than 20 million times per month and republished by hundreds of other media outlets across the world.

Given a deliberate emphasis on research in this volume, you will read many facts and figures in the pages ahead. Because the original articles may have been written in response to a shooting event a few years ago, in many cases we have updated them to remove dated references or to feature more recent data. Whenever possible, we have tried to indicate when a statistic or study was first published or when an event occurred. Regardless of when the articles were originally published, their information remains relevant and will add to your foundational knowledge.

In choosing articles for this volume, I worked with a guest editor, sociologist James Densley of Metro State University, the cofounder of The Violence Project, a nonpartisan, nonprofit research center best known for creating a mass shooter database. He will act as your guide through the book, offering first a preface and then an introductory framing essay at the beginning of each part that brings pertinent facts and research to bear on the theme in the part that follows.

Unfortunately, more shootings are inevitable, and they will lead to more heated discussions over what to do. This book will help you see how the national discussion on guns has evolved over our country's history, understand what policy options are available, and, importantly, learn about the broader societal impact of guns.

Martin LaMonica

Guns in America

An Immigrant's View

ON MARCH 13, 1996, a gunman walked into Scotland's Dunblane Primary School and opened fire, killing 16 children and a teacher in what remains the deadliest mass shooting in British history. I was 13 years old at the time, but I still remember it. Everyone in the United Kingdom does.

I remember how my parents struggled to find the words to explain what had happened to those innocent five- and six-year-olds.

I remember my shell-shocked teachers trying to reassure us that our school was safe.

I remember the newspaper headlines. "HE shot them ALL," read one of them, framed by an image of the balding killer's bespectacled face and a collage of his victims' school pictures.

I remember the grassroots campaign for stricter gun laws. I remember because I was the proud owner of a 410 bolt-action shotgun at the time, a gun club member with a license for clay pigeon shooting under the supervision of my father, a police officer and firearms instructor.

I also remember British politicians taking decisive legislative action. A little over a year after the shooting, Parliament banned private ownership of most handguns.

There hasn't been a school shooting in the United Kingdom since.

Gun laws in the United Kingdom are among the toughest in the world. Very few people, even police officers, carry firearms. Modern semiautomatic weapons, the type of guns that can be fired rapidly without needing to be reloaded, are largely prohibited. That's not to say guns are not a problem in the United Kingdom. When I was all grown up and a graduate student studying gangs and youth violence on the streets of London,[1] I encountered several firearms. Many were converted imitation firearms not even capable of firing, but they looked the part, enough to intimate and signal toughness.

I recall a Bruni Olympic .38 starter pistol, doctored to fire low-velocity ball bearings down a smoothbore barrel, and an Airsoft electric assault rifle, with a magazine capable of firing upwards of 50 BB rounds, converted to shoot one single shotgun cartridge. One gang member in my study blew off three of his fingers when his homemade gun misfired during a point-blank assassination attempt. Nineteen of the 69 gang-involved youth I interviewed reported having previously been threatened with guns. Nine had been shot at, and three had been shot. One teacher I interviewed described confiscating from a student what he thought was a toy gun, only to discover it was real.

Despite this, gun control generally seemed to be working. Black market firearms were prohibitively expensive for most youth gang members, who, in turn, lacked strong ties to the serious organized criminals who trafficked them. This was why my interviewees pooled whatever weapons they had and loaned them to one another. I quickly discovered that when multiple gang members in proximity, including rivals, claimed access to a firearm, they were usually referring to the same shared weapon, which was linked to multiple offenses.

My research on gun crime changed when I moved from the United Kingdom to the United States. Here, the streets were awash with guns, and gang members routinely found themselves staring down the barrel of one. And while I continued to study gangs and everyday gun violence,[2] I decided to research a rarer form of gun crime that claimed fewer lives overall but that loomed large over public opinion and public policy on guns: mass shootings.

Frustrated by the daily drumbeat of gunshots on the nightly news and reactive policy conversations that never seemed to convert into meaningful action, I launched The Violence Project in 2017 with my colleague, psychologist Dr. Jillian Peterson.[3] The Violence Project is a comprehensive database of more than 180 US mass shooters, anyone who had killed four or more people in a public space, starting with the 1966 University of Texas tower shooting, which is widely regarded as the first *modern* mass shooting (albeit not the first recorded one) because it was broadcast live on radio and television.[4] Note that four or more killed in public is a pretty conservative definition of a mass shooting. If we went with four or more people *shot* in any setting, including domestic shootings, the database would include 300–600 cases *every year*, not 185 total over six decades.[5] For comparison, there have been four mass shootings in the United Kingdom since 1966—the 1987 Hungerford massacre, Dunblane in 1996, the Cumbria shootings in 2010, and the Plymouth shooting in 2021.

Our goal with The Violence Project was to establish the root causes of mass shootings and figure out how to stop them by examining hundreds of data points in the life histories of mass shooters—from their childhood and adolescence to their mental health and motives. With funding from the National Institute of Justice, the research arm of the US Department of Justice, we interviewed the living perpetrators of mass shootings and people who knew them, shooting survivors, victims' families, first responders, and leading experts to gain a comprehensive understanding of the real stories behind the bloodshed, rather than the sensationalized media narratives that too often prevail.

Among other things, we learned that mass shootings cause damage beyond what is measured by the lives claimed or changed through death or injury.[6] Survivors may recover physically but never emotionally, or not financially owing to the ongoing costs of treatment. Mass shootings tear at the fabric of close-knit communities, and because they feel random and indiscriminate and they play out on repeat over the media, they needle our anxieties and eat away at our sense of safety.[7] They also help fuel a multi-billion-dollar industry in unproven and quintessentially American mitigation technologies, such as bulletproof backpacks for children.[8]

That's not to say we are helpless against mass shootings. Our research found that school mass shooters, for example, generally got their firearms from home. The implication is that if you have a teenager in the home and you legally own a gun, you should keep it locked and hidden when not being used and remain cautious about who knows you own it. This is something simple we all can do to potentially stop a mass shooting, and it doesn't take an act of Congress.

At the same time, our research found that around half of all mass shooters used at least one weapon they had legally purchased themselves, and about 30% of mass shootings since the infamous Columbine High School massacre in April 1999 have involved firearms that were banned under the now-expired 1994 federal assault-weapons law.[9] This includes the deadliest mass shootings on record: 21 killed and 17 injured at an elementary school in Uvalde, Texas (May 2022); 23 killed and 26 injured at a Walmart in El Paso, Texas (August 2019); 25 killed and 20 injured at a Baptist church in Sutherland Springs, Texas (November 2017); 27 killed and 1 injured at an elementary school in Newtown, Connecticut (December 2012); 49 killed and 53 injured at Pulse nightclub in Orlando, Florida (June 2016); and 58 killed and over 800 injured at a country music festival in Las Vegas, Nevada (October 2017). Rarely do these events provoke the sort of swift political action I grew up with in the United Kingdom. And, the truth is, they are just the tip of the iceberg when it comes to gun deaths in the United States.

The Prevalence of Guns and Gun Violence in the United States

I'm an American by choice. America's approach to gun violence is equally a choice—a policy one. More Americans died of gun-related injuries in 2020 than in any other year on record. According to mortality data from the Centers for Disease Control and Prevention, there were 45,222 firearm-related deaths in the United States in 2020—about 5,000 more than in 2019, a 35% year-on-year increase.[10] Over half of these deaths were suicides, meaning that a little over half of all suicides in 2020 (24,292 out of 45,979 total) involved a gun. At the same time, nearly 8 in 10 murders in 2020 involved a firearm (in the United Kingdom the figure was 4%), the highest percentage on record.[11] The total of 45,222 averages to nearly 124 gun deaths a day across the country, making firearm injury a leading cause of death in America. Guns killed more American children and teens in 2020 than car accidents, overdoses, or cancer.[12]

While 2020 saw the highest total number of gun deaths in the United States, this statistic does not take into account the nation's growing population. On a per capita basis, there were 13.6 gun deaths per 100,000 people in 2020, the highest rate since the mid-1990s but below the peak of 16.3 gun deaths per 100,000 people in 1974. Indeed, gun murder (6.2 per 100,000 people) and gun suicide (7.0 per 100,000 people) rates in the United States both remain below their peak levels recorded in the 1970s (7.2 and 7.7 per 100,000, respectively). However, the increase in US homicides that started in 2014 after two decades of declines has been driven entirely by a rise in firearm-related murders.[13]

Per capita rates also enable state-by-state and country-by-country comparisons. In 2020, the states with the highest rates of gun-related deaths were Mississippi (28.6 per 100,000 people), Louisiana (26.3), Wyoming (25.9), Missouri (23.9), and Alabama (23.6).[14] Not coincidentally, the states with the highest gun death rates are among the ones with the highest rates of gun ownership and the most permissive gun laws.[15] The states with the lowest gun death rates in 2020—Hawaii (3.4 per 100,000 people), Massachusetts (3.7), New Jersey (5.0), Rhode Island (5.1), and New York (5.3)— have some of the lowest gun ownership rates and most restrictive gun laws. These numbers are consistent with research showing greater numbers of gun deaths, especially homicides,[16] in states with higher rates of household gun ownership[17] and where firearms are more easily accessible.[18]

Globally, the gun death rate in the United States is far below the rates in several Latin American countries—Colombia, El Salvador, Guatemala, and Honduras—but much higher than in most comparable developed nations.[19] Not coincidentally, the United States has a lot more guns than these other developed countries. For every 100 Americans, there are an estimated 120 guns, whereas the number is between 5 and 40 for the rest of the developed world.[20] This is partly because the United States is one of the only countries worldwide where the right to bear arms is constitutionally protected. (The others are Guatemala, Haiti, and Mexico.) Still, it is worth noting that America's 400-million-plus guns are not equally distributed. About 30% of US adults say they personally own a gun, while 40% report living in a household with a gun.[21] Republicans, rural residents, men, and southerners are the most likely subgroups to say they own a gun, whereas Democrats, non-white Americans, women, and eastern residents are least likely. Three-quarters of gun owners have two or more guns, and half of all guns in private hands are owned by just 3% of the US adult population. These people, called "super-owners" by researchers, own 17 guns each on average.[22]

The Conversation on Guns

This book is a curated collection of essays full of data and stories about the causes and consequences of gun violence, gun culture in the United States, commonalities in gun crime, and evidence-based solutions to rising gun deaths. These essays, originally published by The Conversation, a nonprofit, independent news organization dedicated to unlocking the knowledge of experts for the public good, are written by some of the leading scholars presently working in the field: historians, psychologists, sociologists, criminologists, lawyers, public health researchers, and more. The chapters are organized under five general themes. The first part examines American gun culture and history for a better understanding of public opinion on guns, the reasons why guns outnumber people in the United States, and how America compares to the rest of the world on this issue.

The second part explores the many forms of gun violence, including community gun violence, which disproportionately affects underserved neighborhoods of color, police shootings, suicides, and mass shootings. This is followed by part III, which details the trends and trauma of school shootings specifically.

The effects of gun violence generally, and how shootings have changed America, are the focus of part IV. This is followed in part V by a discussion of policies meant to address gun violence and an explanation of why it is so difficult to pass gun safety laws in the United States. The book concludes in part VI with a look at the future of gun ownership and the evolution of firearm technology, including "smart guns," which use biometrics to prevent unauthorized use, and unserialized and untraceable "ghost guns," which can be bought online and assembled at home.

Together, this volume aims to connect readers to the demonstrable expertise of its contributors, to answer authoritatively some of the most frequently asked questions about American gun violence, and to create a common and comprehensive understanding of this vexing social problem.

Notes

1. James Densley, *How Gangs Work: An Ethnography of Youth Violence* (New York: Palgrave Macmillan, 2013).
2. Scott Decker, David Pyrooz, and James Densley, *On Gangs* (Philadelphia: Temple University Press, 2022).
3. The Violence Project. https://www.theviolenceproject.org.
4. Jillian Peterson and James Densley, *The Violence Project: How to Stop a Mass Shooting Epidemic* (New York: Abrams, 2021).
5. Gun Violence Archive. https://www.gunviolencearchive.org.
6. Everytown for Gun Safety, *When the Shooting Stops: The Impact of Gun Violence on Survivors in America*, 2022. https://everytownresearch .org/report/the-impact-of-gun-violence-on-survivors-in-america /#introduction.
7. Ali Rowhani-Rahbar, Douglas F. Zatzick, and Frederick P. Rivara, "Long-Lasting Consequences of Gun Violence and Mass Shootings," *Journal of the American Medical Association* 321, no. 18 (1029): 1765–66. https://doi.org/10.1001/jama.2019.5063.
8. John Woodrow Cox, *Children under Fire: An American Crisis* (New York: HarperCollins, 2021).
9. Public Safety and Recreational Firearms Use Protection Act, H.R. 4296, 103rd Cong. (1993–1994). Congress.gov. https://www.congress .gov/bill/103rd-congress/house-bill/4296/text.
10. "Provisional Mortality Statistics, 2018 through Last Month Results," Centers for Disease Control and Prevention. https://wonder.cdc.gov /controller/saved/D176/D260F140.
11. Rosanna Smart, Terry L. Schell, Andrew R. Morral, and Nancy Nicosia, "Geographic Disparities in Rising Rates of Firearm-Related Homicide," *New England Journal of Medicine* 387, no. 2 (2022): 189–91. https://doi.org/10.1056/nejmc2203322.
12. Jason E. Goldstick, Rebecca M. Cunningham, and Patrick M. Carter, "Current Causes of Death in Children and Adolescents in the United States," *New England Journal of Medicine* 386 (2022): 1955–56. https://doi.org/10.1056/nejmc2201761.

13. Smart, Schell, Morral, and Nicosia, "Geographic Disparities in Rising Rates of Firearm-Related Homicide."
14. "Stats of the States—Firearm Mortality," Centers for Disease Control and Prevention, 2019. https://www.cdc.gov/nchs/pressroom/sosmap/firearm_mortality/firearm.htm.
15. Heather Saunders, "Do States with Easier Access to Guns Have More Suicide Deaths by Firearm?," KFF, July 18, 2002. https://www.kff.org/other/issue-brief/do-states-with-easier-access-to-guns-have-more-suicide-deaths-by-firearm/.
16. Michael Siegel, Yamrot Negussie, Sarah Vanture, Jane Pleskunas, Craig S. Ross, and Charles King, "The Relationship between Gun Ownership and Stranger and Nonstranger Firearm Homicide Rates in the United States, 1981–2010," *American Journal of Public Health* 104, no. 10 (2014): 1912–19. https://doi.org/10.2105/ajph.2014.302042.
17. Matthew Miller, Deborah Azrael, and David Hemenway, "Rates of Household Firearm Ownership and Homicide across US Regions and States, 1988–1997," *American Journal of Public Health* 92, no. 12 (2002): 1988–93. https://doi.org/10.2105/ajph.92.12.1988.
18. Matthew Miller, David Hemenway, and Deborah Azrael, "State-Level Homicide Victimization Rates in the US in Relation to Survey Measures of Household Firearm Ownership, 2001–2003," *Social Science & Medicine* 64, no. 3 (2007): 656–64. https://doi.org/10.1016/j.socscimed.2006.09.024.
19. Erin Grinshteyn and David Hemenway, "Violent Death Rates in the US Compared to Those of the Other High-Income Countries, 2015," *Preventive Medicine* 123 (2019): 20–26. https://doi.org/10.1016/j.ypmed.2019.02.026.
20. Aaron Karp, *Estimating Global Civilian-Held Firearms Numbers* (Australia: Small Arms Survey, June 2018). https://www.smallarmssurvey.org/sites/default/files/resources/SAS-BP-Civilian-Firearms-Numbers.pdf.
21. Katherine Schaeffer, "Key Facts about Americans and Guns," Pew Research Center, September 13, 2021. https://www.pewresearch.org/fact-tank/2021/09/13/key-facts-about-americans-and-guns/.
22. Lois Beckett, "Gun Inequality: US Study Charts Rise of Hardcore Super Owners," *Guardian*, September 19, 2016. https://www.theguardian.com/us-news/2016/sep/19/us-gun-ownership-survey.

Part I.

Why America Is a Gun Country

America's love affair with firearms is rooted in the Second Amendment of the US Constitution. The American Revolution was fought—and won—with guns, but with the British army's trampling on Americans' liberties in the 1760s and 1770s still fresh in memory, the Second Amendment was written to assuage the concerns of antifederalists who opposed large standing armies. Today, the United States has five times the population of Britain and 700 times more gun homicides, but that's beside the point. Adopted on December 15, 1791, as part of the first 10 amendments contained in the Bill of Rights, the Second Amendment reads, "A well-regulated militia, being necessary to the security of a free State, the right of the people to keep and bear arms, shall not be infringed."

When Congress passed and the states ratified the Second Amendment, political consensus held that rights and obligations were one and the same. Sir William Blackstone, author of the seminal *Commentaries on the Laws of England*, described the right to bear arms as an "auxiliary right"—a mechanism to protect both the natural or inherent right to freedom from oppression *and* one's civic duty to act in the common defense of the state.[1] The right to bear arms was inextricably linked to a citizen's obligation to serve in a militia and to protect the community from enemies domestic and foreign, including a tyrannical federal government.[2]

As the US Supreme Court ruled in *United States v. Miller, 307 U.S. 174* (1934), the "obvious purpose" of the Second Amendment was to "render possible the effectiveness" of militias; thus the amendment must be "interpreted and applied with that end in view." The "arms" prescribed by the Second Amendment were also, obviously, military weapons, mostly long arms that could discharge only once before they had to be reloaded, very different from the arms of today.[3] Since the 1970s, however, the National Rifle Association (NRA), which was founded in 1871 to promote firearms safety education and marksmanship training,[4] has lobbied extensively for an individual's right to carry a gun as a means of *self-defense*, rather than the people's right to form armed militias to provide for the *common defense*.[5]

The modern American culture of personal weapons began after the American Civil War ended in 1865 when demobilized Union and Confederate troops were permitted to take home their guns. At this time, firearms were critical tools for pioneers in hunting game and fending off varmints, the ultimate expression of rugged individualism forged on the frontier, far from civilization and the reach of laws, where gunslingers took justice into their own hands. The term *gun culture* was coined in 1970 by historian Richard Hofstadter to describe Americans' unique belief in the "notion that the people's right to bear arms is the greatest protection of their individual rights and a firm safeguard of democracy."[6] However, research shows that American gun culture has since evolved from an initial emphasis on hunting, recreational target shooting, and collecting (Gun Culture 1.0) to self-defense alone (Gun Culture 2.0).[7] Firearm manufacturers have played a major role in this shift, tapping into public fears of crime and racial upheaval to build a nearly $20 billion gun industry.[8]

The self-defense narrative of righteous justice is arguably what sets apart the gun rights movement in the United States from similar movements in other countries. It is the number one reason why Americans claim to own a firearm in the first place, a central trope of Hollywood, and a defining feature of American masculinity.[9] It achieved new legal authority in *District of Columbia v. Heller, 554 U.S. 570* (2008), which ruled unconstitutional a Washington, DC, ban on handguns, and *New York State Rifle & Pistol Association, Inc. v. Bruen, 597 U.S.* (2022), which overturned a New York law limiting the concealed carry of handguns in public areas. While there is a long history of restricting places where guns can be, these rulings expanded the scope of the Second Amendment to establish there is a right to possess guns for personal *self-defense*, including outside one's home. This further explains the rapid state expansion of concealed-carry and stand-your-ground laws in recent years, the latter pertaining to an extension of the so-called castle doctrine, exonerating from prosecution anyone who uses deadly force when confronted by an assailant, even if that person could have retreated safely.

The chapters in part I examine the origins of America's obsession with guns, starting with a historian's reading of the Second Amendment and the "five types of gun laws the Founding Fathers loved." The chapters that follow, each written by leading scholars of American culture and history, situate the political debate on guns in America in the enduring stories that Americans tell about them. With guns so closely tied to our national narrative, chapters in this part explore popular culture's role in building these stories, from television and movies about the Wild West to pulpy crime fiction in the early part of the 20th century. Other chapters examine the psychology of firearms ownership, the cultural influence of firearms manufacturers, and the changing nature of the NRA over the years. Collectively, these chapters offer a detailed commentary on the place of guns in US culture.

Recommended Further Reading

- *Gunfight: My Battle against the Industry That Radicalized America* by Ryan Busse
- *Gunfight: The Battle over the Right to Bear Arms in America* by Adam Winkler
- *Misfire: Inside the Downfall of the NRA* by Tim Mak
- *The Second Amendment: A Biography* by Michael Waldman
- *The Second: Race and Guns in a Fatally Unequal America* by Carol Anderson

Notes

1. William Blackstone, *Commentaries on the Laws of England* (Oxford: Clarendon Press, 1765).
2. Michael Waldman, *The Second Amendment: A Biography* (New York: Simon & Schuster, 2015).
3. Jill Lepore, "One Nation, under the Gun," *New Yorker*, April 16, 2012. https://www.newyorker.com/magazine/2012/04/23/battleground -america.

4. Tim Mak, *Misfire: Inside the Downfall of the NRA* (New York: Dutton, 2021).
5. Adam Winkler, *Gunfight: The Battle over the Right to Bear Arms in America* (New York: W. W. Norton, 2013).
6. Richard Hofstadter, "America as a Gun Culture," *American Heritage* 21, no. 6 (1970). https://www.americanheritage.com/america-gun-culture.
7. David Yamane, "The Sociology of U.S. Gun Culture," *Sociology Compass* 11, no. 7 (2017): e12497. https://doi.org/10.1111/soc4.12497.
8. Ryan Busse, *Gunfight: My Battle against the Industry That Radicalized America* (New York: PublicAffairs, 2021).
9. Jennifer Carlson, *Citizen-Protectors: The Everyday Politics of Guns in an Age of Decline* (New York: Oxford University Press, 2015); Katherine Schaeffer, "Key Facts about Americans and Guns," Pew Research Center, September 13, 2021. https://www.pewresearch.org/fact-tank/2021/09/13/key-facts-about-americans-and-guns/.

Chapter 1

Five Types of Gun Laws the Founding Fathers Loved

SAUL CORNELL

THE SECOND AMENDMENT is one of the most frequently cited provisions in the American Constitution, but it is also one of the most poorly understood. The 27 words that make up the Second Amendment seem to baffle modern Americans on both the Left and Right.

Ironically, those on both ends of our contemporary political spectrum cast the Second Amendment as a barrier to robust gun regulation. Gun rights supporters—mostly, but not exclusively, on the Right—seem to believe the Second Amendment prohibits many forms of gun regulation. On the

Left, frustration with the lack of progress in modern gun control leads to periodic calls for the amendment's repeal.

Both of these beliefs ignore an irrefutable historical truth. The framers and adopters of the Second Amendment were generally ardent supporters of the idea of well-regulated liberty. Without strong governments and effective laws, they believed, liberty inevitably degenerated into licentiousness and eventually into anarchy. Diligent students of history, particularly Roman history, the Federalists who wrote the Constitution realized that tyranny more often resulted from anarchy, not strong government.

I have been researching and writing about the history of gun regulation and the Second Amendment for more than two decades.[1] When I began this research, most people assumed that regulation was a relatively recent phenomenon, something associated with the rise of big government in the modern era. Actually, while the founding generation certainly esteemed the idea of an armed population, they were also ardent supporters of gun regulation.[2]

Consider these five categories of gun laws that the Founders endorsed.

1. Registration

Today, American gun rights advocates typically oppose any form of registration—even though such schemes are common in every other industrial democracy—and typically argue that registration violates the Second Amendment. This claim is hard to square with the history of the nation's founding. All of the colonies—apart from Quaker-dominated Pennsylvania, the one colony in which religious pacifists blocked the creation of a militia—enrolled local citizens, white men between the ages of 16 and 60 in state-regulated militias. The colonies and then the newly independent states kept track of the privately owned weapons required for militia service. Men could be fined if they reported to a muster without a well-maintained weapon in working condition.

2. Public Carry

The modern gun rights movement has aggressively pursued the goal of expanding the right to carry firearms in public.

The American colonies inherited a variety of restrictions that had evolved under English Common Law. In 18th-century England, armed travel was limited to a few well-defined occasions such as assisting justices of the peace and constables. Members of the upper classes also had a limited exception to travel with arms. Concealable weapons such as handguns were subject to even more stringent restrictions. The City of London banned public carry of these weapons entirely.

The American Revolution did not sweep away English Common Law. In fact, most colonies adopted Common Law as it had been interpreted in the colonies prior to independence, including the ban on traveling armed in populated areas. Thus, there was no general right of armed travel when the Second Amendment was adopted and certainly no right to travel with concealed weapons.[3] Such a right first emerged in the United States in the slave states of the South decades after the Second Amendment was adopted. The market revolution of the early 19th century made cheap and reliable handguns readily available. Southern murder rates soared as a result.

In other parts of the nation, the traditional English restrictions on traveling armed persisted with one important change. American law recognized an exception to this prohibition for individuals who had a good cause to fear an imminent threat. Nonetheless, by the end of the century, prohibiting public carry without a permit was the legal norm, not the exception.[4]

3. Stand-Your-Ground Laws

Under traditional English Common Law, persons had a duty to retreat, not to stand their ground. Deadly force was justified only if no other alternative were possible. One had to retreat, until retreat was no longer possible, before killing an aggressor.

The use of deadly force was justified only in the home, where retreat was not required under the so-called castle doctrine, or the idea that "a man's home is his castle." The emergence of a more aggressive view of the right of self-defense in public, standing your ground, developed decades after the adoption of the Second Amendment.

4. Safe Storage Laws

Although some gun rights advocates attempt to demonize government power, it is important to recognize that one of the most important rights citizens enjoy is the freedom to elect representatives who can enact laws to promote health and public safety. This is the foundation for the idea of ordered liberty. The regulation of gunpowder and firearms arises from an exercise of this basic liberty.

In 1786, Boston acted on this legal principle, prohibiting the storage of a loaded firearm in any domestic dwelling in the city.[5] Guns had to be kept unloaded, a practice that made sense because the black powder used in firearms in this period was corrosive. Loaded guns also posed a particular hazard in cases of fire because they might discharge and injure innocent bystanders or those fighting fires.

5. Loyalty Oaths

One of the most common claims one hears in the modern Second Amendment debate is the assertion that the Founders included this provision in the Constitution to make possible a right of revolution. But this claim rests on a serious misunderstanding of the role that the right to bear arms played in American constitutional theory.

The Founders, in fact, engaged in large-scale disarmament of the civilian population during the American Revolution. The right to bear arms was conditional on swearing a loyalty oath to the government, and individuals who refused to swear an oath were disarmed. The notion that the Second Amendment was understood to protect a right to take up arms against the government is absurd. Indeed, the Constitution itself defines such an act as treason.

Gun regulation and gun ownership have always existed side by side in American history. Although some of the persons disarmed were deemed dangerous, others such as the Quakers were among the most peaceful and law-abiding citizens in America. To understand the disarmament of Quakers, one needs to understand how radically different American ideas about rights were in this period.

The lesson of the history of firearms regulation is clear: the Second Amendment poses no obstacle to enacting sensible gun laws. The failure to do so is not the Constitution's fault; it is ours.

Notes

1. Saul Cornell, " 'Half Cocked': The Persistence of Anachronism and Presentism in the Academic Debate over the Second Amendment," *Journal of Criminal Law and Criminology* 106, no. 2 (2016). 203–18. https://scholarlycommons.law.northwestern.edu/jclc/vol106/iss2/2.
2. Saul Cornell and Nathan DeDino, "A Well Regulated Right: The Early American Origins of Gun Control," *Fordham Law Review* 73 (2004): 487–528. https://ir.lawnet.fordham.edu/flr/vol73/iss2/3.
3. Eric M. Rube and Saul Cornell, "Firearm Regionalism and Public Carry: Placing Southern Antebellum Case Law in Context," *Yale Law Journal Forum* 125 (2015): 121–35. http://www.yalelawjournal.org/forum/firearm-regionalism-and-public-carry.
4. Saul Cornell, "The Right to Keep and Carry Arms in Anglo-American Law: Preserving Liberty and Keeping the Peace," *Law and Contemporary Problems* 80 (2017): 11–54. http://scholarship.law.duke.edu/lcp/vol80/iss2/2.
5. Cornell and DeDino, "A Well Regulated Right."

Chapter 2

Three Enduring Stories Americans Tell about Guns

GREG DICKINSON and **BRIAN L. OTT**

THE UNITED STATES HAS STRUGGLED with a history of horrific mass shootings and will need to grapple with the implications of the US Supreme Court's 2022 decision to strike down the State of New York's restrictions on carrying concealed firearms, which has consequences beyond the state.

After each tragic mass shooting, people try to make sense of the violence by talking about what happened. The discussion usually gravitates toward two familiar poles: gun control on one end and personal liberty on the other. But despite all the talk, not much changes.

A family poses in front of their sod house in Custer County, Nebraska, in 1887.
Bettmann / Bettmann via Getty Images

We are scholars of communication who study how rhetoric shapes politics and culture, particularly how the stories Americans tell about the country's past continue to shape its present. The nation's failure to prevent frequent mass shootings is, we suggest, partially a product of how American society commemorates guns.

Imagining the "Wild West"

An excellent example of how American culture tells the story of guns is the Cody Firearms Museum in Wyoming: home to "the most comprehensive collection of American firearms in the world" and the subject of an academic article we coauthored with colleague Eric Aoki in 2011.[1] We have continued this research as part of a book project.

Featuring more than 7,000 weapons, the museum is part of the Buffalo Bill Center of the West. The center's namesake, 19th-century rifleman and showman Buffalo Bill, popularized the story of the "Wild West" that remains familiar to Americans today—one where guns were central.[2]

Stories, of course, are never neutral. They include certain details and exclude others; they highlight some aspects of a thing and downplay others. They distill the great complexity of our world into manageable and memorable bits that guide how we understand it.

An especially important kind of storytelling happens at museums. As historians Roy Rosenzweig and David Thelen explain, surveys show that people trust museums more than family members, eyewitnesses, teachers, and history textbooks.[3] So it matters what US museums have to say about guns.

Based on multiple research visits to the Cody Firearms Museum over the past decade, we have identified three foundational narratives about guns—stories that, we argue, get replayed in the present-day rhetoric about firearms.[4]

Story 1: Guns Are Tools

One of the key themes at the Cody Firearms Museum is that guns were central to life on the frontier. Settlers had few possessions, and guns, which were necessary for hunting and fending off dangerous animals, were among the most common household items.

The view of guns as a common tool remains prevalent today, usually through references to hunting. Emphasizing firearms' important role in everyday survival—even though so few people in the United States live that way today—"domesticates" guns, and many Americans continue to treat even assault rifles as ordinary objects of everyday life.

Consider the comment that Colorado representative Ken Buck made to the House Judiciary Committee just days after the 2022 mass shooting in Buffalo, New York: "In rural Colorado, an AR-15 is a gun of choice for killing raccoons before they get to our chickens. It is a gun of choice for killing a fox. It is a gun that you [use to] control predators on your ranch, your farm, your property." Such talk domesticates assault rifles, depicting them as ordinary objects. But they are far from ordinary. One 2017 study found that assault rifles and other high-capacity semiautomatics "account for 22% to 36% of crime guns, with some estimates upwards of 40% for cases involving serious violence including murders of police."[5] They are also used in up to 57% of mass murders involving firearms.

Story 2: Guns Are Wonders

A second key theme on display at the museum is that guns are technological marvels. Visitors can learn, often in painstaking detail, about each advancement in loading systems, ammunition cartridges, and firing mechanisms.

Displays like these frame guns as inert objects of study and fascination, shifting attention from their function and purpose to their design and development. Moreover, the display of thousands of guns in glass cases, physically separated from human beings, turns them into objects that seem almost worthy of veneration.

Gun hobbyists view guns as collectibles. According to a Pew Research Center study, 66% of gun owners own multiple firearms, with 73% saying they "could never see themselves not owning a gun" and half acknowledging that "owning a gun is important to their overall identity."[6] Because gun hobbyists regard guns as collectibles, they often use rhetoric that regards guns as inert objects rather than as machines engineered for violence.

For many gun owners, gun violence is a problem associated with "bad" actors, not with guns. Following the mass shooting in Buffalo, New York, podcaster Graham Allen wrote, "Firearms are LIFELESS objects, they do not think, they do not feel, and they do not take a life on their own. Therefore you CANNOT hold an inanimate object accountable for the actions of the shooter."[7]

Story 3: Guns Are Quintessentially American

The third story American culture tells about guns is that they are central to what it means to be "American." They symbolize the myth of rugged individualism on which the country was founded. Guns are also associated with Manifest Destiny, the belief that white Americans were destined by God to violently "settle" the plains and "civilize" the West, expanding US territory from coast to coast.

Guns served as the primary instrument for westward expansion and the forced removal of Native Americans. As American studies scholar Richard Slotkin explains, many iconic portrayals of the frontier depict white colonizers doing what they believed to be "God's work" with the help of their guns.[8]

Today, national discourse still frames guns as part of a God-given right to eliminate "threats" in a world full of dangerous people. The National Rifle Association has used religiously infused language to argue for gun rights, such as when its executive vice president, Wayne LaPierre, said in 2018 that the right to bear arms is "granted by God to all Americans as our American birthright."

In these arguments, gun ownership is a way of expressing a deep and long-held American desire to protect oneself, one's family, and one's property. Crime data, however, suggests that self-defense with guns is rare, used by victims in 1% or fewer of "crimes in which there is personal contact between the perpetrator and victim."[9] The Greenwood Mall shooting in Indiana in 2022, where a bystander shot and killed the gunman, may be a counterexample since an armed mall-goer killed the gunman; however, according to FBI statistics, out of 101 active shooter cases in 2020 and 2021, only 6 of the shooters were stopped by an armed citizen. Instead of decreasing gun deaths, owning guns increases other dangers like accidental shooting and gun-related suicide.

Joseph Pierre, a psychiatrist at the University of California, Los Angeles, has written that, while fear may be the main reason cited for owning a gun, ownership is also strongly associated with fear of losing of control. Seventy-four percent of gun owners say the right to own guns is essential to their sense of freedom, according to the previously cited survey of the Pew Research Center.

From Talk to Action—or Inaction

How people talk about an object influences how they understand and see it. And once that view hardens into an attitude, it significantly impacts future action.

In the Cody Firearms Museum, and in American culture broadly, guns are portrayed as utilitarian tools of daily life, venerated objects of technological progress, and symbols of what it means to be American. These stories continue to shape and constrain how America talks and thinks about guns, and they help explain why gun policy in the United States looks the way that it does.

Notes

1. Brian L. Ott, Eric Aoki, and Greg Dickinson, "Ways of (Not) Seeing Guns: Presence and Absence at the Cody Firearms Museum," *Communication and Critical/Cultural Studies* 8, no. 3 (2011): 215–39. https://doi.org/10.1080/14791420.2011.594068.
2. Greg Dickinson, Brian L. Ott, and Aoki Eric, "Memory and Myth at the Buffalo Bill Museum," *Western Journal of Communication* 69, no. 2 (2005): 85–108. https://doi.org/10.1080/10570310500076684.
3. Roy Rosenzweig and David Thelen, *The Presence of the Past: Popular Uses of History in American Life* (New York: Columbia University Press, 2000).
4. Ott, Aoki, and Dickinson, "Ways of (Not) Seeing Guns."
5. Christopher S. Koper, William D. Johnson, Jordan L. Nichols, Ambrozine Ayers, and Natalie Mullins, "Criminal Use of Assault Weapons and High-Capacity Semiautomatic Firearms: An Updated Examination of Local and National Sources," *Journal of Urban Health* 95, no. 3 (2017): 313–21, 313. https://doi.org/10.1007/s11524-017-0205-7.
6. Kim Parker et al., *America's Complex Relationship with Guns*, Pew Research Center, June 22, 2017. https://www.pewresearch.org/social-trends/2017/06/22/americas-complex-relationship-with-guns/.
7. Graham Allen, "Guns Don't Kill People. Bad People Kill People," Turning Point USA, May 16, 2022. https://www.tpusa.com/live/guns-dont-kill-people-bad-people-kill-people.
8. Richard Slotkin, *Gunfighter Nation: Myth of the Frontier in Twentieth-Century America* (Norman: University of Oklahoma Press, 1998).
9. David Hemenway and Sara J. Solnick, "The Epidemiology of Self-Defense Gun Use: Evidence from the National Crime Victimization Surveys, 2007–2011," *Preventive Medicine* 79 (2015): 22–27. https://doi.org/10.1016/j.ypmed.2015.03.029.

Chapter 3

How the "Good Guy with a Gun" Became a Deadly American Fantasy

SUSANNA LEE

AT THE END OF MAY 2019, it happened again. A mass shooter killed 12 people, this time at a municipal center in Virginia Beach. Employees had been forbidden to carry guns to work, and some lamented that this policy had prevented "good guys" from taking out the shooter. This trope—"the good guy with a gun"—has become commonplace among gun rights activists.

Where Did the Trope Come From?

On December 21, 2012—one week after Adam Lanza shot and killed 26 people at Sandy Hook Elementary School in Newtown,

Connecticut—the executive vice president of the National Rifle Association, Wayne LaPierre, announced during a press conference that "the only way to stop a bad guy with a gun is a good guy with a gun."

Ever since then, in response to each mass shooting, pro-gun pundits, politicians, and social media users parrot some version of the slogan, followed by calls to arm the teachers, arm the churchgoers, or arm the office workers. And whenever an armed citizen takes out a criminal, conservative media outlets pounce on the story.

But "the good guy with a gun" archetype dates to long before LaPierre's 2012 press conference. There's a reason LaPierre's words resonated so deeply. He had tapped into a uniquely American archetype, one whose origins I trace back to American pulp crime fiction in my book *Hard-Boiled Crime Fiction and the Decline of Moral Authority.*[1] Other cultures have their detective fiction. But it was specifically in America that the "good guy with a gun" became a heroic figure and a cultural fantasy.

"When I Fire, There Ain't No Guessing"

Beginning in the 1920s, a certain type of protagonist started appearing in American crime fiction. He often wore a trench coat and smoked cigarettes. He didn't talk much. He was honorable, individualistic—and armed.

These characters were dubbed *hard-boiled*, a term that originated in the late 19th century to describe "hard, shrewd, keen men who neither asked nor expected sympathy nor gave any, who could not be imposed upon." The word didn't describe someone who was simply tough; it communicated a persona, an attitude, an entire way of being.

Most scholars credit Carroll John Daly with writing the first hard-boiled detective story. Titled "Three Gun Terry," it was published in *Black Mask* magazine in May 1923. "Show me the man," the protagonist, Terry Mack, announces, "and if he's drawing on me and is a man what really needs a good killing, why, I'm the boy to do it." Terry also lets the reader know that he's a sure shot: "When I fire, there ain't no guessing contest as to where the bullet is going."

From the start, the gun was a crucial accessory. Since the detective only shot at bad guys and because he never missed, there was nothing to fear.

Part of the popularity of this character type had to do with the times. In an era of Prohibition, organized crime, government corruption, and rising populism, the public was drawn to the idea of a well-armed, well-meaning maverick—someone who could heroically come to the defense of regular people. Throughout the 1920s and 1930s, stories that featured these characters became wildly popular.

Taking the baton from Daly, authors like Dashiell Hammett and Raymond Chandler became titans of the genre. Their stories' plots differed, but their protagonists were mostly the same: tough-talking, straight-shooting private detectives.

In an early Hammett story, the detective shoots a gun out of a man's hand and then quips that he's a "fair shot—no more, no less."

In a 1945 article, Chandler attempted to define this type of protagonist: "Down these mean streets a man must go who is not himself mean, who is neither tarnished nor afraid. . . . He must be, to use a rather weathered phrase, a man of honor, by instinct, by inevitability, without thought of it, and certainly without saying it."

As movies became more popular, the archetype expanded to the silver screen. Humphrey Bogart played Hammett's Sam Spade and Chandler's Philip Marlowe to great acclaim.

By the end of the 20th century, the fearless, gun-toting good guy had become a cultural hero. He had appeared on magazine covers, movie posters, in television credits, and in video games.

Selling a Fantasy

Gun rights enthusiasts have embraced the idea of the "good guy" as a model to emulate—a character role that just needed real people to step in and play it. The store of the National Rifle Association even sells T-shirts blazoned with LaPierre's slogan and encourages buyers to "show everyone that you're the 'good guy'" by buying the T-shirt.

The problem with this archetype is that it's just that: an archetype. A fictional fantasy.

In pulp fiction, the detectives never miss. Their timing is precise and their motives are irreproachable. They never accidentally shoot themselves or an innocent bystander. Rarely are they mentally unstable or blinded by rage. When they clash with the police, it's often because they're doing the police's job better than the police can.

Another aspect of the fantasy involves looking the part. The "good guy with a gun" isn't just any guy: it's a white one. In "Three Gun Terry," the detective apprehends the villain, Manual Sparo, with some tough words: " 'Speak English,' I says. I'm none too gentle because it won't do him any good now." In Daly's "Snarl of the Beast," the protagonist, Race Williams, takes on a grunting, monstrous immigrant villain.

Could this explain why, in 2018, when a Black man with a gun tried to stop a shooting in a mall in Alabama—and the police shot and killed him—the National Rifle Association, usually eager to champion good guys with guns, didn't comment?

A Reality Check

Most gun enthusiasts don't measure up to the fictional ideal of the steady, righteous, and sure shot. In fact, research has shown that gun-toting independence unleashes much more chaos and carnage than heroism. Studies have shown that right-to-carry laws increase, rather than decrease, violent crime.[2] Higher rates of gun ownership are correlated with higher homicide rates.[3] Gun possession is correlated with increased road rage.

There have been times when a civilian with a gun successfully intervened in a shooting, but these instances are rare. Those who carry guns often have their own guns used against them.[4] And a civilian with a gun is more likely to be killed than to kill an attacker. Even in instances where a person is paid to stand guard with a gun, there's no guarantee that he'll fulfill this duty.

Hard-boiled novels have sold in the hundreds of millions. The movies and television shows they inspired have reached millions more. What started as entertainment has turned into a durable American fantasy. Maintaining it has become a deadly American obsession.

Notes

1. Susanna Lee, *Hard-Boiled Crime Fiction and the Decline of Moral Authority* (Columbus: Ohio State University Press, 2016). https://doi .org/10.2307/j.ctvrxk3t1.

2. John J. Donohue, Abhay Aneja, and Kyle D. Weber, "Right-to-Carry Laws and Violent Crime: A Comprehensive Assessment Using Panel Data and a State-Level Synthetic Control Analysis," *Journal of Empirical Legal Studies* 16, no. 2 (2019): 198–247. https://doi.org/10.1111/jels.12219.
3. Michael Siegel, Craig S. Ross, and Charles King, "The Relationship between Gun Ownership and Firearm Homicide Rates in the United States, 1981–2010," *American Journal of Public Health* 103, no. 11 (2013): 2098–105. https://doi.org/10.2105/ajph.2013.301409.
4. Charles C. Branas, Therese S. Richmond, Dennis P. Culhane, Thomas R. Ten Have, and Douglas J. Wiebe, "Investigating the Link between Gun Possession and Gun Assault," *American Journal of Public Health* 99, no. 11 (2009): 2034–40. https://doi.org/10.2105/ajph.2008.143099.

Chapter 4

American Gun Culture Is Based on Frontier Mythology but Ignores How Common Gun Restrictions Were in the Old West

PIERRE M. ATLAS

IN THE WAKE OF THE BUFFALO AND UVALDE mass shootings in 2022, 70% of Republicans said it was more important to protect gun rights than to control gun violence, while 92% of Democrats and 54% of independents expressed the opposite view, according to an NPR/PBS *NewsHour*/Marist National Poll.[1] Just weeks after those mass shootings, Republicans and gun rights advocates hailed the June 23, 2022, US Supreme Court ruling that invalidated New York State's gun permit law and declared that the Second Amendment guarantees a right to carry a handgun outside the home for self-defense.

Mayor Eric Adams, expressing his opposition to the ruling, suggested that the court's decision would turn New York City into the "Wild West." Contrary to the imagery of the Wild West, however, many towns in the real Old West had restrictions on the carrying of guns that were, I would suggest, stricter than the one invalidated by the Supreme Court.

Support for gun rights among Republicans played an important role in determining the contents of the bipartisan Safer Communities Act of 2022, the first new gun reform bill in three decades. President Joe Biden signed it into law just two days after the Supreme Court's decision was released. To attract Republican support, the law does not include gun control proposals such as an assault weapons ban, universal background checks, or a raised purchasing age of 21 for certain types of rifles. Nevertheless, the bill was denounced by some Republicans in Congress and was opposed by the National Rifle Association.

I have found that for those Americans who see the gun as both symbolizing and guaranteeing individual liberty, gun control laws are perceived as fundamentally un-American and a threat to their freedom. For the most ardent gun rights advocates, gun violence—as horrible as it is—is an acceptable price to pay for that freedom.

In an analysis I did in 2019,[2] I found that gun culture in the United States derives largely from its frontier past and from the mythology of the Wild West,[3] which romanticizes guns, outlaws, rugged individualism, and the inevitability of gun violence. This culture ignores the fact that gun control was widespread and common in the Old West.

Reenactments of Old West gunfights, like this one at a tourist attraction in Texas in 2014, are part of the mythology underpinning the United States' gun culture. *Carol M. Highsmith via Library of Congress*

The Prevalence of Guns

Guns are part of a deep political divide in American society. The more guns a person owns, the more likely they are to oppose gun control legislation, and the more likely they are to vote for Republican candidates.[4] In 2020, 44% of American households reported owning at least one firearm. According to the 2018 international Small Arms Survey, there were approximately 393 million firearms in civilian hands in the United States, or 120.5 firearms per 100 people. That number is likely higher now, given increases in gun sales in 2019, 2020, and 2021.

Americans have owned guns since colonial times, but American gun culture really took off after the Civil War with the imagery, icons, and tales—or mythology—of the lawless frontier and the Wild West. Frontier mythology, which celebrates and exaggerates the amount and significance of gunfights and vigilantism, began with 19th-century western paintings, popular dime novels, and traveling Wild West shows by Buffalo Bill Cody and others. It continues to this day with western-themed shows on television such as *Yellowstone* and *Walker*.

A Marketing Move

Historian Pamela Haag attributes much of the country's gun culture to that western theme. Before the middle of the 19th century, she writes, guns were common in US society, but they were unremarkable tools used by a wide range of people in a growing nation.[5]

But then the gun manufacturers Colt and Winchester started marketing their firearms by appealing to customers' sense of adventure and the romance of the frontier. In the mid-19th century, gun manufacturers began advertising their guns as a way that people all around the country could connect with the excitement of the West, with its Indian wars, cattle drives, cowboys, and gold and silver boomtowns. Winchester's slogan was "The Gun That Won the West," but Haag argues that it was really "the West that won the gun."

By 1878, this theme was so successful that Colt's New York City distributor recommended that the company market the .44-40 caliber version of its model 1873 single-action revolver as the "Frontier Six Shooter" to appeal to the public's growing fascination with the Wild West.

A Different Reality

Gun ownership was commonplace in the Old West after the Civil War, but actual gunfights were rare.[6] One reason for this was that, contrary to the mythology, many frontier towns had strict laws against carrying firearms and other weapons in public, either openly or concealed.[7]

As constitutional law professor Adam Winkler puts it, "Guns were widespread on the frontier, but so was gun regulation. . . . Wild West lawmen took gun control seriously and frequently arrested people who violated their town's gun control laws."[8] *Gunsmoke*, the iconic TV show that ran from the 1950s through the 1970s, would have featured far fewer gunfights had its fictional marshal, Matt Dillon, enforced Dodge City's real laws banning the carrying of any firearms within city limits.

The appeal of this mythology extends to the present day. In August 2021, a Colt Frontier Six Shooter became the world's most expensive firearm when the auction house Bonhams sold "the gun that killed Billy the Kid" at auction for over $6 million. As a mere antique firearm, that revolver would be worth a few thousand dollars. Its astronomic selling price was due to its Wild West provenance.

The historical reality of the American frontier was more complex and nuanced than its popular mythology. But it's the mythology that fuels American gun culture today, which rejects the types of laws that were commonplace in the Old West.

A Particular View of Safety and Freedom

Hardcore gun owners, their lobbyists, and many members of the Republican Party refuse to allow the thousands of annual

gun deaths and the additional thousands of nonfatal shootings to be used as justifications for restricting their rights as
law-abiding citizens. They are willing to accept gun violence
as an inevitable side effect of a free and armed, if violent,
society. Their opposition to new gun reforms as well as their
support of gun rights legislation—such as permitless carry
and the arming of teachers—are but the latest manifestations
of American gun culture's deep roots in frontier mythology.

Wayne LaPierre, executive director of the National Rifle
Association, the country's largest gun rights group, tapped
into imagery from frontier mythology and American gun
culture following the Sandy Hook massacre in 2012. In his call
to arm school resource officers and teachers, LaPierre
adopted language that could have come from a classic
western film: "The only thing that stops a bad guy with a gun
is a good guy with a gun."

This view of a lone armed person who can stand up and
save the day has persisted ever since, and it provides an
answer of its own to mass shootings: guns are not the
problem—they're the solution.

Notes

1. "Gun Violence in the U.S., June 2022," Marist Poll, June 9, 2022.
   https://maristpoll.marist.edu/polls/npr-pbs-newshour-marist
   -national-poll-gun-violence-in-the-united-states-june-2022/.
2. Pierre M. Atlas, "Of Peaceable Kingdoms and Lawless Frontiers:
   Exploring the Relationship between History, Mythology and Gun
   Culture in the North American West," *American Review of Canadian
   Studies* 49, no. 1 (2019): 25–49. https://doi.org/10.1080/02722011
   .2019.1573843.
3. Richard Slotkin, *Gunfighter Nation: The Myth of the Frontier in
   Twentieth-Century America* (Norman: Oklahoma University Press,
   1998).
4. Mark. R. Joslyn, *The Gun Gap* (New York: Oxford University Press,
   2020).

5. Pamela Haag, *The Gunning of America: Business and the Making of American Gun Culture* (New York: Basic Books, 2016).
6. Robert R. Dykstra, "Quantifying the Wild West: The Problematic Statistics of Frontier Violence," *Western Historical Quarterly* 40, no. 3 (2009): 321–47. https://doi.org/10.1093/whq/40.3.321.
7. Robert Spitzer, *Guns across America: Reconciling Rules and Rights* (New York: Oxford University Press, 2017).
8. Adam Winkler, *Gunfight: The Battle over the Right to Bear Arms in America* (New York: W. W. Norton, 2011).

Chapter 5

How the NRA Evolved from Backing a 1934 Ban on Machine Guns to Blocking Nearly All Firearm Restrictions Today

ROBERT SPITZER

INEVITABLY, IF ALSO UNDERSTANDABLY, after mass shootings occur, many Americans blame the National Rifle Association for thwarting stronger gun laws that might have prevented the tragedy and others to come. After spending decades researching and writing about how and why the NRA came to hold such sway over national gun policies,[1] I've seen the narrative about the NRA's influence take unexpected turns in the last few years that raise new questions about the organization's reputation for invincibility.

Three Phases

The NRA's history of more than 150 years spans three distinct eras. At first the group was mainly concerned with marksmanship. It later played a relatively constructive role regarding safety-minded restrictions on gun ownership before turning into a rigid politicized force.

The NRA was formed in 1871 by two Civil War veterans from northern states who had witnessed the typical soldier's inability to handle guns. The organization initially leaned on government support, which included subsidies for shooting matches and surplus weaponry. These freebies, which lasted until the 1970s, gave gun enthusiasts a powerful incentive to join the NRA.

The NRA played a role in fledgling political efforts to formulate state and national gun policy in the 1920s and 1930s after Prohibition-era liquor trafficking stoked gang warfare. It backed measures like requiring a permit to carry a gun and even a waiting period for purchasing a gun.

The NRA helped shape the National Firearms Act of 1934, with two of its leaders testifying before Congress at length regarding this landmark legislation. They supported, if grudgingly, its main provisions, such as restricting gangster weapons, which included a national registry for machine guns and sawed-off shotguns and taxing them heavily. But they opposed handgun registration, which was stripped out of the country's first significant national gun law.

Decades later, in the legislative battle held in the aftermath of President John F. Kennedy's assassination and amid rising concerns about crime, the NRA opposed another national registry provision that would have applied to all firearms. Congress ultimately stripped it from the Gun Control Act of 1968.

Throughout this period, however, the NRA remained primarily focused on marksmanship, hunting, and other recreational activities, although it did continue to voice opposition to new gun laws, especially to its membership.

A Sharp Right Turn

By the mid-1970s, a dissident group within the NRA believed that the organization was losing the national debate over guns by being too defensive and not political enough. The dispute erupted at the NRA's 1977 annual convention, where the dissidents deposed the old guard.

From this point forward, the NRA became ever more political and strident in its defense of so-called gun rights, which it increasingly defined as nearly absolute under the Second Amendment.

One sign of how much the NRA had changed: the Second Amendment right to bear arms never came up in the 166 pages of congressional testimony regarding the 1934 gun law.[2] Today, the organization treats those amendment's words as its mantra, constantly citing them. And until the mid-1970s, the NRA supported waiting periods for handgun purchases. Since then, however, it has opposed them. It fought vehemently against the ultimately successful enactment in 1993 of a five-business-day waiting period and background checks for handgun purchases.

The NRA's influence hit a zenith during George W. Bush's gun-friendly presidency, which embraced the group's

Late actor and former National Rifle Association president Charlton Heston held a rifle aloft at a 2002 get-out-the-vote rally.
AP Photo / Jim Cole

positions. Among other things, his administration let the ban on assault weapons expire, and it supported the NRA's top legislative priority: enactment in 2005 of special liability protections for the gun industry, the Protection of Lawful Commerce in Arms Act.

Having a White House Ally Isn't Everything

Despite past successes, the NRA has suffered a series of mostly self-inflicted blows that have precipitated an existential crisis for the organization.

Most significantly, an investigation by the New York attorney general, filed in 2020, revealed extensive allegations of rampant cronyism, corruption, sweetheart deals, and fraud.

Partly as a result of these revelations, NRA membership has apparently declined to roughly 4.5 million, down from a high of about 5 million.

Despite this trend, however, the grassroots gun community is no less committed to its agenda of opposition to new gun laws. Indeed, the Pew Research Center's findings in 2017 suggested that about 14 million people identify with the group. By any measure, that's a small minority out of nearly 260 million US voters.[3]

Yet support for gun rights has become a litmus test for Republican conservatism,[4] and it is baked into that political party's agenda. This laser-like focus on gun issues continues to enhance the NRA's influence even when the organization faces turmoil. This means that the protection and advancement of gun rights are propelled by the broader conservative movement so that the NRA no longer needs to carry the ball by itself.

Like Bush, Trump maintained a cozy relationship with the NRA. The organization was among his 2016 presidential bid's most enthusiastic backers, contributing $31 million to his presidential campaign. When Trump directed the Justice Department to draft a rule banning bump stocks, and indicated his belated support for improving background checks for gun purchases after the Parkland shooting, he was sticking with NRA-approved positions. He also supported arming teachers, another NRA proposal.

Only one sliver of light opened up between the Trump administration and the NRA: his apparent willingness to consider raising the minimum age for buying assault weapons from 18 to 21 years old, a position he later abandoned. In 2022, a year after Trump left office, 18-year-olds, including the gunmen allegedly responsible for the mass shootings in Uvalde and Buffalo, were able to purchase firearms legally.

In politics, victory usually belongs to whoever shows up. And by showing up, the NRA has managed to strangle every federal effort to restrict guns since the Newtown shooting. Nevertheless, the NRA does not always win. Following the Parkland school shooting at the start of 2018, 27 states had enacted 67 new gun laws by the end of that year. And for the first time in nearly 30 years, Congress passed a modest set of new gun measures in June 2022.

Repercussions of the Supreme Court's ruling

Mass shootings may stir gun safety supporters to mobilize public outrage and turn out voters favoring stricter firearm regulations.

But there is a recent wild card: the US Supreme Court's 2022 ruling in *New York State Rifle & Pistol Club v. Bruen*, the most significant case regarding gun rights the court has considered in years. The court struck down a long-standing New York provision in pistol permit law requiring an applicant to show "proper cause" in order to get a license; this ruling will likely broaden the right to carry guns in public in the United States. It could galvanize gun safety supporters while also emboldening gun rights activists—making the debate about guns in America even more tumultuous.

Notes

1. Robert J. Spitzer, *Guns across America: Reconciling Rules and Rights* (New York: Oxford University Press, 2017).
2. Robert J. Spitzer, "Gun Law History in the United States and Second Amendment Rights," *Law and Contemporary Problems* 80 (2017): 55–83. https://scholarship.law.duke.edu/lcp/vol80/iss2/3; Robert J. Spitzer, "The Second Amendment 'Right to Bear Arms' and *United*

States v. Emerson," *St. John's Law Review* 77 (2003). https://scholarship.law.stjohns.edu/lawreview/vol77/iss1/1/.

3. Ruth Igielnik and Anna Brown, "Key Takeaways on Americans' Views of Guns and Gun Ownership," Pew Research Center, June 22, 2017. https://www.pewresearch.org/fact-tank/2017/06/22/key-takeaways-on-americans-views-of-guns-and-gun-ownership/.

4. Genevieve Quinn, "Do Gun Policy Specifics Matter? Hyper-polarization and the Decline of Vote Splitting in Congress," *Forum* 18, no. 2 (2020): 249–82. https://doi.org/10.1515/for-2020-2007.

Chapter 6

The Key Role Firearms Makers Play in America's Gun Culture

MICHAEL SIEGEL

AMERICANS HAVE BLAMED MANY CULPRITS, from mental illness to inadequate security, for the tragic mass shootings that are occurring with increasing frequency in schools, offices, stores, and movie theaters across the United States. Yet during much of America's ongoing conversation about the root causes of gun violence, the makers of guns have typically escaped scrutiny. As a public health researcher, I find this odd, because evidence shows that the culture around guns contributes significantly to gun violence.[1] And firearm manufacturers have played a major role in influencing American gun culture.

That lack of scrutiny is beginning to change, particularly since the $73 million settlement between the families of victims of the 2012 Sandy Hook Elementary School shooting and the maker of the rifle used in the massacre. This may open the door for more lawsuits against firearm manufacturers.

To help support this much-needed discussion, I'd like to share some critical facts about the firearm industry that I've learned from my research on gun violence prevention.[2]

Surging Handgun Sales

The United States is saturated with guns and has become a lot more so over the past decade. In 2020 alone, US gun manufacturers produced 11.1 million firearms, up from 5.4 million in 2010. Pistols and rifles made up about 75% of the total.

In addition, only a small number of gun-makers dominate the market. The top five pistol manufacturers alone controlled over 70% of all production in 2020: Smith & Wesson; Sig Sauer; Sturm, Ruger & Co.; Glock; and Kimber Manufacturing. Similarly, the biggest rifle manufacturers—Sturm, Ruger & Co.; Smith & Wesson; Springfield; Henry RAC Holding; and Diamondback Firearms—controlled 61% of that market.

But that tells only part of the story. A look at the caliber of pistols manufactured over the past decade reveals a significant change in demand that has reshaped the industry.

The number of manufactured large-caliber pistols able to fire rounds of a size greater than or equal to 9 millimeters has soared over the past 15 years, rising from just over half a

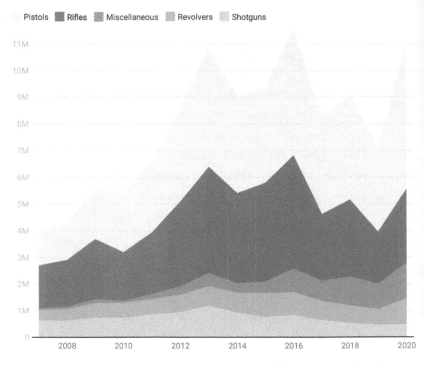

Trends in gun manufacturing. More than 11 million (M) guns were produced in the United States in 2020. *The Conversation, CC BY-ND. Data from the Bureau of Alcohol, Tobacco, Firearms and Explosives*

million in 2005 to more than 3.9 million by 2020. The number of .38-caliber pistols—small handguns designed specifically for concealed carry—jumped to a record 1.1 million in 2016 and totaled 660,000 in 2020, compared with 107,000 in 2005. This indicates a growing demand for more lethal weapons, especially those suited for self-defense and concealed carry.

The production of rifles has also increased, doubling from 1.4 million in 2005 to 2.8 million in 2020, although down from a record 4.2 million in 2016. This is driven primarily by a higher demand for semiautomatic weapons, including assault rifles.

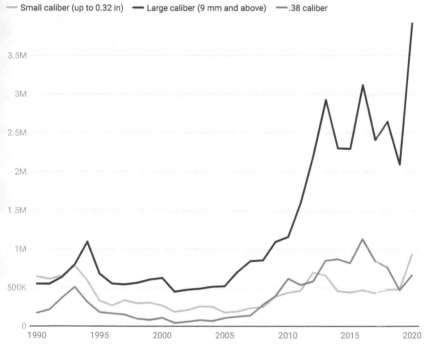

Small caliber (up to 0.32 in) — Large caliber (9 mm and above) — .38 caliber

Pistol manufacturing in the United States. The growing demand for large and .38 caliber pistols shows Americans' increased interest in guns designed specifically for self-defense and concealed carry. K = thousand; M = million. *The Conversation, CC BY-ND. Data from the Bureau of Alcohol, Tobacco, Firearms and Explosives*

Explaining the Stats

So what can explain the jump in the sale of high-caliber handguns and semiautomatic rifles?

Gun-makers have become effective at marketing their wares as necessary tools for self-defense—perhaps in large part to offset a decline in demand for recreational use.[3] For example, in 2005, Smith & Wesson announced a major new marketing campaign focused on "safety, security, protection

Gallup (Change from 2005 to 2021)

Self-defense

0%   20%   40%   60%   80%   100%

88%

Gallup (Change from 2000 to 2019)

Hunting   40%

Sport   11%

0%   20%   40%   60%   80%   100%

Why do Americans own guns? Over the last two decades, fewer Americans have cited hunting and sport as their reasons for owning guns. In 2021, 88% of gun owners said self-defense was a key reason.
The Conversation, CC BY-ND. Data from Gallup, "Guns," https://news.gallup.com/poll/1645/guns.aspx

and sport." The number of guns the company sold soared after the switch, climbing 30% in 2005 and 50% in 2006, led by strong growth in pistol sales. By comparison, the number of firearms sold in 2004 rose 11% over the previous year.

There's strong survey evidence showing that gun owners have become less likely to cite hunting or sport as a reason for their ownership, instead pointing to personal security. The percentage of gun owners who told Gallup that a reason they possessed a firearm was for hunting fell to 40% in 2019, from almost 60% in 2000. The percentage of those who cited sport as a reason fell even more. Meanwhile, Gallup found that 88% of gun owners in 2021 reported self-defense as a reason, up from 67% in 2005.[4]

"Stand Your Ground" Laws Flourish

Another possible explanation for the uptick in handguns could be the widespread adoption of state "stand your ground" laws in recent years. These laws explicitly allow people to use guns as a first resort for self-defense in the face of a threat. Utah enacted the first stand-your- ground measure in 1994. The second law wasn't adopted until 2005 in Florida. A year later, stand-your-ground laws took off, with 11 states enacting one in 2006 alone. Another 15 have passed such laws since then, bringing the total number of states that have them on the books to 28.

These laws were the result of a concerted lobbying campaign by the National Rifle Association. For example, Florida's law, which George Zimmerman used in 2013 to escape charges for killing Trayvon Martin, was drafted by former NRA president Marion Hammer.

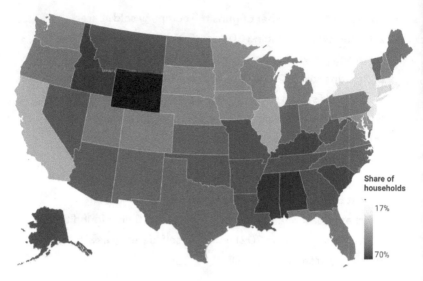

Estimated household gun ownership. Wyoming has the highest rate of home gun ownership, with 70% of households reporting at least one firearm. Hawaii has the lowest at 17%. Data as of 2020. *The Conversation, CC BY-ND. Data from the Centers for Disease Control and Prevention*

It's not clear whether the campaign to promote stand-your-ground laws fueled the surge in handgun production. But it's possible that it's part of a larger effort to normalize the ownership of firearms for self-defense.

This overall picture suggests that a marketing change fueled an increased demand for more lethal weapons. This, in turn, appears to have fostered a change in gun culture, which has shifted away from having guns for hunting, sport, and recreation toward possessing guns as a means of protecting oneself from criminals. Whether and how this change in gun culture is influencing rates of firearms violence are questions I'm currently researching.

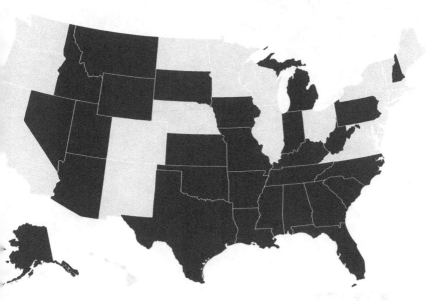

Stand-your-ground laws. From 2004 to 2022, 28 US states (*darker gray*) enacted a stand-your-ground law allowing a person to shoot another if they perceive a threat of bodily harm. *The Conversation, CC BY-ND. Data from the National Conference of State Legislatures*

Notes

1. Bindu Kalesan, Marcos D. Villarreal, Katherine M. Keyes, and Sandro Galea, "Gun Ownership and Social Gun Culture," *Injury Prevention* 22, no. 3 (2015): 216–20. https://doi.org/10.1136/injuryprev-2015 -041586.
2. Victoria M. Smith, Michael Siegel, Ziming Xuan, Craig S. Ross, Sandro Galea, Bindu Kalesan, Eric Fleegler, and Kristin A. Goss, "Broadening the Perspective on Gun Violence: An Examination of the Firearms Industry, 1990–2015," *American Journal of Preventive Medicine* 53, no. 5 (2017): 584–91. https://doi.org/10.1016/j.amepre.2017.05.002.
3. Tom Diaz, *Making a Killing: The Business of Guns in America* (New York: New Press, 2000); Tom Diaz, *The Last Gun: How Changes in the Gun Industry Are Killing Americans and What It Will Take to Stop It* (New York: New Press, 2013).
4. "Guns," Gallup, https://news.gallup.com/poll/1645/guns.aspx.

Chapter 7

Hollywood's Love of Guns Increases the Risk of Shootings—Both on and off Set

BRAD J. BUSHMAN and DAN ROMER

IN A TRAGIC ACCIDENT, actor Alec Baldwin shot dead a cinematographer on October 21, 2021, while discharging a prop gun on set in New Mexico. The incident, in which the film's director was also injured, highlights a simple fact: guns are commonplace in Hollywood films.

As scholars of mass communication and risk behavior, we have studied the growing prevalence of firearms on screen and believe that the more guns there are in movies, the more likely it is that a shooting will occur—the "reel" world relates to the "real" world.

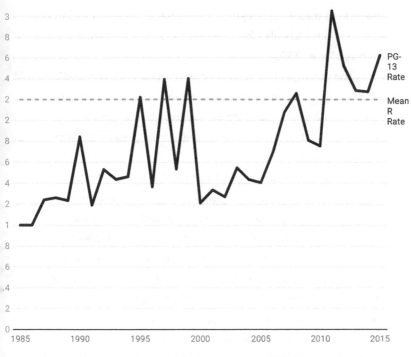

The growth of gun violence in PG-13 movies since 1985. The rate of five-minute film segments with gun violence for the top 30 ranked films rated PG-13 against the mean for R-rated movies between 1985 and 2015. *The Conversation, CC BY-ND. Data from Romer et al (2017)*

Gun violence in Hollywood movies has increased dramatically over time, especially in movies accessible to teens. Indeed, our research shows that acts of gun violence in PG-13 movies nearly tripled over the 30 years between 1985 (the year after the rating was introduced) and 2015.[1] Similar trends have been observed in popular TV dramas, with the rate of gun violence depicted in prime-time dramas doubling between 2000 and 2018.[2]

Of course, depictions of violence in the entertainment industry are nothing new. The use of guns in Hollywood films has a long tradition going back to the gangster movies of the 1930s. Guns were also featured heavily in the western TV shows of the 1950s.

The upsurge in the appearance of guns in movies and TV shows is likely related to the realization that violence draws audiences and that guns are an easy way to dramatize violence.[3] And here, filmmakers have a willing accomplice in the gun industry.

Media outlets are averse to allowing gun advertising on TV or in mass-circulated magazines. But guns are amply displayed in top-grossing movies and popular TV dramas. We know that the gun industry pays production companies to place its products in their movies. The industry is rewarded with frequent appearances of its guns on screen, so much so that, in 2010, the firearm company Glock won a "lifetime achievement award for product placement," with a citation noting that Glocks appeared in 22 box-office number-one films during that year.

The payoff for gun companies can be great: prominent placement in high-profile films can result in a significant bump in sales for gun models.

Making Guns Cool

The potential harm caused by guns in Hollywood goes far beyond the occasional tragic accident on set. Studies show that simply seeing a gun can increase aggression in the viewer through what is called the "weapons effect."[4] Violent movies and TV programs, which often feature guns, can likewise increase aggression and make viewers numb to the pain and suffering of others, numerous studies show.[5]

Children may be especially susceptible to the weapons effect, which makes it all the more notable that the prevalence of guns in PG-13 movies has increased over the decades. Younger viewers often identify movie characters as being "cool" and thus want to imitate their behavior.

A similar effect was seen with smoking on screen: children who see movie characters smoke cigarettes are more likely to smoke themselves. A correlation was also observed with children who watched movie characters drink alcohol.

In a study conducted by one of us,[6] pairs of children ages 8 to 12 years old were first randomly assigned to watch a PG-rated movie clip featuring guns or the same movie clip with the guns edited out. They were then put in a room that contained several toys and games, while being observed through a hidden camera. A cabinet in the room contained a real, but disabled, 9-millimeter handgun that had been modified with a digital counter to record the number of times someone pulled the trigger.

Most children (72%) opened the drawer and found the gun. But children who watched the movie clip with guns in it held the handgun longer—an average of 53.1 seconds compared with 11.1 seconds for those who watched the clip without guns. They also pulled the trigger more times—2.8 times on average compared with 0.01 times for those who watched the movie clip without guns. Some children engaged in flagrantly dangerous behavior with the gun, such as pulling the trigger while pointing it at themselves or their partner. One boy pointed the gun out the laboratory window at people in the street.

The kind of gun violence scripted in Hollywood movies tends to highlight a justified use of the weapon. When characters use a gun to defend themselves or family, that use is portrayed as acceptable.[7] This has the result of encouraging viewers to think that using guns for the protection of self or others is virtuous.

Reflecting or Glamorizing Violence?

The United States is the most heavily armed society in the world. Though making up only about 4% of the world's population, US citizens possess almost half of the world's guns.

By featuring guns so heavily in its movies, Hollywood runs the risk not merely of reflecting society but also of encouraging firearm sales. While incidents of actors or production staff being injured or killed in accidental shootings are thankfully rare, the likelihood of fatal shootings—accidental or otherwise—in the real world goes up with every sale of the kinds of guns presented by Hollywood.

Notes

1. Brad J. Bushman, Patrick E. Jamieson, Ilana Weitz, and Daniel Romer, "Gun Violence Trends in Movies," *Pediatrics* 132, no. 6 (2013): 1014–18. https://doi.org/10.1542/peds.2013-1600; Daniel Romer, Patrick E. Jamieson, and Kathleen Hall Jamieson, "The Continuing Rise of Gun Violence in PG-13 Movies, 1985 to 2015," *Pediatrics* 139, no. 2 (2017). https://doi.org/10.1542/peds.2016-2891
2. Patrick E. Jamieson and Daniel Romer, "The Association between the Rise of Gun Violence in Popular US Primetime Television Dramas and Homicides Attributable to Firearms, 2000–2018," *PLOS One* 16, no. 3 (2021). https://doi.org/10.1371/journal.pone.0247780.
3. International Communication Association, "What Attracts People to Violent Movies?," ScienceDaily, March 2013, www.sciencedaily.com /releases/2013/03/130328091750.htm.
4. Arlin J. Benjamin, Sven Kepes, and Brad J. Bushman, "Effects of Weapons on Aggressive Thoughts, Angry Feelings, Hostile Appraisals, and Aggressive Behavior: A Meta-analytic Review of the Weapons Effect Literature," *Personality and Social Psychology Review* 22, no. 4 (2017): 347–77. https://doi.org/10.1177/1088868317725419.

5. Craig A. Anderson, Brad J. Bushman, Bruce D. Bartholow, Joanne Cantor, Dimitri Christakis, Sarah M. Coyne, Edward Donnerstein, et al., "Screen Violence and Youth Behavior," *Pediatrics* 140, no. Supplement 2 (2017). https://doi.org/10.1542/peds.2016-1758t.
6. Kelly P. Dillon and Brad J. Bushman, "Effects of Exposure to Gun Violence in Movies on Children's Interest in Real Guns," *JAMA Pediatrics* 171, no. 11 (2017): 1057. https://doi.org/10.1001/jamapediatrics.2017.2229.
7. Daniel Romer, Patrick E. Jamieson, Kathleen Hall Jamieson, Robert Lull, and Azeez Adebimpe, "Parental Desensitization to Gun Violence in PG-13 Movies," *Pediatrics* 141, no. 6 (2018). https://doi.org/10.1542/peds.2017-3491.

Chapter 8

If You Give a Man a Gun

The Evolutionary Psychology of Mass Shootings

FRANK T. MCANDREW

MEN COMMIT OVER 85% OF ALL HOMICIDES, 91% of all same-sex homicides, and 97% of all same-sex homicides in which the victim and killer aren't related to each other.[1] These startling statistics are driven home with each new mass shooting.

Meanwhile, politicians and the media trot out the usual suspects to explain the latest tragedy, whether it's the lack of attention paid to mental illness or the easy availability of guns. But these explanations dance around big questions:

Why is it always a man behind the shooting? And why is it almost always a *young* man?

Evolutionary psychology can provide some clues.

Precarious Manhood

Psychologists Joseph Vandello and Jennifer Bosson coined the term *precarious manhood* to describe a predicament that only men seem to face.[2] In a nutshell, they argue that manhood—however an individual male's culture might define it—is a status that must be continually earned. And one's self-worth is tied to being perceived as a "real man." It's precarious because it can be easily lost, especially if the man fails to measure up to the relentless challenges that life throws at him, be they tests of bravery or physical competition with other men for respect and status.

When I introduce this concept to my male students, they instantly recognize what I'm talking about. But when I ask the women if there's a female equivalent, I'm often met with confused looks. (Some do note that the inability to have a child could be a threat to womanhood.) Indeed, it quickly becomes clear in the ensuing class discussion that manhood is more precarious than womanhood.

The roots of this male predicament reside deep in our prehistoric past. Throughout the animal kingdom, the sex that invests the least in the reproduction of offspring (almost always males) competes among themselves for sexual access to mates.

Historically, powerful men have always enjoyed greater sexual access to women than men lower in the pecking order, and violence can often be traced to this grim struggle for status.

Anthropologist Napoleon Chagnon spent years studying the Yanomamo people of South America. He discovered that men who had killed other men acquired significantly more wives than men who hadn't killed anyone. And by all indications, a man's status in the group often depended on how believable were his threats of physical violence.

In different cultures, the male "quest for dominance" may play out in different ways. Regardless, it is clearly a universal motivating principle among males, with the achievement of dominance being satisfying and rewarding for those who attain it. As scholar Jonathan Gottschall put it, "To physically dominate another man is intoxicating."[3]

And so, violence committed against the right people at the right time became a ticket to social success.

Competitive Drives

For sound evolutionary reasons, younger men find themselves especially concerned with status and dominance.

In early human societies, competitive success or failure in early adulthood determined a man's standing in a social group for the rest of his life.[4] It wasn't possible simply to hit the "reset" button and join another group, so what happened during the teen years mattered a lot. For this reason, high-risk competition between young males provided an opportunity for "showing off" the abilities needed to acquire resources and to meet any challenges to one's status. Consequently, heroic or even recklessly daredevil behavior was rewarded with status and respect—assuming, of course, that the young man survived the feat.

Today, the widespread promotion of sport in our culture undoubtedly developed as a constructive alternative for dealing with the proclivities of young males that had evolved in a much different time. In a legally sanctioned gladiatorial arena, young men are able to exhibit the same skills—aiming, throwing, running, tackling, wrestling, clubbing—that would have made them successful hunters or fighters in the ancestral environment.

Young Male Syndrome

It's no secret that most people fear violent behavior from young men more than like behavior from older men. There's a sound basis for this fear. In fact, the tendency of young men to engage in risky, aggressive behavior prompted the Canadian psychologists Margo Wilson and Martin Daly to give it a name: young male syndrome.[5]

The duo studied the relationship among age, sex, and homicide victimization in the United States in 1975. They found that the likelihood of a woman being a murder victim doesn't change dramatically over the course of her life. The pattern for males, on the other hand, is striking. At age 10, males and females have an equal probability of being murdered. But by the time men are in their twenties, they become *six times* more likely to be murdered.

Consistent with Wilson and Daly's data, 87% of the 598 homicide victims in the city of Chicago in 2003 were males, and 64% of the victims were between the ages of 17 and 30. The likelihood of being the victim of lethal violence peaks for men between their late teen years and late twenties, before steadily declining for the rest of their lives.

Nature fuels the fires of male violence by equipping young men with the high levels of testosterone necessary to get the job done. Studies of chimpanzees—our closest primate relative—have shown that high-ranking male chimpanzees exhibit the highest levels of aggression and the highest levels of testosterone. Furthermore, all adult male chimpanzees experience their highest testosterone levels when they're in the presence of females who are ovulating. This peak is associated only with higher levels of aggression, not with significant increases in sexual activity.

Researchers such as me who study the relationship between testosterone and aggression in humans have concluded that testosterone-fueled violence is more likely to occur when males are competing with other males or when the social status of a male is challenged in some way. The increased testosterone facilitates whatever competitive behaviors are needed to meet the challenge, which could mean physical violence.

Many studies have shown that testosterone levels in males rise and fall according to whether an individual wins or loses in competitive sports, like tennis and wrestling and even chess. Sports fans experience the same spike when watching sports, which helps explain the violence and destructive rioting that can take place after big games (win or lose).

Adding Guns to the Mix

So how do guns figure in this violent equation?

In 2006 I coauthored a laboratory study on men's responses to guns, published in the journal *Psychological Science*, with my colleague Tim Kasser and one of our students.[6] We demonstrated that males who interacted with a handgun showed a greater increase in their level of testosterone and more aggressive behavior than males who interacted with the board game *Mouse Trap*.

In the study, each participant dismantled either a gun or the mousetrap used in the game, handled its components, and then wrote instructions for how to assemble the objects. Then we gave them the opportunity to put hot sauce into water that was going to be consumed by another person. The participants who handled the gun put in significantly more hot sauce and were also more likely to express disappointment after learning that no one was actually going to drink the concoction.

Cues tied to threats often won't result in an aggressive response unless testosterone is involved. Elliot Rodger, the disturbed college student whose violent 2014 rampage through Santa Barbara, California, was foretold in a chilling YouTube video, clearly experienced a testosterone surge upon purchasing his first handgun. "After I picked up the handgun," he explained, "I brought it back to my room and felt a new sense of power. Who's the alpha male now, bitches?"

Mass Shooter = Low-Status Loser?

Young male violence is most likely to be initiated by young men who don't command respect from others. They often feel like slighted outcasts, deprived of what they want or feel they deserve.

British clinical psychologist Paul Gilbert developed something he calls social attention holding theory.[7] According to Gilbert, we compete with one another to have other people pay attention to us; when other people take notice, we build status. The increased status that comes from having others attend to us leads to all kinds of positive emotions. But persistently being ignored by others produces dark emotions, especially envy and anger.

It's no mystery why the media often describes mass shooters and terrorists as misfits or loners. In many cases, they are. Nicolas Hénin was a Frenchman who was held hostage by ISIS for 10 months. Here's how he described his young murderous Jihadi captors: "They present themselves to the public as superheroes, but away from the camera are a bit pathetic in many ways: street kids drunk on ideology and power. In France we have a saying—stupid and evil. I found them more stupid than evil. That is not to understate the murderous potential of stupidity."[8]

Apparently, a lack of attention from others results in a lack of status, leading to a lack of access to women. Combined with a young man's testosterone, it creates a toxic, combustible mix. There may not be much we can do to change the structure of the young male mind that evolved over millions of years. To ignore or deny its existence, though, doesn't do us any favors.

Notes

1. Francis T. McAndrew, "The Interacting Roles of Testosterone and Challenges to Status in Human Male Aggression," *Aggression and Violent Behavior* 14, no. 5 (2009): 330–35. https://doi.org/10.1016/j.avb.2009.04.006.
2. Jennifer K. Bosson and Joseph A. Vandello, "Precarious Manhood and Its Links to Action and Aggression," *Current Directions in Psychological Science* 20, no. 2 (2011): 82–86. https://doi.org/10.1177/0963721411402669.
3. Jonathan Gottschall, *The Professor in the Cage: Why Men Fight and Why We Like to Watch* (New York: Penguin Press, 2005), 205.
4. McAndrew, "Interacting Roles of Testosterone and Challenges to Status."
5. Margo Wilson and Martin Daly, "Competitiveness, Risk Taking, and Violence: The Young Male Syndrome," *Ethology and Sociobiology* 6, no. 1 (1985): 59–73. https://doi.org/10.1016/0162-3095(85)90041-x.
6. Jennifer Klinesmith, Tim Kasser, and Francis T. McAndrew, "Guns, Testosterone, and Aggression: An Experimental Test of a Mediational

Hypothesis," *Psychological Science* 17, no. 7 (2006): 568–71. https://doi.org/10.1111/j.1467-9280.2006.01745.x.

7. Paul Gilbert, "The Relationship of Shame, Social Anxiety and Depression: The Role of the Evaluation of Social Rank," *Clinical Psychology & Psychotherapy* 7, no. 3 (2000): 174–89. https://doi.org /10.1002/1099-0879(200007)7:3<174::aid-cpp236>3.0.co;2-u.

8. Nicolas Hénin, "I Was Held Hostage by Isis. They Fear Our Unity More Than Our Airstrikes," *Guardian*, November 16, 2015. https://www .theguardian.com/commentisfree/2015/nov/16/isis-bombs-hostage -syria-islamic-state-paris-attacks?CMP=share_btn_fb.

Chapter 9

Want to Understand Gun Owners?
Watch Their Videos

CONNIE HASSETT-WALKER

IT WAS AN ORDINARY DAY IN 2011 when I found myself watching a YouTube video of a gun owner making a semi-automatic rifle discharge bullets rapidly, as if it were an auto-matic weapon.[1] My husband, a gun owner, would watch firearms videos like this one. But I had never seen one. Intrigued, I sat down on the couch to absorb the imagery. Hooking his thumb through his pants belt loop, the YouTuber demonstrated how pushing the gun forward, rather than pulling the trigger, allowed the gun's recoil to "keep the gun going."

In other words, he was bump firing his rifle.

I'm a criminal justice researcher. At the time, a flurry of thoughts popped into my mind. Aren't citizens forbidden to own automatic weapons? Is it legal to make a video of a semiautomatic rifle performing like an automatic firearm? What about the 1930s machine gun ban? Is there a YouTube loophole of some sort?

This was 2011, seven years before a gunman at a country music festival in Las Vegas used a bump stock to make his shooting spree more effective and deadly, killing 58 people and injuring 851.

Watching that first video led me to spend the next five years exploring online gun videos and gun owner communities. It also led to a moderation in my views on gun-related issues—something I believe resulted from the understanding and empathy I gained from those videos.

Video Opens a Window on a World

My exploration would become the book *Guns on the Internet: Online Gun Communities, First Amendment Protections, and the Search for Common Ground on Gun Control*, published in August 2018.[2]

That first video, and the many videos I subsequently viewed, showed me how gun owners could legally share content that, in the case of bump stocks, could effectively render a particular gun control law moot.[3] This realization led to a question: Is it worth it to pass a law banning the sale of bump stock devices when people can just make and upload a how-to video of bump firing without the device?

I felt like I had accidentally stumbled onto a secret that was hiding in plain sight. I also realized that despite being married to a gun owner, I knew little about gun subculture, either in real life or online. But I could learn.

Guns, Part of the Fabric of Life

For all the noise around gun control versus gun rights, there was a story being missed by non–gun owners like me: how much guns mean to many of those who own them.

Delving into gun subculture online—which in some, though not all, ways reflects gun subculture in real life—can provide a perspective that may be, for non–gun owners, much different from their own. Americans live in a time of political polarization on a variety of social issues, gun rights among them. Both gun control and gun rights supporters would benefit from understanding how those with opposing political and social views see their identity and their culture.

Data from 2017 reported by the Pew Research Center illuminate the extent of gun owner use of the internet and social media.[4] Thirty-five percent of gun owners responding to the Pew survey indicated that they often or sometimes visited websites focused on hunting, shooting sports, or guns. Ten percent participated in gun forums online.

Culture and its smaller subcultures comprise the values and behaviors that define a group of people.[5] A related idea is homophily, that is, the desire to connect with others who have similar characteristics, experiences, and interests. Gun owners engage in this, both in real life—for example, by attending gun shows or joining a shooting club—as well as online.

Gun owners join Facebook groups with words and phrases such as *freedom*, *liberty*, and *duck hunters* in their names. They also join Facebook groups devoted to survival skills, love of the outdoors, and hunting and fishing. They post in the comment sections of gun-related blogs. These are just some of the ways that the subculture of gun enthusiasts flourishes online.

Dissing Politicians and Shooting Old Computers

I learned that gun owners share ideas, images of firearms, and videos signaling to other gun owners and the greater online community the norms, values, and activities of gun subculture. They use hashtags like #freedom or #2A, for the Second Amendment, on a posting. They post keyword phrases such as *take our rights away, Patriot class*, and *lock 'n load*. Gun owners showcase their rapid-fire skills with semiautomatic guns, explain how to clean a firearm, complain about political parties and gun control organizations, and compare one type of gun to another. See, for example, the video "Glock 17 vs. Ruger SR9."[6]

I've observed that gun-owning YouTubers have a lot of fun filming themselves and their friends shooting at all kinds of things: targets, zombies, and old computers. I've come to view firearms as part of the fabric of their owners' lives, complementing other aspects of lifestyle such as rural living, hunting, and camping.

Previously, I had thought about guns mostly as something dangerous, unnecessary, and possibly enabling a homicide or suicide in someone's home.

Not anymore.

I came to have some favorite videos,[7] as well as YouTubers I liked.[8] Having peered into part of these gun owners' worlds, I felt a sense of familiarity despite not knowing any of them in person. This gave me an idea. If I felt a connection to particular YouTubers and videos, would others experience something similar?

How to Bridge a Divide

Research suggests that individuals can form attachments to media personalities whom they do not know in real life.[9] If feelings of connectedness could be deliberately cultivated between gun control advocates and gun owners, might it be possible to parlay that into a better understanding of the perspectives of those sitting on the other side of the gun controversy? Could this lead to a productive conversation about gun rights and gun control in the United States?

Some research suggests that it is possible to shift people's opinions, even strongly held ones, and to enhance empathy for others who hold very different opinions.[10] Other scholarship has connected familiarity with reduced prejudice. So while a reversal of opinion isn't likely when trying to bring opposing viewpoints closer, small movement on a seemingly intractable issue might be possible.

Through the process of watching hundreds of videos made by and for gun owners, I find that my views on guns have shifted away from unquestioning support for gun control toward a more neutral, even gun-friendly, perspective. I'm also much more aware of what I don't know, including the particulars of all things related to gun (parts, accessories).

The deadlock between proponents of gun rights and of gun control is frustrating. To that end, I conclude my book by proposing that both gun control and gun rights supporters watch 100 YouTube videos featuring content from the opposing camp. Viewers should approach their watching with an open mind. They will see a slice of the other's life in the context of their world.

Notes

1. LifeLibertyEtc, "Bump Fire Academy," YouTube, March 13, 2010. https://www.youtube.com/watch?v=yRJyHEU3mkE.
2. Connie R. Hassett-Walker, *Guns on the Internet Online Gun Communities, First Amendment Protections, and the Search for Common Ground on Gun Control* (New York: Routledge, 2018).
3. Kentucky Ballistics, "Testing a Transparent Shield," YouTube, May 21, 2020. https://www.youtube.com/watch?v=Ka6OFphBBpl.
4. Kim Parker, Juliana Menasce Horowitz, Ruth Igielnik, J. Baxter Oliphant, and Anna Brown, "America's Complex Relationship with Guns," Pew Research Center's Social & Demographic Trends Project, Pew Research Center, February 5, 2022. https://www.pewresearch.org/social-trends/2017/06/22/americas-complex-relationship-with-guns/.
5. T. V. Reed, *Digitized Lives: Culture, Power, and Social Change in the Internet Era* (New York: Routledge, 2019).
6. mmatt, "Glock 17 vs. Ruger SR9," YouTube, February 9, 2014. https://www.youtube.com/watch?v=ysokL6pHf1I.
7. theARMORYchannel, "Gun Shop Manners," YouTube, July 13, 2012. https://www.youtube.com/watch?v=tLgegXWm_CQ.
8. HeathersVlogs, "What in the Heck Was He Doing? The Southern Life with Heather and Jeff," YouTube, June 6, 2012. https://www.youtube.com/watch?v=_k04PoEcni8.
9. Cynthia A. Hoffner and Bradley J. Bond, "Parasocial Relationships, Social Media, & Well-Being," *Current Opinion in Psychology* 45 (2022): 101306. https://doi.org/10.1016/j.copsyc.2022.101306.
10. Boaz Hameiri, Roni Porat, Daniel Bar-Tal, Atara Bieler, and Eran Halperin, "Paradoxical Thinking as a New Avenue of Intervention to Promote Peace," *Proceedings of the National Academy of Sciences* 111, no. 30 (2014): 10996–1001. https://doi.org/10.1073/pnas.1407055111.

Chapter 10

Why Were Medieval Weapons Laws at the Center of a US Supreme Court Case?

JENNIFER TUCKER

IN THE OPENING SCENE OF *THE LAST DUEL*, a film set in 14th-century France, a herald announces the rules for conduct at a tournament to the death. He declares that no members of the public—whatever their social background— are allowed to bring weapons to the event. This scene might seem far removed from 21st-century America. But medieval weapons laws—including a 1328 English statute prohibiting the public carry of edged weapons without royal permission— were at the center of dueling legal opinions in a landmark

2022 case heard by the US Supreme Court, *New York State Rifle and Pistol Association v. Bruen*.

The plaintiffs challenged New York's "proper cause" gun law, which tightly restricted the public carry of firearms. Following the ruling, similar laws in several other states have been called into question. That means that concealed-carry licensing laws could be liberalized for millions of Americans currently living in more restrictive jurisdictions.

Few people realize how big a role history has played in the battle over gun rights. It was the topic of a 2019 collection of essays titled *A Right to Bear Arms? The Contested Role of History in Contemporary Debates on the Second Amendment*, which I coedited with Barton Hacker and Margaret Vining, curators of the Smithsonian Museum of American History.[1] The book explores how courts in the United States have turned to history for instruction in how guns should be treated—decrees, laws, and interpretations of the past that were at the forefront of the case before the Supreme Court in 2022.

Scalia Points to the English Bill of Rights

The United States' legal system grew out of the English legal tradition. This connection, which is often referenced by originalists, is crucial to making sense of the arguments around gun rights in America today. Originalism is an approach to interpreting legal texts, including the Constitution, based on what justices think is their original meaning.

An important victory for gun rights advocates took place in the case of *District of Columbia v. Heller*. In that 2008 decision, the Supreme Court for the first time ruled that the

A gun rights advocate walks through the rotunda of the Kentucky Capitol. Some lawyers argue that the 1689 English Bill of Rights created the legal basis for public carry of weapons in the United States. *Bryan Woolston / Getty Images*

Second Amendment protects an individual's right to possess a firearm for personal self-defense in the home.

Justice Antonin Scalia, author of the five-to-four majority opinion in *Heller*, claimed that there was a long tradition of the English state's granting freedom to possess weapons dating back to the 1689 English Bill of Rights, which includes a clause that reads, "the subjects which are Protestant may have arms for their defence suitable to their conditions and as allowed by law." Scalia's argument relied heavily on the work of historian Joyce Malcolm, the author of *To Keep and Bear Arms: The Origins of an Anglo-American Right*,[2] and a Second Amendment scholar at the Antonin

Scalia Law School at George Mason University. Malcolm and lawyers who support the expansion of gun rights argue that this clause created the legal basis for having weapons for personal self-defense in colonial America.

Having prevailed in *Heller*, gun rights activists are seeking the liberalization of restrictions on the public carrying of guns outside the home. As for the New York case, some lawyers and other parties are now arguing that medieval statutes restricted only public carry that "terrified" the public and that such statutes were never actually enforced to prevent "normal" public carry.

Historians Object

Most scholars of English and American history, however, vigorously dispute the accuracy of this claim.[3] In fact, since the *Heller* decision, the history of firearms regulation in England and the United States has been the focus of what Fordham University law professor Saul Cornell has called an "explosion of empirical research." Many of these findings appeared in an amicus brief presented to the court in *New York State Rifle and Pistol Association v. Bruen*.

Signed by 17 professors of law, English history, and American history—including me—the brief demonstrates through a review of historical evidence that "neither English nor American history supports a broad Second Amendment right to carry firearms or other dangerous weapons in public based on a generic interest in self-defense."[4] It highlights 700 years of transatlantic weapons regulations, from the English tradition of restricting public carry through the American tradition of doing the same. The brief makes clear that limitations on the public carry of dangerous weapons, including firearms, are a centuries-old legal and cultural norm.

Early royal proclamations dating as far back as the 13th century regularly prohibited citizens going armed in public without special permission. In 1328, the Statute of Northampton banned the public carry of swords and daggers, open or concealed—this was before the invention of firearms—without express permission from the authorities.

As legal scholar and historian Geoffrey Robertson, an expert on the English Bill of Rights, put it, "There was never any absolute 'right' to carry guns. As the Bill of Rights (1689) made clear, this was only 'as allowed by law.'"[5]

An American Tradition of Limiting Public Carry

The English tradition of broad public carry restrictions continued across the Atlantic in the colonies. During periods of heightened risk of attack, some colonies required certain individuals to carry guns to church or when working in fields away from fortified or populated areas. This obligation was not understood, however, as establishing a right to carry firearms in public.

After the American Revolution, states continued to adopt regulations echoing the Statute of Northampton. Recent scholarship has uncovered that early-to-mid-19th-century firearms regulations varied considerably by jurisdiction and geography, but 19 states had restrictions for public carry on the books.[6] After the Civil War, as the lethality of firearms increased exponentially through technological advances, municipalities and states like Texas imposed even broader prohibitions on public carry.

By 1900, there was a legal consensus that states and localities generally had the authority to limit public carry. While the American approach to restricting public carry was fluid—varying across time and jurisdiction based on social and political changes—there is a consistent history and tradition of many American colonies, states, territories, and municipalities imposing broad prohibitions on carrying dangerous weapons in public, particularly without a specific need for self-defense.

An Invented Tradition?

So how did the 1689 English Bill of Rights, which never gave any absolute right to carry guns, turn into a key justification for that very right in the United States?

Patrick Charles, the author of the 2019 book *Armed in America: A History of Gun Rights from Colonial Militias to Concealed Carry*, argues that pro-gun advocates have selectively interpreted the historical record to justify a personal right to possess and carry weapons in public. Essentially, they invented a tradition.

"Invented traditions," a concept highlighted in the 1983 book *The Invention of Tradition*, edited by historians Eric Hobsbawm and Terence Ranger, are cultural practices that are thought to have emerged long ago but that are actually grounded in a much more recent past. A classic example is the Scottish tartan kilt, once believed to derive from the ancient garb of the Scottish Highlanders but actually invented in the 18th century by an Englishman.

The "individual right" to carry firearms in public seems to be another.

Notes

1. Jennifer Tucker, Barton C. Hacker, and Margaret Vining, *A Right to Bear Arms? The Contested Role of History in Contemporary Debates on the Second Amendment* (Washington, DC: Smithsonian Institution Scholarly Press, 2019).
2. Joyce Lee Malcolm, *To Keep and Bear Arms: The Origins of an Anglo-American Right* (Cambridge, MA: Harvard University Press, 1996).
3. Saul Cornell, *A Well-Regulated Militia: The Founding Fathers and the Origins of Gun Control in America* (New York: Oxford University Press, 2006).
4. *New York State Rifle and Pistol Association v. Bruen*. Brief for Amici Curiae Professors of History and Law in Support of Respondents, p. 1. https://www.supremecourt.gov/DocketPDF/20/20-843/193309 /20210921191001002_20-843%20bsacProfessorsOfHistoryAnd Law.pdf.
5. Quoted in Jack Taylor, "The Pursuit of Global Justice: Interview with Geoffrey Robertson," *Harvard Political Review*, May 9, 2020. https://harvardpolitics.com/interview-with-geoffrey-robertson-qc/.
6. Robert J. Spitzer, "Gun Law History in the United States and Second Amendment Rights," *Law and Contemporary Problems* 80 (2017): 55–83. https://scholarship.law.duke.edu/lcp/vol80/iss2/3.

Part II.

The Many Forms of Gun Violence

Part II critically examines the many forms of gun violence in America, because there is not one gun problem but multiple gun *problems* to address.[1] As I discussed in the preface to this book, suicide by firearm and community gun violence, which includes interpersonal conflicts and shootings related to gangs/groups or to underlying crime, are the most pressing in terms of overall gun deaths, but domestic violence, unintentional shootings, police-involved shootings, and mass shootings demand our attention and action too.

Researchers know the most about fatal shootings, the majority of which are suicides, and the least about nonfatal shootings, most of which are assaults, but there are also unintentional shootings, about 95% of which the victim survives.[2] This incomplete picture has to do with a lack of government investment in gun research. For over 20 years, the so-called Dickey Amendment to annual appropriations legislation prohibited the use of federal funds to advocate for gun control;[3] compounding the problem are simple data limitations (for instance, nonfatal shootings may or may not be treated in hospitals or reported, whereas every fatal shooting is documented by coroners, medical examiners, police departments, and other sources). As William Shakespeare famously wrote, "Truth will come to sight; murder cannot be hid long."[4]

That said, there is no federal government repository for police shootings, and the FBI tracks only the 400 to 500 homicides each year determined to be legally "justified," which is defined as "the killing of a felon by a peace officer in the line of duty."[5] Media and watchdog groups, by contrast, consistently document about 1,000 fatal police shootings annually,[6] which means that police officers' use of lethal force is far more common than the justified statistics suggest. One recent study extrapolated that more than half of all deaths from police violence from 1980 to 2018 were unreported in US government data.[7] Another analysis of fatal and nonfatal shootings from the country's 50 largest police departments found that for every person shot and killed between 2010 and 2016, officers shot at two more people who survived—meaning that the actual number of civilians shot by the police each year may be upward of 3,000.[8]

Guns underlie the tension between police and communities in America. Two-thirds of people shot and killed by police were found to be carrying firearms,[9] and in 1989 the US Supreme Court in *Graham v. Connor, 490 U.S. 386* (1989) deemed it constitutionally permissible for police to use deadly force in cases where they reasonably perceive imminent and grave harm. Killings excused under this reasonable belief standard may fall short of norms in other wealthy nations—for example, the European Convention on Human Rights permits only deadly force that is *absolutely necessary* to achieve a lawful purpose[10]—and the data show that a fatal police shooting typically occurs when there is a threat of violence to an officer or another citizen.[11] Higher rates of gun ownership and gun homicide combined make many police fearful for their lives and prone to misidentify or magnify threats—like cellphones or screwdrivers in the hands of suspects—especially if those suspects are Black and the officers are under mental stress.[12]

It seems obvious to say *no guns, no gun violence*, but the evidence is clear: where there are more guns, there are more gun deaths. And, as I noted in the preface to this book, this is true at both the state and country level. The United States is actually not more prone to violent crime than other developed countries. A landmark 1997 study by criminologists Franklin E. Zimring and Gordon Hawkins of the University of California, Berkeley, found that American crime is simply more *lethal*.[13] A New Yorker and a Londoner were equally likely to be robbed, for instance, but the New Yorker was 50 times more likely to be killed in the process. After controlling for other possible factors, Zimring and Hawkins found that the discrepancy came down to guns.

Guns turn domestic disputes deadly and public assaults into homicides. Research shows that a firearm in the home is a proximate risk factor for intimate partner homicide and familicide.[14] Likewise, felons often claim to carry guns for "protection," but guns intended to protect are liable to endanger. People who fire a gun in the commission of a crime overwhelmingly claim to have had no prior intent to fire one, suggesting that the presence of a gun alone greatly increases the chances of using it.[15] This is partly explained by what social psychologists call the "weapons effect," a concept derived from an experimental study that found heightened aggression among participants whenever a revolver was placed on the table in front of them.[16] A meta-analysis of 78 independent studies of the weapons effect from 1967 to 2017, involving 7,668 participants, concluded that merely having a weapon on hand increased aggression in people, particularly people already aroused.[17]

When guns are around, swearing and shoving can escalate into shooting. Likewise, suicide tends to be an impulsive act, and in a moment of crisis, people are more likely to attempt suicide if a firearm is available.[18] A suicide attempt is also far more likely to succeed with a firearm than by any other means.[19] This explains why a 2010 study of the Israeli army found that requiring soldiers to leave their weapons on base over the weekend, as opposed to taking them home, reduced the suicide rate among troops by almost 40%.[20] Importantly, the relationship between household gun ownership and suicide exists not just for the firearm owner but for all other household members. Firearm prevalence and unsafe storage practices (that is, storing firearms loaded and unlocked) are also associated with higher rates of unintentional firearm deaths, especially accidents involving children.[21]

Part II goes beyond the horrific headlines about mass shootings to provide a broader view of gun violence in America, examining how it affects different communities, how it causes children's injuries and deaths, and how criminals get their guns. There are chapters on accidental shootings and suicides written by leading public health researchers. Other chapters address gun use in policing, including racial disparities in officer-involved shootings and different protocols and solutions that police forces around the world use to reduce gun violence.

Recommended Further Reading

- *Ghettoside: A True Story of Murder in America* by Jill Leovy

- *Policing the Second Amendment* by Jennifer Carlson
- *The Condemnation of Blackness* by Khalil Gibran Muhammad
- *When Police Kill* by Franklin E. Zimring

Notes

1. *Reducing Gun Violence: What Works, and What Can Be Done Now* (Washington, DC: Police Executive Research Forum, 2019). https://www.policeforum.org/assets/reducinggunviolence.pdf.
2. Catherine Barber, Philip J. Cook, and Susan T. Parker, "The Emerging Infrastructure of US Firearms Injury Data," *Preventive Medicine* 165, Part A (December 2022): 107129. https://doi.org/10.1016/j.ypmed.2022.107129.
3. Allen Rostron, "The Dickey Amendment on Federal Funding for Research on Gun Violence: A Legal Dissection," *American Journal of Public Health* 108, no. 7 (2018): 865–67. https://doi.org/10.2105/ajph.2018.304450.
4. William Shakespeare, *The Merchant of Venice* (1600), act 2, scene 2.
5. "Expanded Homicide," FBI: Uniform Crime Reporting, 2019. https://ucr.fbi.gov/crime-in-the-u.s/2019/crime-in-the-u.s.-2019/topic-pages/expanded-homicide.
6. Frank Edwards, Michael H. Esposito, and Hedwig Lee, "Risk of Police-Involved Death by Race/Ethnicity and Place, United States, 2012–2018," *American Journal of Public Health* 108, no. 9 (2018): 1241–48. https://doi.org/10.2105/ajph.2018.304559.
7. GBD 2019 Police Violence US Subnational Collaborators, "Fatal Police Violence by Race and State in the USA, 1980–2019: A Network Meta-regression," *Lancet* 398, no. 10307 (2021): 1239–55. https://doi.org/10.1016/S0140-6736(21)01609-3.
8. "Get Data on Nonfatal and Fatal Police Shootings in the 50 Largest U.S. Police Departments," Vice News, December 10, 2017. https://news.vice.com/en_us/article/a3jjpa/nonfatal-police-shootings-data.
9. Joseph Cesario, David J. Johnson, and William Terrill, "Is There Evidence of Racial Disparity in Police Use of Deadly Force? Analyses of Officer-Involved Fatal Shootings in 2015–2016," *Social Psychological and Personality Science* 10, no. 5 (2018): 586–95. https://doi.org/10.1177/1948550618775108.
10. Franklin E. Zimring, *When Police Kill* (Cambridge, MA: Harvard University Press, 2017).
11. M. James Lozada and Justin Nix, "Validity of Details in Databases Logging Police Killings," *Lancet* 393, no. 10179 (2019): 1412–13. https://doi.org/10.1016/s0140-6736(18)33043-5.

12. Zimring, *When Police Kill.*

13. Franklin E. Zimring and Gordon Hawkins, *Crime Is Not the Problem: Lethal Violence in America* (New York: Oxford University Press, 1997).

14. Jacquelyn C. Campbell, Daniel Webster, Jane Koziol-McLain, Carolyn Block, Doris Campbell, Mary Ann Curry, Faye Gary, et al., "Risk Factors for Femicide in Abusive Relationships: Results from a Multisite Case Control Study," *American Journal of Public Health* 93, no. 7 (2003): 1089–97. https://doi.org/10.2105/ajph.93.7.1089; Neil Websdale, Kathleen Ferraro, and Steven D. Barger, "The Domestic Violence Fatality Review Clearinghouse: Introduction to a New National Data System with a Focus on Firearms," *Injury Epidemiology* 6, no. 1 (2019). https://doi.org/10.1186/s40621-019-0182-2.

15. James D. Wright and Peter H. Rossi, *The Armed Criminal in America: A Survey of Incarcerated Felons* (Washington DC: National Institute of Justice, 1985).

16. Leonard Berkowitz and Anthony Lepage, "Weapons as Aggression-Eliciting Stimuli," *Journal of Personality and Social Psychology* 7, no. 2, pt. 1 (1967): 202–7. https://doi.org/10.1037/h0025008.

17. Arlin J. Benjamin, Sven Kepes, and Brad J. Bushman, "Effects of Weapons on Aggressive Thoughts, Angry Feelings, Hostile Appraisals, and Aggressive Behavior: A Meta-analytic Review of the Weapons Effect Literature," *Personality and Social Psychology Review* 22, no. 4 (2017): 347–77. https://doi.org/10.1177/1088868317725419.

18. Deborah Azrael and Matthew Miller, "Reducing Suicide without Affecting Underlying Mental Health: Theoretical Underpinnings and a Review of the Evidence Base Linking the Availability of Lethal Means and Suicide," in *The International Handbook of Suicide Prevention: Research, Policy and Practice*, 2nd ed., ed. Rory O'Connor and Jane Pirkis (Chichester, UK: Wiley Blackwell, 2016), 637–62.

19. Matthew Miller, Deborah Azrael, and Catherine Barber, "Suicide Mortality in the United States: The Importance of Attending to Method in Understanding Population-Level Disparities in the Burden of Suicide," *Annual Review of Public Health* 33, no. 1 (2012): 393–408. https://doi.org/10.1146/annurev-publhealth-031811-124636.

20. Gad Lubin, Nomi Werbeloff, Demian Halperin, Mordechai Shmushkev-itch, Mark Weiser, and Haim Y. Knobler, "Decrease in Suicide Rates after a Change of Policy Reducing Access to Firearms in Adolescents: A Naturalistic Epidemiological Study," *Suicide and Life-Threatening Behavior* 40, no. 5 (2010): 421–24. https://doi.org/10.1521/suli.2010.40.5.421.

21. David C. Grossman, Beth A Mueller, Christine Riedy, M. Denise Dowd, Andres Villaveces, Janice Prodzinski, Jon Nakagawara, John Howard, Norman Thiersch, and Richard Harruff, "Gun Storage Practices and Risk of Youth Suicide and Unintentional Firearm Injuries." *Journal of the American Medical Association* 293, no. 6 (2005): 707–14. https://doi.org/10.1001/jama.293.6.707.

Chapter 11

Norway and Finland Have Similar Levels of Gun Ownership as the US but Far Less Gun Crime

PETER SQUIRES

AS THE INDEPENDENT US NONPROFIT ORGANIZATION the Children's Defense Fund has pointed out, gun violence was the leading cause of children's deaths in the United States in 2018. It reported that there were nine fatal shootings of children per day; that's one killing every two hours and 36 minutes. A minority of these killings involved school or mass shootings; the majority were killings of individual children and linked to routine crime and gang violence, and overwhelmingly these shootings resulted in the deaths of African American and minority children.

The United States stands as an extreme outlier among high-income countries: the number of children killed by guns is 36.5 times higher in the United States compared with many other high-income countries including Austria, Australia, Sweden, England, and Wales, according to an analysis published in 2018 by the *New England Journal of Medicine*.[1] International research has also proven conclusively that greater levels of gun ownership are closely associated with higher rates of gun violence.[2]

An audit of all 50 US states by the Democrat-leaning policy and research organization the Center for American Progress found a close correlation between the states with the toughest gun laws and states with the lowest gun crime rates. Meanwhile, international research has compared national gun laws, rates of firearm ownership, and gun violence rates. The results are striking, as the chart suggests.[3]

International Levels of Gun Crime

Interestingly, some European societies come close to US rates of gun ownership, in terms of gun-owning households per 100, but with hunting rifles and shotguns rather than handguns. Yet countries such as Finland and Norway are among the safest societies internationally with respect to gun violence.[4]

Researchers talk about "civilized" and "de-civilizing" gun cultures: cultures where gun ownership is associated with traditional values of respect and responsibility versus cultures where gun availability largely empowers the criminally minded and unstable, adding to the violence and chaos. High levels of social cohesion, low crime rates, and internationally high levels

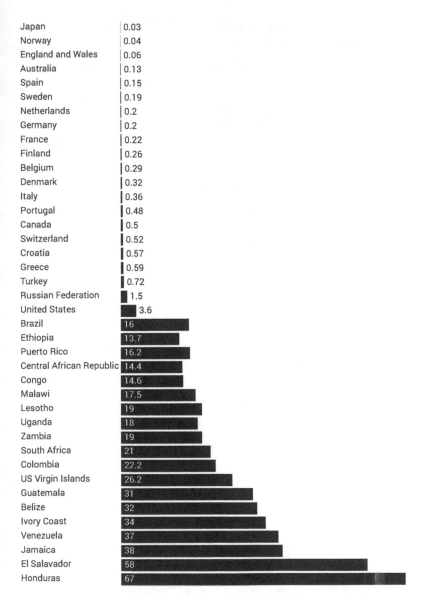

Japan	0.03
Norway	0.04
England and Wales	0.06
Australia	0.13
Spain	0.15
Sweden	0.19
Netherlands	0.2
Germany	0.2
France	0.22
Finland	0.26
Belgium	0.29
Denmark	0.32
Italy	0.36
Portugal	0.48
Canada	0.5
Switzerland	0.52
Croatia	0.57
Greece	0.59
Turkey	0.72
Russian Federation	1.5
United States	3.6
Brazil	16
Ethiopia	13.7
Puerto Rico	16.2
Central African Republic	14.4
Congo	14.6
Malawi	17.5
Lesotho	19
Uganda	18
Zambia	19
South Africa	21
Colombia	22.2
US Virgin Islands	26.2
Guatemala	31
Belize	32
Ivory Coast	34
Venezuela	37
Jamaica	38
El Salvador	58
Honduras	67

Rate of firearm homicide per 100,000 population. The United States has a higher rate of homicide by firearm than many other countries. *Compiled by Peter Squires, University of Brighton* of trust and confidence in police and social institutions do appear to reduce levels of gun homicide.

The flipside to this finding, however, is that countries with high rates of gun ownership such as Finland, Sweden, and Switzerland do have significantly higher rates of suicide committed with a gun. The United Kingdom and Japan, with some of the toughest gun laws in the world, always record the lowest rates of gun homicide, chiefly by virtue of their virtual prohibition of handguns, the criminal weapon of choice. The death tolls in many US mass shootings were much exacerbated by perpetrators using assault rifles, with larger magazines and rapid-fire capabilities far exceeding handguns.

Society as a Factor

There was a time when the only academic research on firearms took place in the United States, with a large part of it funded, directly and indirectly, by the influential US lobbying group the National Rifle Association. As a result of a new international focus in gun control research, wider questions came under the spotlight. Researchers started to focus less on the gun as an independent variable and instead began to address contexts and the different cultures of gun use. They also began to acknowledge, as criminologists have always known, that introducing new laws seldom changes anything on its own, as offenders break laws.

Gun researchers now focus increasingly on wider "gun control regimes," which have a big part to play in increasing or reducing levels of gun violence. These regimes include policing and criminal justice systems, systems of political accountability, welfare safety nets, comprehensive education provision, and cultures of trust and confidence. As the comparative chart suggests, the United States may be an exceptional gun culture compared with affluent democratic nations, yet its death rate by gun violence is dwarfed by those of many poorer countries with more internal conflict, such as South Africa, Jamaica, and Honduras.

Attempts in the United States to confront shootings—without restricting gun ownership in recent years—include scaling up surveillance, especially in schools where pupils, parents, and teachers form a network keeping a watchful eye on pupils. They look for signs of trouble and are able to sound the alarm. More ambitiously, The Violence Project has compiled evidence profiles, learning from past rampage shootings and trying to predict where individuals' behavior, social media engagement, and utterances might ring alarm bells.

It is significant that the immediate reaction to the 2022 Uvalde school massacre tended to focus on narrow questions of school security and an apparent delay in police intervention, rather than the many underlying factors that make the United States such a comparatively dangerous place for children.

Notes

1. Rebecca M. Cunningham, Maureen A. Walton, and Patrick M. Carter, "The Major Causes of Death in Children and Adolescents in the United States," *New England Journal of Medicine* 379, no. 25 (2018): 2468–75. https://doi.org/10.1056/nejmsr1804754.
2. Sripal Bangalore and Franz H. Messerli, "Gun Ownership and Firearm-Related Deaths," *American Journal of Medicine* 126, no. 10 (2013): 873–76. https://doi.org/10.1016/j.amjmed.2013.04.012; John N. van Kesteren, "Revisiting the Gun Ownership and Violence Link: A Multilevel Analysis of Victimization Survey Data," *British*

Journal of Criminology 54, no. 1 (2013): 53–72. https://doi.org/10
.1093/bjc/azt052.

3. Peter Squires, *Gun Crime in Global Contexts* (London: Routledge,
    2015)

4. David Pérez Esparza, Carlos A. Pérez Ricart, and Eugenio Weigend
    Vargas, eds., *Gun Trafficking and Violence: From the Global Network
    to the Local Security Challenge* (Basingstoke: Palgrave Macmillan,
    2022).

Chapter 12

The Facts on US Children and Teens Killed by Firearms

MARC A. ZIMMERMAN, PATRICK CARTER,
and REBECCA CUNNINGHAM

INJURY IS THE LEADING CAUSE OF DEATH for US children and adolescents, accounting for over 60% of all deaths in this age group. Many of these deaths occur by accident in everyday activities, like swimming in the backyard pool or taking a family car ride. But a disproportionate and disturbing number of these deaths in the United States occur as a result of firearms.

Rates of injury and death due to motor vehicle crashes have steadily declined over the last 20 years, but death and

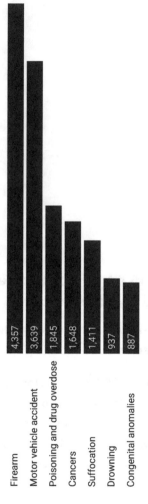

Firearm | 4,357
Motor vehicle accident | 3,639
Poisoning and drug overdose | 1,845
Cancers | 1,648
Suffocation | 1,411
Drowning | 937
Congenital anomalies | 887

Leading causes of child and adolescent death. Firearm-related injuries were the leading cause of death for children between 1 and 19 years old in 2020 in the United States. *Centers for Disease Control and Prevention* injury due to firearms have remained about the same over the same period. As of 2020, firearms are the leading cause of death among US children and adolescents. Firearm deaths occur at a rate over three times higher than drownings.

We have dedicated our careers to understanding violence and injury prevention, including how firearm injury and death happen and how they can be prevented.

Firearm Death Rates

Since 2013, fatal firearm injuries for children and teens have risen unabated.

Rates of death from firearms among youth aged 14 to 17 are now 43.3% higher than motor vehicle–related death rates. In the United States, children of middle and high school age are now more likely to die as the result of a firearm injury than from any other single cause of death. For Americans between the ages of 1 and 19, over 60% firearm-related deaths in 2020 were homicides. Another 29.7% of firearm-related deaths in this age group were suicides, while the rest resulted from unintentional injuries or undetermined causes.

What's more, the United States has had over 2,000 school shootings since 1970. The number of these tragic events has increased, with 48% of the total occurring in the nine years after the 2012 shooting at Sandy Hook Elementary School in Newtown, Connecticut. School shootings are a focus of media attention and raise awareness about the problem of firearm deaths among children and teens. But they remain the smallest proportion of deaths, accounting for only a few percent of all homicides among 5- to 18-year-olds.

Death Disparities

African American children and teens are over eight times more likely to die from firearm homicide than their white counterparts. Firearms have been the leading cause of death for African American youth for well over a decade.

Firearm suicide rates are highest among American Indian/Alaskan Native and white children and teens, compared with other racial/ethnic groups. Researchers have limited information on the reasons for these racial disparities.[1] We suspect they are likely a result of a number of factors, including socioeconomic status;[2] historical structural factors at the community and societal level such as economic disinvestment, racial segregation, and redlining; firearm availability and accessibility; and a lack of access to mental health services.

Although firearm-related rates of death for children and teens living in urban, suburban, and rural communities are similar, rural rates of firearm suicide are twice as high, and unintentional firearm injuries are four times higher than in urban communities. Meanwhile, firearm homicide rates are twice as high in urban than in rural communities.

A Uniquely American Epidemic

The United States stands out among high-income countries: more than 90% of all the firearm deaths among children and adolescents that occur in industrialized nations occur in this country.[3] Furthermore, the United States has more privately owned firearms—not including military firearms—than it does citizens.

In a Pew Research Center survey of US adults in 2021,[4] about 30% reported owning a firearm, and 41% reported living in a household with firearms. Two-thirds of households have more than one firearm, and almost one-third have five or more firearms. Firearms may have different purposes—deer hunting, shooting competitions, target practice, and so on—which may explain why so many households own more than one gun. Pew's data indicates that 54% of firearm owners with children under 18 living in the home have their firearms locked away.[5] This suggests to us that many young children and teens may have relatively easy access to unsecured firearms.

Digging into the Data

Research on firearms is limited in the United States. Government sponsorship of research focused on firearms has been virtually eliminated by an annual appropriations amendment, first added by Arkansas congressman Jay Dickey in 1996.

In recent years, academics, the National Institutes of Health (NIH), state governments, and private foundations have begun to renew the focus on research to prevent firearm injuries and fatalities. This is due largely to changes in public opinion about firearms as mass shootings keep occurring.

Established in 2017 with NIH funding, the Firearm Safety Among Children and Teens (FACTS) consortium is one of these efforts, with a focus on conducting research into firearm injury prevention while respecting legal and safe firearm ownership. We lead FACTS, in which academics from 14 universities around the country are involved. Members of this consortium are investigating the best methods for health care providers to counsel families about safe firearm storage, interventions to decrease the risk of firearm suicide among teens living in rural households, and the effect of state firearm laws on school shootings.

Just as other public health problems have turned to scientific evidence to prevent injuries, we feel that the United States should use evidence to inform policies that protect children and teens from gun violence. Much more can be done to address this vital public health problem.

Notes

1. Rebecca M. Cunningham, Maureen A. Walton, and Patrick M. Carter, "The Major Causes of Death in Children and Adolescents in the United States," *New England Journal of Medicine* 379, no. 25 (2018): 2468–75. https://doi.org/10.1056/nejmsr1804754.
2. Catherine Cubbin, Felicia LeClere, and Gordon Stephen Smith, "Socioeconomic Status and the Occurrence of Fatal and Nonfatal Injury in the United States," *American Journal of Public Health* 90, no. 1 (2000): 70–77. https://doi.org/10.2105/ajph.90.1.70.
3. Erin Grinshteyn and David Hemenway, "Violent Death Rates: The US Compared with Other High-Income OECD Countries, 2010," *American Journal of Medicine* 129, no. 3 (2016): 266–73. https://doi.org/10.1016/j.amjmed.2015.10.025.
4. Katherine Schaeffer, "Key Facts about Americans and Guns," Pew Research Center, September 13, 2021. https://www.pewresearch.org/fact-tank/2021/09/13/key-facts-about-americans-and-guns/.
5. Kim Parker, Juliana Menasce Horowitz, Ruth Igielnik, J. Baxter Oliphant, and Anna Brown, "America's Complex Relationship with Guns," Pew Research Center's Social & Demographic Trends Project, Pew Research Center, February 5, 2022. https://www.pewresearch.org/social-trends/2017/06/22/americas-complex-relationship-with-guns/.

Chapter 13

How Easy Access to Guns at Home Contributes to America's Youth Suicide Problem

MATTHEW MILLER and DEBORAH AZRAEL

SCHOOL SHOOTINGS IN THE UNITED STATES are national tragedies, and the toll they take in lives cut short and traumatized distinguishes the United States from other high-income countries. But there is another way that guns are killing American children, and in far greater numbers: suicide.

Between 2011 and 2020, the most recent decade for which data is available, 14,763 children ages 5–17 died by suicide in the United States, a rate of approximately four deaths every day.[1] Over 40% of these suicides involved a firearm. Suicide rates among children have trended upward over the past decade, as they have for adults. For children ages 5–17, suicides have climbed by around 50%, from 1,129 children in 2011 to 1,679 in 2020. That equates to a jump in the suicide rate from 2.1 deaths per 100,000 children in America to 3.1 per 100,000. Half of this increase—0.5 deaths per 100,000 children—was due to suicide by guns.

Although suicides affect all racial and ethnic groups in America, the suicide rate is highest among Native communities, while recent increases have disproportionately hit Asian/Pacific Islanders and Black communities.

The great majority of guns involved in youth suicides come from the victim's home or the home of a relative.[2] As scholars who have studied firearm violence and suicide prevention, we know that the exceptionally high rate of gun suicides by US youths is directly linked to the easy access many young people have to guns in and around the home.

Studies show that the risk of death by suicide is more than four times higher in households with firearms.[3] Consistent with this elevated risk in gun-owning households, studies that compared rates of suicide in different cities and across the 50 states show that, in places where there are more guns, there are more suicide deaths overall due to there being more firearm suicides.[4]

Reducing the Risk

The suicide risk associated with the presence of firearms in homes with children can be reduced, though not eliminated, by storing firearms locked, unloaded, and separated from ammunition.

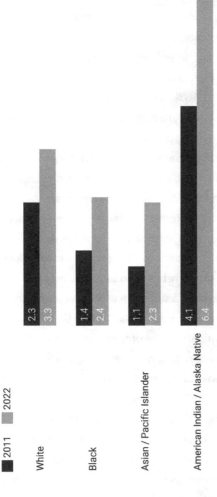

2011 **2022**

White
2.3
3.3

Black
1.4
2.4

Asian / Pacific Islander
1.1
2.3

American Indian / Alaska Native
4.1
6.4

Suicide rates of US children ages 5–17. The overall suicide rate for the age group has gone from 2.1 per 100,000 in 2011 to 3.1 per 100,000 in 2020—an increase of 50%. For Black, Asian/Pacific Islander, and American Indian/Alaska Native children, the increase has been steeper—71%, 109%, and 56%, respectively. *The Conversation, CC BY-ND. Data from the Centers for Disease Control and Prevention, National Center for Injury Prevention and Control*

Today, approximately 40% of US households with children contain firearms.[5] This means that around 30 million children under the age of 18 currently live in a home with at least one firearm, of whom roughly 5 million live in homes where at least one firearm is both loaded and unlocked.

A recent simulation study estimated that approximately 100 suicides a year among youths ages 5 to 19 could be prevented if the proportion of unlocked firearms in households with children were to decrease from 50%, as is roughly the percentage today, to 40%.[6] Research also suggests that when clinicians provide counseling to parents that emphasizes the importance of making guns inaccessible to their children, a substantial minority of parents improve storage by locking previously unloaded guns, especially when the counseling is supplemented with free firearm storage devices.[7]

For youths at particularly high risk of suicide who are seen in the emergency department for a mental or behavioral health crisis, training clinicians to counsel parents to reduce access to firearms—often referred to as "lethal means counseling"—can result in a substantial increase in the proportion of parents spoken to about firearm risk in the emergency department and, critically, in the proportion of parents who lock previously unloaded guns after returning home.

Storing guns unloaded and locked up does not necessarily, or in itself, prevent children's access to firearms. The evidence that having a firearm in a child's home substantially increases that child's risk of death by suicide is overwhelming. Locking and unloading all household firearms and storing firearms separately from ammunition substantially mitigates, but does not eliminate, this risk.

In a recent nationally representative study of parents and their adolescent children, all of whom lived in a home with firearms, more than one-third of adolescents reported being able to independently access a loaded household firearm in less than five minutes, and half said they could do so within an hour.[8] Although this proportion was lower in homes where parents locked away all their guns, even here one-quarter of children said they were able to access and fire a loaded gun within five minutes.

Meanwhile, only 3 in 10 parents acknowledged that their child could independently access a household firearm, suggesting that many either do not fully appreciate the risk that access to firearms confers or do not believe that the risk pertains to their child. Moreover, nearly 1 in 4 children whose parents indicated that their child could not independently access a household gun reported being able to access and fire a gun in their home within five minutes.

We believe that rigorously evaluating how to effectively communicate the importance of making household firearms inaccessible to children is an urgently needed next step if we are to prevent the loss of so many young lives year after year to suicide.

Notes

1. "WISQARS™—Web-Based Injury Statistics Query and Reporting System," Centers for Disease Control and Prevention, December 2, 2021. https://www.cdc.gov/injury/wisqars/.
2. David C. Grossman, Donald T. Reay, and Stephanie A. Baker, "Self-Inflicted and Unintentional Firearm Injuries among Children and Adolescents," *Archives of Pediatrics & Adolescent Medicine* 153, no. 8 (1999): 875–78. https://doi.org/10.1001/archpedi.153.8.875; Catherine Barber, Deborah Azrael, Matthew Miller, and David Hemenway, "Who Owned the Gun in Firearm Suicides of Men, Women,

and Youth in Five US States?," *Preventive Medicine*, 2022, 107066. https://doi.org/10.1016/j.ypmed.2022.107066.

3. David A. Brent, Joshua A. Perper, Grace Moritz, Marianne Baugher, Joy Schweers, and Claudia Roth, "Firearms and Adolescent Suicide A Community Case- Control Study," *American Journal of Diseases of Children* 147, no. 10 (1993): 1066–71. https://doi.org/10.1001/archpedi.1993.02160340052013.

4. Mathew Miller, Deborah Azrael, and David Hemenway, "Firearm Availability and Unintentional Firearm Deaths, Suicide, and Homicide among 5–14 Year Olds," *Journal of Trauma and Acute Care Surgery* 52, no. 2 (2002): 267–75. https://doi.org/10.1097/00005373-200202000-00011.

5. Matthew Miller and Deborah Azrael, "Firearm Storage in US Households with Children," *JAMA Network Open* 5, no. 2 (2022). https://doi.org/10.1001/jamanetworkopen.2021.48823.

6. Michael C. Monuteaux, Deborah Azrael, and Matthew Miller, "Association of Increased Safe Household Firearm Storage with Firearm Suicide and Unintentional Death among US Youths," *JAMA Pediatrics* 173, no. 7 (2019): 657–62. https://doi.org/10.1001/jamapediatrics.2019.1078.

7. Matthew Miller, Carmel Salhi, Catherine Barber, Deborah Azrael, Elizabeth Beatriz, John Berrigan, Sara Brandspigel, Marian E. Betz, and Carol Runyan, "Changes in Firearm and Medication Storage Practices in Homes of Youths at Risk for Suicide: Results of the SAFETY Study, a Clustered, Emergency Department–Based, Multisite, Stepped-Wedge Trial," *Annals of Emergency Medicine* 76, no. 2 (2020): 194–205. https://doi.org/10.1016/j.annemergmed.2020.02.007.

8. Carmel Salhi, Deborah Azrael, and Matthew Miller, "Parent and Adolescent Reports of Adolescent Access to Household Firearms in the United States," *JAMA Network Open* 4, no. 3 (2021). https://doi.org/10.1001/jamanetworkopen.2021.0989.

Chapter 14

How Dangerous People Get Their Weapons in America

PHILIP J. COOK

INVARIABLY TWO QUESTIONS ARISE in the wake of mass shootings: How do dangerous people get their guns? And what should the police and courts be doing to make those transactions more difficult?

Gun violence is becoming almost routine in many American neighborhoods. The guns carried and misused by youths, gang members, and active criminals are more likely than not obtained by transactions that violate federal or state law.[1] And, as I've learned from my decades of researching the

Weapons used in the attack in San Bernardino in 2015. *Photo by San Bernardino County Sheriff's Department via Getty Images*

topic, rarely do the people who provide these guns to the eventual shooters face any legal consequences.

How can this illicit market be policed more effectively?

Undocumented and Unregulated Transactions

The vast majority of gun owners say they obtained their weapons in transactions that are documented and for the most part legal.

When asked where and how they acquired their most recent firearm in a 2015 survey, about 64% of a cross-section of American gun owners reported buying it from a gun store, where the clerk would have conducted a background check and documented the transfer in a permanent record required by federal law.[2] Another 14% were transferred their guns in some other way but still underwent a background check. The remaining 22% said they got their guns without a background check.

The same is not true for criminals, however; most of whom obtain their guns illegally.

A transaction can be illegal for several reasons, but of particular interest are transactions that involve disqualified individuals—those banned from purchase or possession of a firearm owing to their criminal record, age, adjudicated mental illness, illegal alien status, or some other reason. Convicted felons, teenagers, and other people who are legally barred from possession would ordinarily be blocked from purchasing a gun from a gun store because they would fail the background check or lack the permit or license required by some states.

Anyone providing the gun in such transactions would be culpable if he or she had reason to know that the buyer was disqualified, was acting as a straw purchaser, or had violated state regulation pertaining to such private transactions.

The importance of the informal (undocumented) market in supplying criminals is suggested by the results of inmate surveys and data gleaned from guns confiscated by the police. A 2015 national survey of inmates in state prisons found that just 10% of youthful (ages 18–40) male respondents who admitted to having a gun at the time of their arrest had obtained it from a gun store. The other 90% had obtained them through a variety of off-the-book means, for example, as gifts or sharing arrangements with fellow gang members.[3]

Similarly, a study of how Chicago gang members get their guns found that only a trivial percentage obtained them by direct purchase from a store.[4] To the extent that gun dealers

Also important are "street" sources, such as gang members and drug dealers, which may result from a prior relationship. Thus, social networks play an important role in facilitating transactions, and an individual (such as a gang member) who tends to hang out with people who have guns will find it relatively easy to obtain one.

Effective policing of the underground gun market could help to separate guns from everyday violent crime. Currently, those who provide guns to offenders seldom face any legal consequences, and changing that situation will require additional resources to penetrate the social networks of gun offenders. Needless to say, that effort won't be cheap or easy and will require that both the police and the courts have the necessary authority and give this sort of gun enforcement high priority.

Notes

1. Philip J. Cook, Susan T. Parker, and Harold A. Pollack, "Sources of Guns to Dangerous People: What We Learn by Asking Them," *Preventive Medicine* 79 (2015): 28–36. https://doi.org/10.1016/j.ypmed.2015.04 .021.
2. Matthew Miller, Lisa Hepburn, and Deborah Azrael, "Firearm Acquisition without Background Checks," *Annals of Internal Medicine* 166, no. 4 (2017): 233–39. https://doi.org/10.7326/m16-1590.
3. Cook, Parker, and Pollack, "Sources of Guns to Dangerous People."
4. Philip J. Cook, Richard J. Harris, Jens Ludwig, and Harold A. Pollack, "Some Sources of Crime Guns in Chicago: Dirty Dealers, Straw Purchasers, and Traffickers," *Journal of Criminal Law and Criminology* 104, no. 4 (2014): 717–60. https://scholarlycommons.law.northwestern.edu/jclc /vol104/iss4/2.
5. Philip J. Cook and Kristin A. Goss, *The Gun Debate: What Everyone Needs to Know* (New York: Oxford University Press, 2014).
6. Philip J. Cook, Jens Ludwig, Sudhir Venkatesh, and Anthony A. Braga, "Underground Gun Markets," *Economic Journal* 117, no. 524 (2007). https://doi.org/10.1111/j.1468-0297.2007.02098.x.

Chapter 15

Gun Violence in the US Kills More Black People and Urban Dwellers

MOLLY PAHN, ANITA KNOPOV, and MICHAEL SIEGEL

ON NOVEMBER 5, 2017, just 35 days after the deadly Las Vegas shooting, a man walked into a church in a small Texas town and murdered 26 people with an assault rifle. The coverage dominated the news. But the day before, even more people—43—were shot to death in cities and towns around the country. And nobody really seemed to notice.

As of 2020, shootings killed more than 45,000 Americans each year, and every day, gun violence causes about 123 deaths and more than 250 injuries.[1] Unlike terrorist acts, the mundane gun violence that impacts our communities is

A man lowers a flag to half-staff near the First Baptist Church of Sutherland Springs, where a man opened fire inside the church in November 2017. *AP Photo / Eric Gay*

accepted as a part of life. Of all firearm homicides in 23 high-income countries, 82% occur in the United States.[2] An American is 25 times more likely to be fatally shot than a resident of other high-income nations.

As public health scholars who study firearm violence, we believe that our country is unique in its acceptance of gun violence. Although death by firearms in America is a public health crisis, it is a crisis that legislators accept as a societal norm. Some have suggested this is due to the fact that Blacks and not whites are predominantly the victims, and our data support this striking disparity.

Urban and Racial Disparities

Within the United States, the odds of dying from firearm homicide are much higher for Americans who reside in cities.

Twenty percent of all firearm homicides in the United States occur in the country's 25 largest cities, even though they contain just over one-tenth of the US population. Data from the Centers for Disease Control and Prevention show that of the more than 19,000 firearm homicides in 2020, 89% occurred in urban areas.[3]

There is even more to the story: CDC data also show that within our nation's cities, Black Americans are, on average, eight times more likely to be killed by firearms than are white Americans. The rate of death by gun homicide for Black people exceeds those for white people in all 50 states, but there is great variation in the magnitude of this disparity. In 2015, a Black person living in Wisconsin was 26 times more likely to be fatally shot than a white person living in that state. At the same time, a Black person in Arizona was "only" 3.2 times more likely than a white person to be killed with a gun. The combination of being Black and living in an urban area is even more deadly. In 2015 the Black homicide rate for urban areas in Missouri was higher than the total death rate from any cause in New York State.

These differences across states occur primarily because the gap between levels of disadvantage among white and Black Americans differs sharply by state. For example, Wisconsin—the state with the highest disparity between Black and white firearm homicide rates—has the second-highest gap of any state between Black and white incarceration rates,[4] and it has the second-highest gap between Black and white unemployment rates.[5] Racial disparities in advantage translate into racial disparities in firearm violence victimization.

Americans are 128 times more likely to be killed in every-day gun violence than by any act of international terrorism.

And a Black person living in an urban area is almost 500 times more likely to be killed by everyday gun violence than by terrorism. From a public health perspective, efforts to combat firearm violence need to be every bit as strong as those to fight terrorism.

The first step in treating the epidemic of firearm violence is declaring that the everyday gun violence devastating the nation is unacceptable. Mass shootings and terrorist attacks should not be the only incidents of violence that awaken Americans to threats to our freedom and that spur politicians to action.

Notes

1. "WISQARS™—Web-Based Injury Statistics Query and Reporting System," Centers for Disease Control and Prevention, December 2, 2021. https://www.cdc.gov/injury/wisqars/.
2. Erin Grinshteyn and David Hemenway, "Violent Death Rates: The US Compared with Other High-Income OECD Countries, 2010," *American Journal of Medicine* 129, no. 3 (2016): 266–73. https://doi.org/10.1016/j.amjmed.2015.10.025.
3. "WISQARS™," Centers for Disease Control and Prevention.
4. "U.S. Incarceration Rates by Race and Ethnicity, 2010," Prison Policy Initiative, accessed October 4, 2022. https://www.prisonpolicy.org/graphs/raceinc.html.
5. Janelle Jones, "State Unemployment Rates by Race and Ethnicity at the End of 2016 Show Progress but Not Yet Full Recovery," Economic Policy Institute, accessed October 4, 2022. https://www.epi.org/publication/state-unemployment-rates-by-race-and-ethnicity-at-the-end-of-2016-show-progress-but-not-yet-full-recovery/.

Chapter 16

Why Do American Cops Kill So Many Compared to European Cops?

PAUL HIRSCHFIELD

CHICAGO POLICE OFFICER JASON VAN DYKE was charged with first-degree murder on November 24, 2015, in the death of Laquan McDonald. A video released by police shows Van Dyke shooting the teenager 16 times. Van Dyke is an extreme example of a pattern of unnecessary deadly force used by US police. American police kill a few people each day, making them far more deadly than police in Europe.[1]

Historical rates of fatal police shootings in Europe suggest that American police in 2014 were 18 times more lethal than Danish police and 100 times more lethal than

Finnish police; plus they killed significantly more frequently than police in France, Sweden, and other European countries. In another analysis looking at the period from 2018 to 2021, I found that rates of fatal police violence in the United States were 10 to 15 higher than in Belgium, France, England and Wales, and the Netherlands.

As a scholar of sociology and criminal justice, I set out to understand why rates of police lethality in the United States are so much higher than rates in Europe.[2]

More Guns and Aggression

Such massive disparities defy a simple explanation, but America's gun culture is clearly an important factor. Unlike European nations, most US states make it easy for adults to purchase handguns for self-defense and to keep them handy at nearly all times. Acquiring guns illegally in the United States is not much harder.

American police are primed to expect guns. About 58% of deadly force victims in 2022 were allegedly armed with actual, toy, or replica guns. The specter of gun violence may make police prone to misidentifying or magnifying threats like cell phones and screwdrivers. It makes American policing more dangerous and combat-oriented. It also fosters police cultures that emphasize bravery and aggression.

Americans armed with less deadly weapons like knives—and even those known to be unarmed—are also more likely to be killed by police. Wielders of bladed or blunt objects made up only about 21% of deadly force victims in the United States in 2021. Yet the rates of these deaths alone exceed total known deadly force rates in any European country.

Knife violence is a big problem in England, yet British police fatally shot only six people wielding bladed weapons from 2008 to mid-2022. By contrast, US police, according to the *Washington Post*, fatally shot 1,292 such people from 2015 to mid-2022.[3]

Racism helps explain why African Americans and Native Americans are particularly vulnerable to police violence.[4] Racism, along with a prevailing American ideology of individualism and limited government, partly accounts for why white citizens and legislators give more support to controversial police shooters and aggressive police tactics and less to criminals and poor people.[5]

Not Racism Alone

But racism alone can't explain why non-Latino white Americans are many times more likely to die by police gunfire than Europeans. And racism alone doesn't explain why states like Montana, West Virginia, and Wyoming—where both perpetrators and victims of deadly force are almost always white—exhibit relatively high rates of police lethality.

An explanation may be found in a key distinguishing characteristic of American policing: its localism. Each of America's 15,500 municipal and county departments is responsible for screening applicants, imposing discipline, and training officers when a new weapon like the Taser is adopted. Some under-resourced departments may perform some of these critical tasks poorly. To make matters worse, cash-strapped local governments may see tickets, fines, impounding fees, and asset forfeitures as revenue sources and push for more involuntary police encounters.

Dangers in Small Places

In an article I published in 2015, I noted that more than a quarter of deadly force victims were killed in towns with fewer than 25,000 people, despite the fact that only 17% of the US population lives in such towns.

By contrast, as a rule, towns and cities in Europe do not finance their own police forces. The municipal police that do exist are sometimes unarmed and not routinely involved in apprehending felons and fugitives. As a result, most armed police forces that citizens encounter in Europe are provincial (the counterpart to state police in the United States), regional (Swiss cantons), or national. Centralized policing makes it possible to train and judge all armed officers according to the same use-of-force guidelines. It also facilitates the rapid translation of insights about deadly force prevention into enforceable national mandates.

In the United States, the only truly national behavioral mandates for using deadly force are set by the US Supreme Court, which in 1989 deemed it constitutionally permissible for police to use deadly force when they "reasonably" perceive imminent and grave harm. State laws regulating deadly force—in the 38 states where they exist—are almost always as permissive as Supreme Court precedent allows, or more so.

A Different Standard

By contrast, national standards in most European countries conform to the European Convention on Human Rights, which impels its 47 signatories to permit deadly force only when it is "absolutely necessary" to achieve a lawful purpose. Killings excused under America's "reasonable belief" standards often violate Europe's "absolute necessity" standards.

For example, in the high-profile 2014 shooting in Ferguson, Missouri, where former police officer Darren Wilson fatally shot Michael Brown, Wilson's unfounded fear that Brown was armed would likely not have absolved him in Europe. This is also the case when police officers shot a mentally ill Dallas man in 2015 out of fear he would stab them with the screwdriver in his hand.

In Europe, killing is considered unnecessary if alternatives exist. For example, national guidelines in Spain would have prescribed that Wilson incrementally pursue verbal warnings, warning shots, and shots at nonvital parts of the body before resorting to deadly force. Wilson's six shots that hit Brown would likely be deemed disproportionate to the threat that Brown, unarmed and wounded, allegedly posed. Denmark, Germany, the Netherlands, Spain, Sweden, and Switzerland prescribe or encourage warning and leg shots.

In the United States, only eight states require verbal warnings (when possible), while warning and leg shots are typically prohibited. In contrast, Finland and Norway require, in certain controlled situations, that police obtain permission from a superior officer before shooting anyone.

Not only do centralized standards in Europe make it easier to restrict police behavior, but centralized training centers also efficiently teach police officers how to avoid using deadly weapons. Sweden, Norway, and Finland, for example, require that police attend a national academy—essentially a college for cops—for three years. In Norway, 4,264 applicants competed for 400 spots in 2021. Three years' training affords police ample time to learn how better to understand, communicate with, and calm distraught individuals.

By contrast, in 2013, US police academies provided an average of 21 weeks of classroom instruction.[6] Under such time constraints, the average recruit in the United States spends almost 20 times as many hours of training in using force than in conflict de-escalation. Most states require fewer than eight hours of crisis intervention training.

Desperate and potentially dangerous people in Europe are, therefore, more likely than their American counterparts to encounter well-educated and restrained police officers.

Explanations of elevated police lethality in the United States should focus on more than police policy and behavior, however. The charged encounters that give rise to deadly force by American police also result from weak gun controls, social and economic deprivation and injustice, inadequate mental health care, and harsh terms of imprisonment for convicts.

Future research should examine not only whether American police behave differently from European police but also whether more generous, supportive, and therapeutic policies in European countries ensure that fewer people become desperate enough to summon, provoke, or resist their less dangerous police.

Notes

1. "2021 Police Violence Report," Mapping Police Violence, accessed October 4, 2022. https://policeviolencereport.org/.
2. Paul J. Hirschfield, "Lethal Policing: Making Sense of American Exceptionalism," *Sociological Forum* 30, no. 4 (2015): 1109–17. https://doi.org/10.1111/socf.12200.

3. "Fatal Force: Police Shootings Database," *Washington Post*, January 22, 2020. https://www.washingtonpost.com/graphics/investigations/police -shootings-database/.

4. Brad W. Smith and Malcolm D. Holmes, "Police Use of Excessive Force in Minority Communities: A Test of the Minority Threat, Place, and Community Accountability Hypotheses," *Social Problems* 61, no. 1 (2014): 83–104. https://doi.org/10.1525/sp.2013.12056.

5. Michael T. Costelloe, Ted G. Chiricos, and Marc Gertz, "Punitive Attitudes toward Criminals: Exploring the Relevance of Crime Salience and Economic Insecurity," *Punishment and Society* 11, no. 1 (2009): 25–49. https://doi.org/10.1177/1462474508098131.

6. Brian A. Reaves, "State and Local Law Enforcement Training Academies, 2013 (Re-issue)," US Department of Justice Office of Justice Programs, 2016. https://www.ojp.gov/ncjrs/virtual-library /abstracts/state-and-local-law-enforcement-training-academies -2013-re-issue.

Chapter 17

Police Are More Likely to Kill Men and Women of Color

FRANK EDWARDS

MICHAEL BROWN WAS KILLED BY POLICE in Ferguson, Missouri, in 2014. Since then, US police have killed more than 6,000 people. Researchers and activists know about these deaths only because journalists do what the federal government has not: collect detailed information on police-involved fatalities.[1] Because the government has not collected systematic data on police killings, the public doesn't have definitive numbers that, once interpreted, will show how likely people are to be killed by police.

In a study published on August 5, 2019, sociologist Hedwig Lee, social scientist Michael Esposito, and I used unofficial data to show how the risk of dying at the hands of police varies by age, sex, and race or ethnicity in the United States.[2]

Measuring Police Violence

My colleagues and I relied on data provided by Fatal Encounters, a data set maintained by journalist and former newspaper editor D. Brian Burghart. Burghart conducts systematic searches of online news, social media, and public records to provide a close-to-comprehensive and up-to-date archive of police killings. The database documents about 1,000 to 1,200 deaths a year since 2000.

Police are responsible for a very small share of deaths overall—about 0.05% of all male deaths and 0.003% of all female deaths—yet police are responsible for a substantial proportion of all deaths of young people. For young men, police violence ranked as the sixth leading cause of death between 2015 and 2019, as classified by the National Vital Statistics System, after accidents, which include drug overdoses, motor vehicle accidents, and other accidental deaths; suicides; other homicides; heart disease; and cancer. In that period, police were responsible for 1.6% of all deaths of Black men between the ages of 20 and 24.

Our analysis found that about 52 of every 100,000 men and boys, and about 3 of every 100,000 women and girls, will be killed by police.

For comparison, among the general population, the lifetime risk of a person being killed in a motor vehicle accident is about 970 per 100,000, and the lifetime risk of

	Men	Women
African American	96.0	3.7
American Indian / Alaska Native	54.7	4.2
Latinx	52.7	2.2
Total	51.7	2.7
White	39.1	2.7
Asian / Pacific Islander	14.4	0.6

Lifetime risk of being killed by the police. Between 2013 and 2018, about 51.7 in 100,000 men and 2.7 in 100,000 women were killed by police in the United States. *The Conversation, CC BY–ND. Data from the* Proceedings of the National Academy of Sciences of the United States of America *(2019)*

being killed by a firearm in a homicide is about 350 per 100,000.

People who are American Indian / Alaska Native, Black, or Latino are more likely to be killed by police than people who are white. About 1 in 1,000 Black men and boys are killed by police. For American Indian and Alaska Native men and boys, the lifetime risk of being killed by police is about 1 in 2,000.

Young men and women are at greater risk of being killed by police. Between the ages of 25 and 29, about 2 of every 100,000 young men in the United States are killed by police, while about 0.1 of every 100,000 women are killed by police. That risk is greatest for young men and women of color.

Policy Implications

Based on our results, I believe that the United States urgently needs to reduce the rates at which police kill civilians and to reduce inequalities in the exposure of men and women to police violence.

In my view, some commonsense interventions would likely drive down rates of death. For example, investment in community-based mental health and social services would reduce the use of police, jails, and prisons as catch-all responses to social problems.[3] Moreover, accountability and effective reform demand better data. High-quality data will provide policy makers and activists with better sets of tools to hold police departments accountable for reducing the number of deaths caused by their officers.

Notes

1. Brian Karl Finch, Audrey Beck, D. Brian Burghart, Richard Johnson, David Klinger, and Kyla Thomas, "Using Crowd-Sourced Data to Explore Police-Related-Deaths in the United States (2000–2017): The Case of Fatal Encounters," *Journal of Open Health Data* 6, no. 1 (2019). https://doi.org/10.5334/ohd.30.
2. Frank Edwards, Hedwig Lee, and Michael Esposito, "Risk of Being Killed by Police Use of Force in the United States by Age, Race–Ethnicity, and Sex," *Proceedings of the National Academy of Sciences* 116, no. 34 (2019): 16793–98. https://doi.org/10.1073/pnas.1821204116.
3. Alex S. Vitale, *The End of Policing* (London: Verso, 2017); Ruth Wilson Gilmore, *Golden Gulag: Prisons, Surplus, Crisis, and Opposition in Globalizing California* (Berkeley: University of California Press, 2007).

Chapter 18

Don't Shoot

When Dallas Police Draw Their Guns,
They Usually Choose Not to Fire

ANDREW P. WHEELER

THE PUBLIC HAS A RIGHT TO QUESTION whether police are
biased when they shoot and kill unarmed people of color. To
do this, the public needs data about when police shootings
occur, but that kind of data isn't collected nationally. That's
why several news outlets, such as the *Washington Post* and
the *Guardian*, have begun collecting news and crowd-sourced
data on police shootings and killings.

Analyses of these data by researchers have suggested
that African Americans are more frequently shot by police

than whites.[1] Researchers have inferred that the difference is likely due to what's called implicit racial bias. This kind of bias exists outside our conscious awareness and so may impact our decisions without our realizing it.

Such databases have a fundamental limitation, however. They only collect negative outcomes—when an officer-involved shooting occurs—and omit cases when officers choose not to shoot at a suspect.

Based on a study of data from 2013 through 2016 from the Dallas Police Department—data not only on when Dallas police shot but also when they didn't shoot—my colleagues and I have suggestions for police departments, policy makers, and the public on how to determine if there is racial bias in officer-involved shootings, as well as how to identify factors to reduce excessive shootings.

What Influences the Decision to Shoot?

My colleagues and I are criminologists, and we wanted to understand whether a suspect's race influenced an officer's decision to shoot. So we examined data from the Dallas Police Department from 2013 through 2016.[2] Officers in Dallas are required to submit a report when they draw their firearm and point it at a suspect but decide not to fire. We compared these instances with the 56 times officers decided to shoot. This comparison helped us identify aspects of the situation and suspects that might explain why officers decide not to pull the trigger, including the race of the suspect.

We found that officers were less likely to shoot at African American suspects compared with white suspects. In our sample, white suspects were shot at 4% of the time (11 out of 250), Latinos 5% of the time (22 out of 476), and African

Americans were shot at 2% of the time (23 out of 1,005). The differences in the suspect's race were not significant. This suggests that race is not a factor in an officer's decision to shoot and that officers are not racially biased in their decision to shoot African Americans.

It also suggests that factors other than race have a much greater influence on when officers decide to shoot at a suspect.

When suspects were armed with a firearm, officers fired at the suspect in 23% of the cases across all races, compared with only 1% when they were unarmed. When an officer was injured, they fired at a suspect 11% of the time, compared with only 3% of the time when they were not injured. Using regression analysis that controlled for multiple factors, we found that a suspect being armed and an officer being injured were the factors with the strongest relationship to whether an officer decided to shoot.

Our finding that African Americans were less likely to be shot is possibly the result of officers being more likely to draw their firearm when the suspect is a minority, even if the situation does not call for it. That would be consistent with our Dallas data showing that African Americans were much more likely to have a firearm pointed at them.

Another potential explanation, though, is simply geographic. That is, minorities are more likely to come into contact with police because of the way crime rates and police resources are currently distributed. Crimes often repeatedly take place in the same neighborhoods, so police departments frequently channel extra resources to those particular locations. Minorities tend to disproportionately make up the resident population of those locations.[3] This approach to policing could explain why African Americans have an officer point a gun at them more frequently.

Policy Implications

To be clear, existing databases of police shootings can demonstrate the magnitude of racial disparity in police shootings. African Americans represent a higher proportion of officer-involved shootings compared with the proportion of African Americans living in the United States. However, our findings shed light on why this alone is not enough to show that police shootings are a result of racial bias.

To assess whether police officers are racially biased in their use of deadly force, researchers need to collect information on when officers choose not to use deadly force, too. Instead of constructing a database consisting only of officer-involved shootings, all levels of use of force—including shootings—could be regularly collected and made public by police agencies. That would allow for assessments of racial bias at all levels of decision-making, such as when using a Taser or simply an officer's hands.

In additional research, we found that officers with a greater number of complaints of mistreatment made by the public were more likely to shoot at suspects.[4] This suggests that identifying officers who behave badly could help reduce the number of police shootings, at least in Dallas.

Police departments may be more likely to prevent excessive use of force against the public either through better training of such officers or, in more serious cases, firing an officer.

Limitations

Our findings have important limitations. Our study examined officer-involved shootings in only one city: Dallas. We cannot make the generalization that all police in the United States are unbiased in their decision-making based on findings for one police department.

Also, our study looked at only one decision—when officers decide whether to shoot after they've drawn their weapons. Our research cannot show whether officers are racially biased in other instances. For example, we did not look at bias when officers use other types of force or when they decide to draw their gun in the first place.

Identifying racial bias in the decision to shoot is important, but lower levels of force are much more regular occurrences. Monitoring their use will have more power to identify problem behavior by individual officers or disparity in the use of force toward any particular racial group.

Other researchers have used the Dallas Police Department's use-of-force database to examine lesser levels of force and have come to similar conclusions.[5] These conclusions and ours depend, of course, on officers reliably reporting their behavior and on departments disseminating that information to the public.

Notes

1. Justin Nix, Bradley A. Campbell, Edward H. Byers, and Geoffrey P. Alpert, "A Bird's Eye View of Civilians Killed by Police in 2015: Further Evidence of Implicit Bias," *Criminology & Public Policy* 16, no. 1 (2017): 309–40. https://doi.org/10.1111/1745-9133.12269.
2. Andrew P. Wheeler, Scott W. Phillips, John L. Worrall, and Stephen A. Bishopp, "What Factors Influence an Officer's Decision to Shoot? The Promise and Limitations of Using Public Data," *Justice Research*

and Policy 18, no. 1 (2017): 48–76. https://doi.org/10.1177
/1525107118759900.

3. Tammy Rinehart Kochel, "Constructing Hot Spots Policing: Unexamined Consequences for Disadvantaged Populations and for Police Legitimacy," *Criminal Justice Policy Review* 22, no. 3 (2010): 350–74. https://doi.org/10.1177/0887403410376233.

4. John L. Worrall, Stephen A. Bishopp, Scott C. Zinser, Andrew P. Wheeler, and Scott W. Phillips, "Exploring Bias in Police Shooting Decisions with Real Shoot/Don't Shoot Cases," *Crime & Delinquency* 64, no. 9 (2018): 1171–92. https://doi.org/10.1177/0011128718756038.

5. Katelyn K. Jetelina, Wesley G. Jennings, Stephen A. Bishopp, Alex R. Piquero, and Jennifer M. Reingle Gonzalez, "Dissecting the Complexities of the Relationship between Police Officer–Civilian Race/Ethnicity Dyads and Less-Than-Lethal Use of Force," *American Journal of Public Health* 107, no. 7 (2017): 1164–70. https://doi.org/10.2105/ajph.2017 .303807.

Chapter 19

Are Mass Shootings an American Epidemic?

LACEY WALLACE

MASS SHOOTINGS ARE TRAUMATIC FOR VICTIMS, families, communities, and the nation as a whole. But despite the despair, they are actually uncommon incidents that account for just 0.2% of firearm deaths in the United States each year.

Killings are not the only kind of gun violence and are in fact a relative rarity when compared with other forms of gun violence in the United States. According to the National Crime Victimization Survey, 470,840 people were victims of crimes that involved a firearm in 2018, and in 2019, 481,950. Each person is counted separately, even if several of them were part of the same incident, and this tally does not require that the gun be fired or anyone killed.

When it comes to people killed by firearms, police data reported to the FBI estimates that guns were used in 10,258 of the 13,927 homicides that occurred in 2019.

That's much higher than even the uppermost count of mass shootings in 2019: the 417 deaths recorded by the Gun Violence Archive. That group counts all incidents in which at least four people are shot, excluding the shooter, regardless of whether the shooter is killed or injured. It also includes events that involve gang violence or armed robbery, as well as shootings that occurred in public or in private homes, as many domestic violence shootings do.

A *Mother Jones* magazine database that defines mass shootings more restrictively lists only 10 for 2019. Even the FBI's own data set—which applies yet another set of criteria focused on people who continue to shoot more people over the course of an incident—records just 28 active shooter incidents in 2019.

A study from 2018 on the frequency of mass shootings found that they are becoming more common,[1] though the exact number each year can vary widely.

But not all experts agree. Some argue that mass shootings have not increased and that reports of an increase are due to differences in research methods, such as determining which events to count in the first place. Speaking specifically about school shootings in a 2018 interview, two researchers who study gun violence said that those events have not become more common but rather that people have become more aware of them.[2]

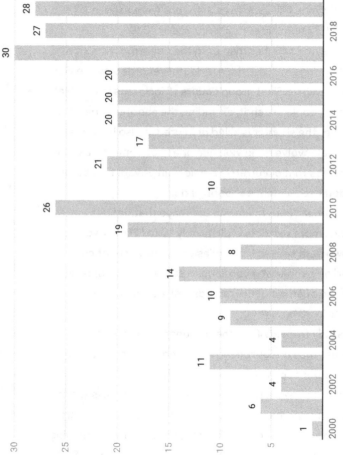

Active shooters are more common now than they used to be. Each year, the FBI releases data on what it classifies as "active shooter incidents," in which one or more attackers continue to shoot people over time, as opposed to targeting just one victim. Though there is no clear trend, these events are more frequent now than 20 years ago. *The Conversation, CC BY-ND. Data from the Federal Bureau of Investigation*

The same may be true of mass shootings generally. In any case, some researchers have found that mass shootings are becoming more deadly,[3] with more victims in recent attacks.

Suicide Is the Leading Form of Gun Death

In 2019, the 417 mass shootings tallied by the Gun Violence Archive resulted in 465 deaths. By contrast, 14,414 people were killed by someone else with a gun in 2019. And 23,941 people intentionally killed themselves with a gun in 2019, according to the Centers for Disease Control and Prevention. Every year, homicides—one person killing another—make up about 35% of gun deaths. More than 60% of gun deaths are suicides.

Mass shootings get more attention than these other, more common types of firearm deaths both because of human nature and the news media. People are naturally curious about violent events that appear to happen at random, having no clear explanation. Those incidents often spark fears in people about whether something similar could happen to them; as a result, they desire to know more in an effort to understand. In addition, cases with higher death counts or unusual characteristics, such as a shooter manifesto or video footage, are more likely to get press attention and extensive coverage.[4]

Americans' opinions are split on whether mass shootings are isolated incidents or part of a broader societal problem. And Americans are divided about how to reduce their frequency. A 2017 poll found that 47% of adults believed that reducing the number of guns in the United States would reduce the number of mass shootings.[5] But a follow-up question revealed that 75% of American adults believed that someone who wants to

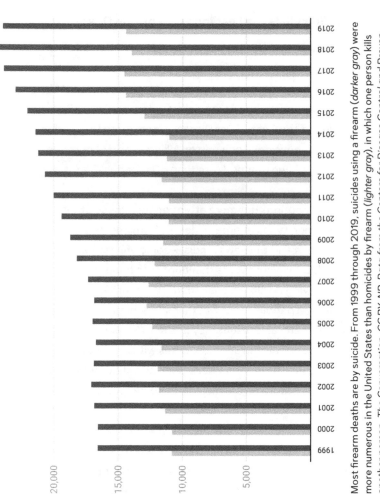

Most firearm deaths are by suicide. From 1999 through 2019, suicides using a firearm (*darker gray*) were more numerous in the United States than homicides by firearm (*lighter gray*), in which one person kills another person. *The Conversation, CC BY-ND. Data from the Centers for Disease Control and Prevention, National Center for Health Statistics*

hurt or kill others will find a way to do it whether they have access to a firearm or not.

With those diverging views, it will be hard to develop solutions that prove effective nationwide. That doesn't mean nothing will change, but it does mean the political debates will likely continue.

Notes

1. Ping-I Lin, Lin Fei, Drew Barzman, and M. Hossain, "What Have We Learned from the Time Trend of Mass Shootings in the U.S.?," *PLOS One* 13, no. 10 (2018). https://doi.org/10.1371/journal.pone.0204722.
2. Martin Kaste, "Despite Heightened Fear of School Shootings, It's Not A Growing Epidemic," National Public Radio, March 15, 2018. https://www.npr.org/2018/03/15/593831564/the-disconnect -between-perceived-danger-in-u-s-schools-and-reality.
3. Adam Lankford and James Silver, "Why Have Public Mass Shootings Become More Deadly?," *Criminology & Public Policy* 19, no. 1 (2019): 37–60. https://doi.org/10.1111/1745-9133.12472.
4. James N. Meindl and Jonathan W. Ivy, "Mass Shootings: The Role of the Media in Promoting Generalized Imitation," *American Journal of Public Health* 107, no. 3 (2017): 368–70. https://doi.org/10.2105/ajph.2016 .303611.
5. Kim Parker, Juliana Menasce Horowitz, Ruth Igielnik, J. Baxter Oliphant, and Anna Brown, "Views of Guns and Gun Violence," Pew Research Center's Social & Demographic Trends Project, Pew Research Center, June 22, 2017. https://www.pewresearch.org/social-trends/2017/06 /22/views-of-guns-and-gun-violence/.

Part III.

The Trauma of School Shootings

When the Columbine High School massacre took place in April 1999, it was seen as a watershed moment in the United States—the worst mass shooting at a school in the country's history.

Now, it ranks fourth. The three school shootings to surpass its toll of 13 deaths—12 students, 1 teacher—have all taken place within the last decade: the 2012 attack on Sandy Hook Elementary, in which a gunman killed 26 children and school staff; the 2018 shooting at Marjory Stoneman Douglas High School in Parkland, Florida, which claimed the lives of 17 people; and the 2022 Robb Elementary School assault in Uvalde, Texas, where 19 children and 2 adults were murdered.

There have been 13 school mass shootings in which four or more victims were shot and killed on campus in the United States; the first occurred on January 17, 1989, when a gunman armed with an AK-47-style weapon shot and killed five schoolchildren in a Stockton, CA., schoolyard.[1] The majority of these attacks were perpetrated by a lone gunman, with just two—Columbine and the 1998 shooting at Westside School in Jonesboro, Arkansas—carried out by two gunmen working together. The Jonesboro shooters, an 11-year-old and a 13-year-old, are still the youngest mass shooters in history.

The choice of *gunmen* to describe the perpetrators is accurate: all 13 mass shootings at US schools were carried out by men or boys, with an average age of 18. Most of these shooters also shared a connection to the schools they targeted. Thirteen of the 15 perpetrators were either current or former students of the school. Over half of them died on the scene, nearly all by suicide, the lone exception being the Robb Elementary shooter, who was shot dead by police.

Plus, nearly all the school mass shooters foretold of their attacks by leaving posts, messages, or videos warning of their intent. Many did this because it is what other school shooters had done, starting with the Columbine killers, who created diaries and home movies of their preparations in hopes that their story would outlive them. Unfortunately, it did. One 2015 study found "significant evidence of contagion in school shootings." Specifically, it found that a school shooting is "contagious for an average of 13 days" and incites other school shootings.[2] Columbine in particular became a blueprint for school shooters, inspiration for perpetrators searching for meaning for their motives and notoriety for their actions.[3]

Between 2018 and 2022, more people died in mass shootings in US schools than in the previous 18 years after Columbine combined. Mass shootings, however, are the exception, not the rule, when it comes to gun violence in schools. Since 2010, there have been more than 900 shootings in or around K–12 schools in the United States according to the K–12 School Shooting Database.[4] Around three-quarters of all victims were shot at a location outside the school building—on the athletic fields, in the parking lot, on a school bus, or at an off-campus school event—but that still translates to an average of more than one school-related shooting incident every week.

Many school shootings were an extension of the everyday gun violence that plagues communities across the United States—disputes that escalated simply because of the prevalence of firearms. Half of all victims were students (the rest included staff members, parents, and hundreds more with no connection to the school), and about 100 of them suffered gunshot wounds that proved to be fatal. Most of those in-school student fatalities were associated with the six mass shootings that occurred during this time period: 20 students at Sandy Hook Elementary School in Connecticut; 19 students in Uvalde, Texas; 14 students at Marjory Stoneman Douglas High School in Florida; 8 students at Santa Fe High School in Texas; 4 students at Marysville High School in Washington; and 4 students at Oxford High School in Michigan.

This amounts to an average of 8 student fatalities per year, out of more than 50 million children attending one of more than 130,000 public or private K–12 schools nationwide, which means that students face a roughly 1-in-10 million chance of death by gunfire at school. These are long odds. Yet no matter how unlikely probability says it is, there is something especially gut wrenching about a child dying in a classroom that moves us more than almost any other form of gun violence. Indeed, it was after the horrific school shooting in Uvalde, Texas, that the US Congress passed, in June 2022, the most significant firearms legislation in nearly 30 years.[5] The bill included tougher background checks for buyers younger than 21 years old, US$15 billion in federal funding for mental health programs and school security upgrades, and funding to encourage states to implement "red flag" laws to remove firearms from people considered a threat, among other measures. It enjoyed bipartisan support, with 14 Republicans joining Democrats in the House to approve the bill by 234 to 193 votes and 15 Republican senators voting alongside their 50 Democratic colleagues in the Senate.

Still, there is much work left to do. A majority of US teens say they worry about a shooting happening at their school,[6] and one study of more than 2,000 teens found that fear of school shootings predicted increases in anxiety and panic six months later.[7] Active shooter drills, which are now a routine part of American schooling, and almost fortress-like security do little to assuage these concerns.[8] Students who are constantly worried about impending gun violence devote more mental resources to emotions and fewer to executive functions like learning, memory, and sustained attention.[9] Which perhaps also explains why school shootings increase absenteeism, reduce high school and college graduation rates, and decrease retention of teachers.[10]

The chapters in part III examine the causes and consequences of school shootings in the United States and potential solutions to reduce their number. Written by educators, criminologists, and public health professionals, the chapters address the research needed to make sound policy decisions as well as specific proposals for addressing one of the most traumatic uses of guns in the United States today.

Recommended Further Reading

- *The Violence Project: How to Stop a Mass Shooting Epidemic* by Jillian Peterson and James Densley
- *How to Stop School Rampage Killing: Lessons from Averted Mass Shootings and Bombings* by Eric Madfis
- *School Shooters: Understanding High School, College, and Adult Perpetrators* by Peter Langman

Notes

1. James Densley and Jillian Peterson, "What We Know about Mass School Shootings in the US—and the Gunmen Who Carry Them Out," The Conversation, May 25, 2022. https://theconversation.com/what -we-know-about-mass-school-shootings-in-the-us-and-the-gunmen -who-carry-them-out-183812.
2. Sherry Towers, Andres Gomez-Lievano, Maryam Khan, Anuj Mubayi, and Carlos Castillo-Chavez, "Contagion in Mass Killings and School Shootings," *PLOS One* 10, no. 7 (2015): e0117259. https://doi.org/10 .1371/journal.pone.0117259.
3. Jillian Peterson and James Densley, "How Columbine Became a Blueprint for School Shooters," The Conversation, April 17, 2019. https://theconversation.com/how-columbine-became-a-blueprint -for-school-shooters-115115.
4. David Riedman, K–12 School Shooting Database. https://k12ssdb.org
5. Bipartisan Safer Communities Act, 117th Congress (2021–2022). https://www.congress.gov/bill/117th-congress/senate-bill/2938/text
6. Nikki Graf, "A Majority of U.S. Teens Fear a Shooting Could Happen at Their School, and Most Parents Share Their Concern," Pew Research Center, April 18, 2018. https://www.pewresearch.org/fact-tank/2018 /04/18/a-majority-of-u-s-teens-fear-a-shooting-could-happen-at -their-school-and-most-parents-share-their-concern/.
7. Kira E. Riehm, Ramin Mojtabai, Leslie B. Adams, Evan A. Krueger, Delvon T. Mattingly, Paul S. Nestadt, and Adam M. Leventhal, "Adolescents' Concerns about School Violence or Shootings and Association with Depressive, Anxiety, and Panic Symptoms," *JAMA Network Open* 4, no. 11 (2021): e2132131. https://doi.org/10.1001 /jamanetworkopen.2021.32131.
8. Everytown for Gun Safety, *The Impact of Active Shooter Drills in Schools: Time to Rethink Reactive School Safety Strategies*, updated December 29, 2021. https://everytownresearch.org/report/the -impact-of-active-shooter-drills-in-schools/

9. Amanda M. Dettmer and Tammy L. Hughes, "This Is What Happens to a Student's Brain When Exposed to Gun Violence," *Education Week*, June 27, 2022. https://www.edweek.org/leadership/opinion-this is-what-happens-to-a-students-brain-when-exposed-to-gun -violence/2022/06.
10. Marika Cabral, Bokyung Kim, Maya Rossin-Slater, Molly Schnell, and Hannes Schwandt, "Trauma at School: The Impacts of Shootings on Students' Human Capital and Economic Outcomes," Discussion Papers 13998, Institute of Labor Economics Discussion Papers, December 1, 2020. https://ideas.repec.org/p/iza/izadps/dp13998 .html.

Chapter 20

Why There's So Much Inconsistency in School Shooting Data

LACEY WALLACE

HOW MANY SCHOOL SHOOTINGS HAPPEN IN THE UNITED STATES in a single school year? The answer is surprisingly hard to figure out.

In April 2018, the US Department of Education released a report on the 2015–2016 school year, stating that "nearly 240 schools (0.2% of all schools) reported at least 1 incident involving a school-related shooting."[1] The nonprofit Everytown for Gun Safety's database, however, lists only 29 school shootings for the same period.[2]

People hold a vigil for the victims of the Saugus High School shooting in Santa Clarita, California, in 2019. *Hans Gutknecht/MediaNews Group/Los Angeles Daily News via Getty Images*

When National Public Radio investigated the inconsistency, it found that 161 of the Department of Education's 240 shootings either did not occur or could not be confirmed by the school districts involved.[3] Similarly, the American Civil Liberties Union contacted each school that allegedly had a shooting and found that 138 of the reported shootings were errors.[4]

So where does school shooting information come from? How could these counts be so far apart?

The Laws on Guns in Schools

Students are legally prohibited from bringing guns to school. That means they can be in serious trouble when they do, even if they never fire the gun.

The Gun-Free Schools Act of 1994 requires that schools in any state receiving certain federal funding implement a one-year expulsion rule for students who bring a firearm to school. Students found in possession of a firearm must also be referred to the criminal justice or juvenile justice system.

Each year, schools must report any firearm-related expulsions. Those can include shootings, but they also include firearm possession and other firearm crimes. Schools report firearm offenses like these to the Civil Rights Data Collection (CRDC), which is operated by the Department of Education.

In a biennial survey, the CRDC asks schools and other public educational agencies like charter schools this question: "For the regular . . . school year, not including intersession or summer, was there at least one incident at the school that involved a shooting (regardless of whether anyone was hurt)?" The US Department of Education used the answers to this question to estimate the number of school shootings for 2015–2016. In addition to shootings, schools report the number of incidents that involved possession of a firearm, as well as the number of robberies, homicides, physical attacks, and physical fights that involved a "firearm or explosive device."

Room for Error

A closer look at this survey shows why the US Department of Education's data was so inaccurate.

First, there are problems with the definition of the term *shooting*. Nowhere in the CRDC survey is that word clearly defined. Is it a shooting if a student has a gun that accidentally goes off? Could the term *shooting* refer to incidents involving toy guns?

Schools are asked to provide counts of various crimes involving firearms or explosive devices, so some counts of possession or attacks may be due to weapons other than firearms. The CRDC's definitions of various terms may differ from those used by state agencies or even the school districts themselves. If schools don't record disciplinary actions using the same terms, uniform reporting becomes difficult.

Second, there's the issue of the burden on school administrators. Schools already report a great deal of information to state agencies. Locating the required information or re-reporting information to multiple agencies can be time-consuming, possibly leading to errors or confusion about what to report. The CRDC made some changes to its 2017–2018 data collection effort to reduce this burden.

It's also easy to make mistakes. A school administrator might accidentally type a 9 rather a 0. Or they might accidentally enter the number of offenses for one crime category in the space allotted for another category. These errors may not be spotted until after the results of the survey are made public. There's currently no procedure in place to verify that reported shootings are, in fact, shootings.

Why Getting the Count Right Is So Important

Errors in data reporting can have major consequences, especially if the number is inflated.

A Pew Research Center poll from April 2018 found that 57% of teens were somewhat or very worried that a school shooting could happen in their school. Parents of teens were even more likely to report worry over school shootings, especially those with low incomes. Some families were considering homeschooling their children out of fear of school shootings.[5]

School shooting counts can sway policy. In 2018 alone, 26 states considered bills or resolutions related to arming school personnel. Even more introduced bills or resolutions related to guns in K–12 schools more generally.

Some sources of school shooting data, like Everytown, rely on a different resource: the media. They look for news mentions of school shootings instead of reports from the schools themselves. These counts, however, can also be inaccurate. Not all firearm-related offenses come to the attention of the media. Some media mentions must be verified with law enforcement to ensure the details are accurate.

Combining methods may be our best option. As a researcher who has studied criminal justice, I believe that verifying school shooting reports with a media search may reduce errors without placing undue burden on schools. Double-checking each reported shooting is time-consuming and costly. Unfortunately, so are the consequences of getting the count incorrect.

Notes

1. *2015–16 Civil Rights Data Collection: School Climate and Safety* (Washington, DC: US Department of Education Office for Civil Rights, 2018). https://www2.ed.gov/about/offices/list/ocr/docs/school -climate-and-safety.pdf.
2. "Gunfire on School Grounds in the United States," Everytown Research & Policy, accessed October 4, 2022. https://everytown research.org/maps/gunfire-on-school-grounds/.
3. Anya Kamenetz, "The School Shootings That Weren't," National Public Radio, August 27, 2018. https://www.npr.org/sections/ed/2018/08 /27/640323347/the-school-shootings-that-werent.
4. "Race, Discipline, and Safety at U.S. Public Schools," American Civil Liberties Union. https://www.aclu.org/issues/juvenile-justice/school

-prison-pipeline/race-discipline-and-safety-us-public-schools
?redirect=schooldiscipline.

5. Nikki Graf, "A Majority of U.S. Teens Fear a Shooting Could Happen at
    Their School, and Most Parents Share Their Concern," Pew Research
    Center, April 18, 2018. https://www.pewresearch.org/fact-tank/2018
    /04/18/a-majority-of-u-s-teens-fear-a-shooting-could-happen-at
    -their-school-and-most-parents-share-their-concern/.

Chapter 21

School Shootings Are at a Record High—but They Can Be Prevented

JAMES DENSLEY and JILLIAN PETERSON

WHENEVER A SCHOOL SHOOTING TAKES PLACE like the one at Oxford High School in suburban Detroit on November 30, 2021, it is typically followed by a familiar chorus of questions. How could such a thing happen? Why doesn't the government do more to stop these shootings from occurring?

Those questions are even more urgent in light of the fact that the shooting at Oxford High School was 1 of 250 school shootings in 2021, an all-time high according to the Center for Homeland Defense and Security's K–12 School Shooting Database. There were more school shootings in 2021 than in

2019 and 2018 combined, which at the time of this writing are the second- and third-worst years on record, with 119 and 118 shootings, respectively.

School shootings claimed 42 lives in 2021 and changed countless more. Nine of the 250 incidents that year were "active shooter" attacks in which one or more shooters killed or attempted to kill multiple people. In the Oxford High School case, a 15-year-old boy armed with a semiautomatic handgun was accused of killing four students and injuring six others and a teacher.

As shown in our 2021 book, *The Violence Project: How to Stop a Mass Shooting Epidemic*, school mass shooters tend to be current or former students of the school. They are almost always in a crisis of some sort before their attack, as indicated by a noticeable change in their usual behavior. They often are inspired by other school shooters, and they also tend to leak their plans for violence in advance to their peers. And school shooters usually get their guns from family and friends who failed to store them safely and securely.[1]

News reports suggest that a lot of this holds true for the Oxford High School shooter. For instance, the suspect's father allegedly purchased the handgun used in the shooting just four days prior. The shooter reportedly exhibited "concerning" behavior at school and posted pictures of the gun alongside threats of violence on social media.

The question now is how to translate these findings into policy and practice in order to prevent the next school shooting.

Trouble from the Start

The data we use to track school shootings is a comprehensive database that includes information on "each and every

People bring flowers to a makeshift memorial outside Oxford High School in Oxford, Michigan, in 2021 following a shooting by a 15-year-old student. *Scott Olson/Getty Images*

instance a gun is brandished, is fired, or a bullet hits school property for any reason, regardless of the number of victims, time of day, or day of week" going back to 1970.[2]

Working with its cocreator David Riedman, we uncovered a record 151 school shooting threats in the "back-to-school" month of September 2021, up from a three-year average of 29. Actual school shootings also more than doubled in September 2021 compared with the same month in previous years. There were 55 school shootings in September 2021, up from 24 in September 2020 and 14 in September 2019. But the school carnage began well before the 2021 school year got under way for most students, as evidenced by the August 13 fatal shooting of 13-year-old Bennie Hargrove at Washington Middle School in Albuquerque, New Mexico.

These trends are part of an overall rise in shootings and murders in 2020 and 2021, tied in part to record gun sales. More guns in more hands increases the likelihood that a firearm will find its way into a school.

Local Responses

Schools are struggling to respond to the overwhelming number of shootings and shooting threats. At high school sporting events alone, there were a staggering 38 shootings in 2021.

A "State of Emergency" meeting was held after nine teens were shot in two separate shootings in Aurora, Colorado, in November 2012. Public schools in the area prohibited students from leaving for lunch in an effort to keep them safe. One school in Phoenix, Arizona, banned backpacks and food deliveries after a student was shot in the bathroom on November 29. The Newburgh Enlarged City School District in New York State offered remote learning following two separate shooting incidents near its schools on November 22. Schools across the country increased safety measures, canceled classes, or even initiated police escorts for students coming onto campus.

These localized responses stand in stark contrast to the national legislative action taken in Finland, Germany, and other countries when they experienced deadly school shootings.

Response in the United Kingdom

Twenty-five years ago, in March 1996, a gunman walked into Scotland's Dunblane Primary School and opened fire, killing 16 children and a teacher. A successful campaign for gun regulation followed, laws were changed, handguns were banned, and the United Kingdom hasn't had a school shooting since.

Yet in America, the best schoolchildren can hope for are active shooter drills to rehearse for a real shooting incident and armed guards to respond to one.[3] There is a US$3 billion "homeroom security" industry, and some parents send their children to school wearing bulletproof backpacks.

Searching for Solutions

For a study published in the *Journal of the American Medical Association* in November 2021, we searched public records for 170 mass shooters who killed four or more people from 1966 to 2019 for any communication of an intent to do harm. That included posting a threat on social media or telegraphing future violence to a loved one in person. We found that 79 mass shooters—nearly half of them—leaked their plan in advance. Communication was most common among school shooters and younger shooters. The fact that it was most strongly associated with suicidal tendencies or attempts, as well as prior mental health counseling, suggests it may best be characterized as a cry for help.[4]

Threats of violence circulated on campus before the Oxford High School shooting, with some students staying home out of an abundance of caution. Following a school shooting, there will be questions about whether threats were disclosed to authorities and handled appropriately, in ways consistent with best practices for threat assessment, or what we like to call "crisis response" systems. Our research clearly shows that all threats must be investigated and treated seriously as an opportunity for real intervention.

There are further implications from our research. If a school shooter is nearly always a student of the school, educators and others who work with students need training to identify a student in crisis and to know how to report something they see or hear indicative of violent intent.

Schools also need counselors, social workers, and other resources so that they can respond appropriately and holistically to students in crisis. This means not unduly punishing students with expulsion or criminal charges—things that could escalate the crisis or any grievance with the institution.

And for parents of school-age children, safe gun storage at home is paramount.

School shootings are not inevitable. They're preventable. But practitioners and policy makers must act quickly because each school shooting feeds the cycle for the next one, causing harm far beyond that which is measured in lives lost. We believe the steps outlined above can help address that harm, promoting school security while safeguarding student well-being.

Notes

1. Jillian Peterson and James Densley, *The Violence Project: How to Stop a Mass Shooting Epidemic* (New York: Abrams Press, 2021).
2. "CHDS School Shooting Safety Compendium," Center for Homeland Security and Defense, accessed October 4, 2022. https://www.chds.us/ssdb/.
3. Jillian Peterson, James Densley, and Gina Erickson, "Presence of Armed School Officials and Fatal and Nonfatal Gunshot Injuries during Mass School Shootings, United States, 1980–2019," *JAMA Network Open* 4, no. 2 (February 16, 2021). https://doi.org/10.1001/jamanetworkopen.2020.37394.
4. Jillian Peterson, Gina Erickson, Kyle Knapp, and James Densley, "Communication of Intent to Do Harm Preceding Mass Public Shootings in the United States, 1966 to 2019," *JAMA Network Open* 4, no. 11 (November 4, 2021). https://doi.org/10.1001/jamanetworkopen.2021.33073.

Chapter 22

Five Ways to Reduce School Shootings

PAUL BOXER

AFTER THE SCHOOL SHOOTING in Parkland, Florida, in 2018, my colleagues and I reviewed research to see what could be learned from what we refer to as the "science of violence prevention."[1] In the wake of the May 24, 2022, massacre at Robb Elementary School in Uvalde, Texas, we revisited that research anew—and other research conducted since then—for insights into what can be done to reduce the risk of school shootings in the future. Here are five policy changes, based on our findings, that can be implemented to achieve that end.

1. Dramatically Limit Access to Guns

Gun regulation matters.

When my colleagues and I looked at gun regulations on a state-by-state basis, we found that more restrictive gun laws were associated with lower rates of homicides with guns.[2] This relation held even after we took demographic, economic, and educational factors into account. Other researchers have found that "permissive firearm laws and higher rates of gun ownership" were linked with higher rates of school shootings.[3]

What these results essentially mean is that in states where it is more difficult to acquire a gun, fewer people are killed with guns. Examples of these restrictions are raising the age for legal purchase, imposing lengthy waiting periods before access, and requiring meaningful background checks. These and similar measures—for example, eliminating access for individuals at a high risk of committing violence, such as the perpetrators of domestic violence—all move toward making it significantly harder to access guns, which would reduce gun violence substantially. Research has shown that greater access to guns is associated with higher numbers of gun deaths.[4]

Moreover, placing meaningful restrictions or outright bans on firearm equipment associated with greater lethality, such as assault-style rifles and high-capacity magazines, should also lower the number of people being killed by firearms.

2. Use More Violence Risk Assessments in Schools

In the years since the Columbine shooting in 1999, researchers and federal law enforcement agencies have studied school shootings and developed risk assessments to gauge the likelihood of violence by a young person identified as a possible risk.[5] These assessments are to be conducted by professionals that include police officers, school officials, and teachers. They also involve mental health professionals, such as school counselors and psychologists. Together, these professionals all consult with one another to determine a young person's risk for violence.

These teams may not be able to prevent every possible incident. Still, this sort of approach is critical to improving the process of identifying and stopping potential shooters overall. Guidance on how to use these assessments is freely available and based in extensive applied research. For example, in one 2015 study, the Virginia Student Threat Assessment Guidelines—a set of guidelines for the investigation of a reported threat, thorough assessment of the individual making the threat, and preventive or protective measures to be taken in response—were shown to reduce rates of student aggression. They were also shown to lower out-of-school suspension rates while improving teacher and student perceptions of safety.[6]

3. Expand Evidence-Based Strategies to Reduce Violent Behavior

To help reduce the number of youths who grow up to become violent, governmental agencies could increase the availability and use of evidence-based interventions in schools.

Aggressive and violent behavior has been shown by research to emerge from a mix of personal and environmental risk factors. The factors include impulsivity, callousness, exposure to violence, and victimization.[7]

In light of this research, effective approaches were developed to prevent aggression by teaching students to problem-solve for better responses to peer conflict. They also teach students to think carefully about others' motivations when they feel provoked. Programs shown to reduce aggressive behavior typically train youths who already have exhibited some aggression on developing new and better coping skills for managing stress and anger. And for youths who have become seriously violent, treatments teach new, constructive behavioral and communication skills to the youths and their caregivers. The treatments also help young people develop better relationships with family members and school personnel.

4. Make School Buildings Safer

The Robb Elementary School shooter entered the school building through a door that reportedly had malfunctioned. This highlights the absolute importance for schools to take and maintain physical security measures.

In the wake of shootings, schools often turn to solutions such as upgraded camera surveillance or increased law enforcement. These measures can have mixed effects on students' perceptions of safety and support: cameras posted outside appear to increase felt safety, whereas cameras posted inside seem to promote unease.[8] Increased presence by law enforcement might make teachers feel safer in school. But it also might criminalize student misbehavior without actually making schools safer.

Still, there are a number of ways for schools to improve physical security without increasing student anxiety or needlessly deploying law enforcement. For example, in one large study, students were less likely to skip school because of safety concerns when metal detectors were used at school entry points. In that study, those metal detectors also reduced the likelihood of weapons being brought into schools.[9]

5. Reduce Exposure to Violence through Media and Social Media

Entertainment media and social media are saturated with violent images of physical assaults, gun violence, and gore. Exposure to and participation in virtual violence might not lead to aggressive behavior for all children and adolescents. But watching violent programs and playing violent video games can lead to increased hostility, aggressive feelings, emotional desensitization to violence, and, ultimately, aggressive behavior.[10] These effects can potentially be lessened by reducing the amount of screen violence to which children and adolescents are exposed over time, particularly early in their development.

Notes

1. Brad J. Bushman, Sarah M. Coyne, Craig A. Anderson, Kaj Björkqvist, Paul Boxer, Kenneth A. Dodge, Eric F. Dubow, et al., "Risk Factors for Youth Violence: Youth Violence Commission, International Society for Research on Aggression (ISRA)," *Aggressive Behavior* 44, no. 4 (June 17, 2018): 331–36. https://doi.org/10.1002/ab.21766.
2. John F. Gunn, Paul Boxer, Tracy Andrews, Michael Ostermann, Stephanie L. Bonne, Michael Gusmano, Elizabeth Sloan-Power, and Bernadette Hohl, "The Impact of Firearm Legislation on Firearm Deaths, 1991–2017," *Journal of Public Health* 44, no. 3 (2022): 614–24. https://doi.org/10.1093/pubmed/fdab047.
3. Paul M. Reeping, Louis Klarevas, Sonali Rajan, Ali Rowhani-Rahbar, Justin Heinze, April M. Zeoli, Monika K. Goyal, Marc A. Zimmerman, and Charles C. Branas, "State Firearm Laws, Gun Ownership, and K–12 School Shootings: Implications for School Safety," *Journal of School Violence* 21, no. 2 (2022): 132–46. https://doi.org/10.1080/15388220.2021.2018332.
4. Richard Stansfield, Daniel Semenza, and Trent Steidley, "Public Guns, Private Violence: The Association of City-Level Firearm Availability and Intimate Partner Homicide in the United States," *Preventive*

Medicine 148 (2021): 106599. https://doi.org/10.1016/j.ypmed.2021
.106599.

5. Marisa Reddy, Randy Borum, John Berglund, Bryan Vossekuil, Robert
    Fein, and William Modzeleski, "Evaluating Risk for Targeted Violence in
    Schools: Comparing Risk Assessment, Threat Assessment, and Other
    Approaches," *Psychology in the Schools* 38, no. 2 (2001): 157–72.
    https://doi.org/10.1002/pits.1007; Erin K. Nekvasil and Dewey G.
    Cornell, "Student Threat Assessment Associated with Safety in Middle
    Schools," *Journal of Threat Assessment and Management* 2, no. 2
    (2015): 98–113. https://doi.org/10.1037/tam0000038.

6. E. K. Nekvasil and D. G. Cornell, "Student Threat Assessment Associ-
    ated with Safety in Middle Schools," *Journal of Threat Assessment
    and Management* 2, no. 2 (2015): 98–113. https://doi.org/10.1037
    /tam0000038.

7. Kenneth A. Dodge, Mark T. Greenberg, Patrick S. Malone, and
    Conduct Problems Prevention Research Group, "Testing an Idealized
    Dynamic Cascade Model of the Development of Serious Violence
    in Adolescence," *Child Development* 79, no. 6 (2008): 1907–27.
    https://doi.org/10.1111/j.1467-8624.2008.01233.x.

8. Sarah Lindstrom Johnson, Jessika Bottiani, Tracy E. Waasdorp, and
    Catherine P. Bradshaw, "Surveillance or Safekeeping? How School
    Security Officer and Camera Presence Influence Students' Perceptions
    of Safety, Equity, and Support," *Journal of Adolescent Health* 63, no. 6
    (2018): 732–38. https://doi.org/10.1016/j.jadohealth.2018.06.008.

9. Rachana Bhatt and Tomeka Davis, "The Impact of Random Metal
    Detector Searches on Contraband Possession and Feelings of Safety
    at School," *Educational Policy* 32 no. 4 (2018): 569–97. https://doi
    .org/10.1177/0895904816673735.

10. Robert Busching, Johnie J. Allen, and Craig A. Anderson, "Violent Media
    Content and Effects," *Oxford Research Encyclopedia of Communica-
    tion,* March 3, 2016. https://doi.org/10.1093/acrefore/9780190228613
    .013.1.

Chapter 23

Most School Shooters Get Their Guns from Home—and during the Pandemic, the Number of Firearms in Households with Teenagers Went Up

PATRICK CARTER, MARC A. ZIMMERMAN, and REBECCAH SOKOL

FOUR DAYS BEFORE a 15-year-old sophomore killed four students and wounded others at a high school shooting in Michigan in 2021, his father had purchased the firearm used in the attack. That the teenager used a weapon from home during the attack is not unusual. Most school shooters obtain the firearm from home. Since the onset of the public health crisis brought on by COVID-19, firearm sales have spiked.

As experts on firearm violence and firearm injury prevention, we know that active shooter events in school settings in the United States increased substantially in the years running up to the pandemic. Our research indicates, moreover, that in the early months of the public health crisis, more families with teenage children purchased firearms,[1] which raised the potential risk that a teen could gain unsupervised access to a firearm. Having more access to firearms at home increases the probability of accidental or intentional injury or fatalities, or death by suicide.[2] This fact highlights the importance of locking firearms and keeping them unloaded in the home.

Access to Unsecured Firearms around the House

While school shootings represent a small fraction of the total number of firearm injuries and deaths that occur each year, they can devastate a community, as was seen in the shooting at Oxford High School in Oxford Township, Michigan.

Around half of school shootings are carried out by current or past students who attended the school. In around 74% of incidents, the firearm used was obtained from the student's home or from that of a friend or relative.

While firearm purchases have been increasing for decades, they accelerated during the pandemic. In the three months from March through May 2020, an estimated 2.1 million firearms were purchased, for a 64.3% increase in the expected volume.[3] In the first two years of the pandemic, about one in five households purchased a firearm.

To understand how increased firearm availability affected firearm access among high school–age teens, investigators from the University of Michigan Institute for Firearm Injury Prevention conducted a national survey of nearly 3,000 parents and their teenage children. We found that 10% of households with teens reported purchasing additional firearms between March and July 2020. Around 3% were first-time buyers.[4] This means that more teenagers were being exposed to firearms around the home and also that the number of firearms in households with teenage children had increased. In all, estimates are that one-third of all households with children up to age 18 contain at least one firearm.[5]

While many firearm owners look after their guns responsibly by keeping them locked, unloaded, and inaccessible to teens, access to unsecured firearms remains the single biggest contributor to teen firearm injury and death.[6] Our survey indicated that in the midst of increased firearm purchasing during the COVID pandemic, more firearms were being kept unsecured in homes with teenagers.

Some 5% of firearm-owning parents reported having changed their firearm storage method since the beginning of the pandemic in order to make them more accessible. Firearm-owning parents we spoke to reported leaving them in unlocked cabinets or within easier reach—say, in a bedside cabinet—and with the firearm loaded.

Households that already kept firearms unlocked and loaded were also those whose members were more likely to have purchased firearms during the pandemic, we found. Parents said they were largely motivated to make firearms easier to access out of fear and a need for greater protection.

This also means, though, that others may have easy access to the firearms. During the pandemic, many people, especially youths, experienced stress and isolation, which increases the potential risk of violence against self or others. This tendency emphasizes the importance of securing firearms in a locked safe and storing ammunition separately in the home to prevent unsupervised access during a moment of crisis.

One clear action that parents can take to help reduce the likelihood of future tragic school shootings and to keep their teens safe is to ensure that any firearms present in the home are secured safely, locked up and unloaded, and out of the reach of teens.

Notes

1. Rebeccah L. Sokol, Marc A. Zimmerman, Laney Rupp, Justin E. Heinze, Rebecca M. Cunningham, and Patrick M. Carter, "Firearm Purchasing during the Beginning of the COVID-19 Pandemic in Households with Teens: a National Study," *Journal of Behavioral Medicine* 44, no. 6 (July 9, 2021): 874–82. https://doi.org/10.1007/s10865-021-00242-w.
2. Sonja A. Swanson, Mara Eyllon, Yi-Han Sheu, and Matthew Miller, "Firearm Access and Adolescent Suicide Risk: Toward a Clearer Understanding of Effect Size," *Injury Prevention* 27, no. 3 (May 14, 2020): 264–70. https://doi.org/10.1136/injuryprev-2019-043605.
3. Julia P. Schleimer, Christopher D. McCort, Veronica A. Pear, Aaron Shev, Elizabeth Tomsich, Rameesha Asif-Sattar, Shani Buggs, Hannah S. Laqueur, Garen J. Wintemute, "Firearm Purchasing and Firearm Violence in the First Months of the Coronavirus Pandemic in the United States," medRxiv, July 11, 2020. https://www.medrxiv.org /content/10.1101/2020.07.02.20145508v2.
4. Julia P. Schleimer, Christopher D. McCort, Aaron B. Shev, Veronica A. Pear, Elizabeth Tomsich, Alaina De Biasi, Shani Buggs, Hannah S. Laqueur, and Garen J. Wintemute, "Firearm Purchasing and Firearm Violence during the Coronavirus Pandemic in the United States: A Cross-Sectional Study," *Injury Epidemiology* 8, no. 1 (2021). https://doi .org/10.1186/s40621-021-00339-5.
5. Deborah Azrael, Joanna Cohen, Carmel Salhi, and Matthew Miller, "Firearm Storage in Gun-Owning Households with Children: Results of a 2015 National Survey," *Journal of Urban Health* 95, no. 3 (2018): 295–304. https://doi.org/10.1007/s11524-018-0261-7.
6. Rocco Pallin, Sarabeth A. Spitzer, Megan L. Ranney, Marian E. Betz, and Garen J. Wintemute, "Preventing Firearm-Related Death and Injury," *Annals of Internal Medicine* 170, no. 11 (June 4, 2019). https://doi.org/10.7326/aitc201906040.

Chapter 24

Arming Teachers

An Effective Security Measure or a False Sense of Security?

AIMEE DINNÍN HUFF and MICHELLE BARNHART

IN THE WAKE OF THE MAY 2022 MASS SHOOTING at Robb Elementary School in Uvalde, Texas, some elected officials made renewed calls for teachers to be armed and trained to use firearms to protect the nation's schools. We have studied the ins and outs of putting guns in the hands of the nation's teachers as a way to protect students. Here are answers to common questions.

1. What Does the Public Think about Arming Teachers?

According to a 2021 poll, 43% of Americans supported policies that allow school personnel to carry guns in schools. The polling data shows that most of that support came from Republicans and gun owners. For instance, 66% of Republican respondents expressed support for such policies versus just 24% of Democratic respondents. And 63% of gun owners supported allowing school personnel to carry guns versus just 33% of non–gun owners.[1]

As of this writing, the majority of teachers, parents, and students oppose allowing teachers to carry guns.[2] The largest teachers' unions, including the National Education Association, also oppose arming teachers, arguing that bringing more guns into schools "makes schools more dangerous and does nothing to shield our students and educators from gun violence." These teachers' unions advocate a preventive approach that includes more gun regulations.

While the public is justifiably concerned with eliminating school shootings, there is disagreement over the policies and actions that would be most effective. A 2021 study found that 70% of Americans supported the idea of armed school resource officers and law enforcement in schools, but only 41% supported the idea of training teachers to carry guns in schools.[3]

In our research on how Americans think about the rights and responsibilities related to armed self-defense, we find disagreement even among conservative gun owners over how to best protect schoolchildren. Some advocate arming teachers, while other gun owners believe guns in schools

The idea of arming teachers surfaced as a viable policy following the 1999 Columbine shooting in Colorado and gained momentum after the 2018 Parkland shooting in Florida. *RichLegg/Getty Images*

ultimately make children less safe. These conservative opponents of arming teachers instead support fortifying the building's design and features.

After the massacre in Uvalde, some politicians renewed previous calls to arm teachers and provide them with specialized training. At the same time, there remain questions about whether armed teachers would make a difference. Police acknowledged that they didn't enter the school even as kids frantically dialed 911.

Given that there were also armed officers present at the Columbine and Parkland school massacres in 1999 and 2018, respectively, the public justifiably wonders whether armed teachers can effectively neutralize a shooter.

2. What Are the Potential Drawbacks of Arming Teachers?

Arming teachers introduces risks to students and staff, as well as to school districts. These include the risk of teachers accidentally shooting themselves or students and fellow staff. There are also moral and legal risks associated with improper or inaccurate defensive use of a firearm—even for teachers who have undertaken specialized firearms training.

One study found that highly trained police in gunfights hit their target only 18% of the time. Even if teachers, who would likely have less training, achieve the same accuracy, four or five of every six bullets fired by a teacher would hit something or someone other than the shooter. Furthermore, a teacher responding with force to a shooter may be mistaken for the perpetrator by law enforcement or by armed colleagues.

Introducing guns into the school environment also poses everyday risks.[4] Armed teachers may unintentionally discharge their firearm. For instance, an armed police officer accidentally discharged his weapon in his office at a school in Alexandria, Virginia, in 2018. Guns can also fall into the wrong hands. Research on shootings that took place in hospital emergency rooms found that in 23% of the cases, the weapon used was a gun the perpetrator took from a hospital security guard.

Students could access firearms that are improperly stored or mishandled. Improper storage is a common occurrence among American gun owners. In a school setting, this has resulted in students finding a teacher's misplaced firearm, sometimes taking it or reporting it to another school official. News reports show that guns carried into schools have fallen out of teachers' clothing and have been left in bathrooms and locker rooms. There have also been reports of students stealing guns from teachers. Insurance companies see concealed guns on school grounds as creating a heightened liability risk.

Other drawbacks to arming teachers involve the learning environment. In particular, owing to structural racism and discriminatory school security policies, Black high school students are less supportive than white students of arming teachers—16% versus 26%—and report feeling less safe if teachers are carrying firearms.[5]

3. What Are the Arguments for Arming Teachers?

Proponents emphasize that teachers, as Americans, have a right to use firearms to defend themselves against violent crime, including a school shooter. Our research shows that some people interpret their right to armed self-defense as a moral obligation, and they argue that teachers have both a right and a responsibility to use firearms to protect themselves and their students.[6]

Parents who regularly carry handguns to protect themselves and their children may take comfort in knowing that their child's teacher could perform the role of protector at school. In a school shooting, where lives can be saved or ended in a matter of seconds, some people may feel more secure believing a shooter would immediately meet armed resistance from a teacher rather than acting unimpeded until an armed school officer responds.

4. Have Any School Districts Allowed Teachers to Arm Themselves?

As of May 2022, teachers were allowed to carry guns at school in districts in at least 19 states. The idea surfaced as a viable policy after the 1999 Columbine shooting and gained momentum after the 2018 Parkland shooting.

The number of school districts that permit teachers to be armed is difficult to ascertain. Policies vary across states. New York bars school districts from allowing teachers to carry guns, while Missouri and Montana authorize teachers to carry firearms.

5. What Were the Results?

There are documented incidents of school staff using their firearm to neutralize a shooter. Researchers have not found evidence, however, that arming teachers increases school safety. Rather, arming teachers may contribute to a false sense of security for teachers, students, and the community.

Notes

1. Ted Van Green, "Wide Differences on Most Gun Policies between Gun Owners and Non-owners, but Also Some Agreement," Pew Research Center, August 4, 2021. https://www.pewresearch.org/fact-tank /2021/08/04/wide-differences-on-most-gun-policies-between-gun -owners-and-non-owners-but-also-some-agreement/.
2. Faraneh Shamserad, Timothy McCuddy, and Finn-Aage Esbensen, "Pistol Packing Teachers: What Do Students Think?," *Journal of School Violence* 20, no. 2 (December 13, 2020): 127–38. https://doi .org/10.1080/15388220.2020.1858424.
3. Cheryl Lero Jonson, Alexander L. Burton, Francis T. Cullen, Justin T. Pickett, and Velmer S. Burton Jr., "An Apple in One Hand, a Gun in the Other: Public Support for Arming Our Nation's Schools," *Criminology & Public Policy* 20, no. 2 (January 15, 2021): 263–90. https://doi.org /10.1111/1745-9133.12538.

4. Michelle Barnhart, Aimee Dinnin Huff, Brandon McAlexander, and James H. McAlexander, "Preparing for the Attack: Mitigating Risk through Routines in Armed Self-Defense," *Journal of the Association for Consumer Research* 3, no. 1 (December 18, 2017): 27–45. https://doi.org/10.1086/695762.
5. Faraneh Shamserad, "Race Differences in Youths' Attitudes toward Arming Teachers: Investigating the Role of Procedural Justice," *Youth & Society*, September 22, 2021. https://doi.org/10.1177/0044118x211046637.
6. Michelle Barnhart, Aimee Dinnin Huff, and Inara Scott, "Relating Americans' Responses to the Marketization of Armed Self-Defense to Their Understandings of the Second Amendment," *Advances in Consumer Research* 47 (2019): 135–41. https://www.acrwebsite.org/volumes/2552033/volumes/v47/NA-47.

Part IV.

The Effects of Gun Violence

Different gun violence problems have different underlying dynamics, and they affect people differently based on who they are and where they live. For example, Black males have a far greater lifetime chance of being shot and killed by police, in part because, for reasons including structural racism, they are more likely to encounter police, period.[1] Likewise, 42% of firearm homicide victims in 2020 were Black males between the ages of 15 and 34, a group that accounts for only 2% of the US population. These Black male homicide victims are often survived by Black female romantic partners—wives, girlfriends, mothers of their children—who, in turn, disproportionately shoulder the emotional and economic burden of loss: grief, funeral arrangements, debts, and caring for those left behind.[2]

About 1 in 10 Americans will lose a loved one to homicide during their lifetime, but the "law of crime concentration"[3] further reveals a deep "murder inequality" at the neighborhood level, affecting residents whether or not they themselves are a shooting victim.[4] Witnessing a shooting, or having a friend or loved one become a victim, can be deeply traumatic, leading to mental health problems, difficulty concentrating at school or work, and other issues.[5] Few services specifically address survivors' needs, and while police and court advocates can help, low clearance rates for solving crimes of gun violence, lengthy investigations, and trials may cause further ("secondary") trauma. Gun crime can even drive businesses away from a community, limiting access to important services like health care and banking and contributing to depopulation and abandonment.[6]

Gun violence concentrates not just *spatially* but *socially*, especially among groups of serious offenders. In the city of St. Louis, for example, the age-adjusted rate of homicide mortality for young Black men identified by law enforcement as gang members was a staggering 950 per 100,000—three times greater than that of the average young Black male in the city.[7] Another study of more than 20 cities found that, on average, less than 1% of residents were involved in gangs, drug crews, and other criminally active groups, but they were connected to over 50% of shootings and homicides.[8] In one high-crime Boston community, 85% of all fatal and nonfatal gunshot injuries occurred in a single social network of people with criminal records that constituted less than 5% of the community's total population.[9] Similarly, 70% of all nonfatal shootings in the entire city of Chicago occurred in a co-offending network composed of less than 6% of the city's population.[10] Just being in the network with another gunshot victim increased an individual's probability of victimization by 900%.

It seems obvious to say that living under the constant threat of gun violence is traumatic, but even studies of random mass shootings have documented increases in post-traumatic stress disorder, major depression, anxiety disorders, substance use disorder, and other conditions among people who have survived them.[11] The schools, workplaces, and other institutions in the communities that have experienced a mass shooting have even been described as "co-victims" because they are so deeply affected by the event.[12] Fear of mass shootings has left a large majority of Americans feeling stressed, including the third of adults who say they now avoid certain public places and events as a result of gun violence.[13] Persistent worry about gun violence is fueled in part by the overwhelming amount of media coverage that mass shootings generate.[14]

The trauma of gun violence doesn't end when the shooting stops, nor do the economic costs of long-term physical and mental health care, forgone earnings, criminal justice costs, and lost quality of life.[15] The chapters in part IV discuss some of the many devastating consequences of American gun violence and describe how the United States is a nation of gun violence survivors. They explore why Americans are buying more guns now than ever before and how these guns traumatize people and rend the social fabric of communities.

Recommended Further Reading

- *Children under Fire: An American Crisis* by John Woodrow Cox
- *Another Day in the Death of America: A Chronicle of Ten Short Lives* by Gary Younge
- *A Peculiar Indifference* by Elliott Currie
- *Reducing Gun Violence in America: Informing Policy with Evidence and Analysis*, edited by Daniel Webster and Jon Vernick

Notes

1. Aldina Mesic, Lydia Franklin, Alev Cansever, Fiona Potter, Anika Sharma, Anita Knopov, and Michael Siegel, "The Relationship between Structural Racism and Black-White Disparities in Fatal Police Shootings at the State Level," *Journal of the National Medical Association* 110, no. 2 (2018): 106–16. https://doi.org/10.1016/j.jnma.2017.12.002.
2. Brooklynn Hitchens, "Second Killings: The Black Women and Girls Left Behind to Grieve America's Growing Gun Violence Crisis," Rockefeller Institute of Government, July 26, 2022. https://rockinst.org/blog/second-killings-the-black-women-and-girls-left-behind-to-grieve-americas-growing-gun-violence-crisis/.
3. David Weisburd, "The Law of Crime Concentration and the Criminology of Place," *Criminology* 53, no. 2 (2015): 133–57. https://doi.org/10.1111/1745-9125.12070.
4. Daniel Kay Hertz, "The Debate over Crime Rates Is Ignoring the Metric That Matters Most: 'Murder Inequality,'" The Trace, July 25, 2016. https://www.thetrace.org/2016/07/murder-inequality-urban-violence-statistics/.
5. Alyssa A. Rheingold and Joah L. Williams, "Survivors of Homicide: Mental Health Outcomes, Social Support, and Service Use among a Community-Based Sample," *Violence and Victims* 30, no. 5 (2015): 870–83. https://doi.org/10.1891/0886-6708.vv-d-14-00026.
6. Patrick Sharkey, *Uneasy Peace: The Great Crime Decline, the Renewal of City Life, and the Next War on Violence* (New York: W. W. Norton, 2018).
7. David C. Pyrooz, Ryan K. Masters, Jennifer J. Tostlebe, and Richard G. Rogers, "Exceptional Mortality Risk among Police-Identified Young Black Male Gang Members," *Preventive Medicine* 141 (December 2020): 106269. https://doi.org/10.1016/j.ypmed.2020.106269.

8. Stephen Lurie, "There's No Such Thing as a Dangerous Neighbor-hood," CityLab, February 25, 2019. https://www.citylab.com/perspective/2019/02/broken-windows-theory-policing-urban-violence-crime-data/583030/.

9. Andrew V. Papachristos, Anthony A. Braga, and David M. Hureau, "Social Networks and the Risk of Gunshot Injury," *Journal of Urban Health* 89, no. 6 (2012): 992–1003. https://doi.org/10.1007/s11524-012-9703-9.

10. Andrew V. Papachristos, Christopher Wildeman, and Elizabeth Roberto, "Tragic, but Not Random: The Social Contagion of Nonfatal Gunshot Injuries," *Social Science & Medicine* 125 (January 2015): 139–50. https://doi.org/10.1016/j.socscimed.2014.01.056.

11. Sarah R. Lowe and Sandro Galea, "The Mental Health Consequences of Mass Shootings," *Trauma, Violence & Abuse* 18, no. 1 (2016): 62–82. https://doi.org/10.1177/1524838015591572.

12. Ali Rowhani-Rahbar, Douglas F. Zatzick, and Frederick P. Rivara, "Long-Lasting Consequences of Gun Violence and Mass Shoot-ings," *Journal of the National Medical Association* 321, no. 18 (2019): 1765–66. https://doi.org/10.1001/jama.2019.5063.

13. "One-Third of US Adults Say Fear of Mass Shootings Prevents Them from Going to Certain Places or Events," American Psychological Association, August 15, 2019. https://www.apa.org/news/press/releases/2019/08/fear-mass-shooting.

14. James Alan Fox, Madison Gerdes, Grant Duwe, and Michael Rocque, "The Newsworthiness of Mass Public Shootings: What Factors Impact the Extent of Coverage?," *Homicide Studies*, November, 2020. https://doi.org/10.1177/1088767920974412.

15. Everytown for Gun Safety, *When the Shooting Stops: The Impact of Gun Violence on Survivors in America*, February 3, 2022. https://everytownresearch.org/report/the-impact-of-gun-violence-on-survivors-in-america/.

Chapter 25

The Lasting Consequences of School Shootings on the Students Who Survive Them

MARIKA CABRAL, BOKYUNG KIM, MAYA ROSSIN-SLATER, MOLLY SCHNELL, and HANNES SCHWANDT

ON MAY 24, 2022, a gunman opened fire at Robb Elementary School in Uvalde, Texas. As the United States reeled from another school shooting, much of the public discussion centered on the lives lost: 19 children and 2 adults. Indeed, the Uvalde massacre was the second deadliest such incident on record, after the shooting at Sandy Hook Elementary School in 2012. From the Columbine massacre in 1999—in which 2 teenagers killed 12 students and 1 teacher—to the Uvalde shooting in 2022, at least 185 children, educators, and others were killed by gun violence at American schools, according to figures compiled by the *Washington Post*.

But this death toll captures only one part of the immense cost of gun violence in American schools. We have studied the long-term effects of school shootings on the health, education, and economic futures of those who survive such incidents. Our research shows that despite often escaping without physical harm, the hundreds of thousands of children and educators who survive these tragedies carry scars that affect their lives for many years to come.[1]

Deterioration in Mental Health

In a 2020 study, part of our team (Rossin-Slater, Schnell, and Schwandt) in collaboration with Sam Trejo and Lindsey Uniat analyzed 44 school shootings that took place in the United States between 2008 and 2013 to assess the impact the incidents had on students' mental health. Using a unique data set documenting antidepressant prescriptions in the surrounding areas, we found that antidepressant use among youth near schools that had experienced shootings increased by more than 20% following the event. This increased usage of antidepressants persisted for over three years after the shooting, indicating that the deterioration in mental health among adolescents was not temporary.

The effects were more pronounced when the school shootings had fatalities, suggesting that events like the massacre in Uvalde are likely to result in long-lasting health effects for survivors that extend beyond the physical injuries some receive.

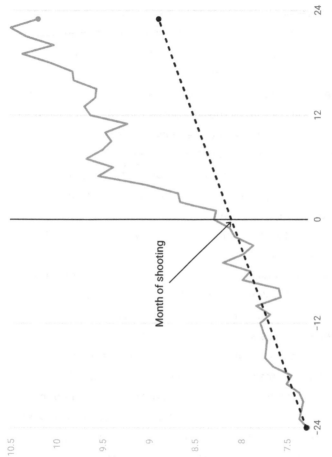

— Antidepressant prescriptions per thousand - - Pre-shooting trend

10.5

10

9.5

9

8.5

8

7.5

-24   -12   0   12   24

Month of shooting

Local use of antidepressants climbed after school shootings. Antidepressant prescriptions for youth per 1,000 (vertical axis) increase in the months after a school shooting (horizontal axis). *The Conversation, CC BY-ND. Data from Rossin–Slater, Schnell, Schwandt, Trejo, and Uniat (2020)*

Educational and Economic Trajectories

But the mental health impacts of mass school shootings tell only part of the story. While deadly massacres like the one in Uvalde receive widespread media and public attention, many more acts of gun violence at schools are less fatal and less highly publicized. Indeed, figures from the Center for Homeland Defense and Security show that, in 2021 alone, there were 240 incidents in which a gun was either brandished or used in a school. Of all shootings that took place at US schools in 2018 and 2019, nearly three-quarters had no fatalities. But that doesn't mean they don't have an impact.

To assess their effects, we studied fatal and nonfatal school shootings in Texas, taking a wider lens and considering acts of gun violence that frequently take place at schools but are unlikely to make national news.[2] Between 1995 and 2016, 33 Texas public schools experienced a shooting on school grounds during school hours; some schools had more than one.

Using detailed educational and labor market data, we compared the trajectories of students at schools that experienced shootings with those of students at schools that were similar in institutional and student characteristics, such as demographic makeup and percentage of students from low-income backgrounds, but that did not have a shooting over our study period. We found that students who had been exposed to a shooting at school were more likely to be chronically absent and to be held back a grade in the two years after the event.

They were also significantly less likely to graduate high school or go to or graduate college. The impacts extended into their early adult life. In their mid-twenties, they were less likely to be employed and had lower earnings than their peers who had not been exposed to a shooting at school.

Eighteen of the 33 shootings we included in the study resulted in no fatalities, and no shootings resulted in more than one death. Yet the negative impacts on people's lives were profound. Our results reveal that each student exposed to a shooting could expect to earn $115,550 less over the course of their lifetime.

Living with the Consequences

The tragedy of the lives lost to gun violence in America's schools cannot be overstated. But the data indicate that even those who escape these horrific events alive and without physical injury are also victims.

These adverse impacts are observed in students exposed to mass shootings but also to the more routine acts of gun violence in schools that rarely make the news. With an average of nearly 50,000 American students experiencing an act of gun violence at their school annually in recent years, our findings suggest that the aggregate cost of school gun violence measured in lost lifetime earnings is nearly $5.8 billion. The full costs in terms of detriment to the mental health of tens of thousands of young people are harder to quantify.

So as we mourn the lives lost in school shootings, we must not forget about the hundreds of other students who are at school when these events occur. These students will be forced to live with the consequences of what happened for decades to come.

Notes

1. Maya Rossin-Slater, Molly Schnell, Hannes Schwandt, Sam Trejo, and Lindsey Uniat, "Local Exposure to School Shootings and Youth Antidepressant Use," *Proceedings of the National Academy of Sciences* 117, no. 38 (September 8, 2020): 23484–89. https://doi.org/10.1073/pnas.2000804117.
2. Marika Cabral, Bokyung Kim, Maya Rossin-Slater, Molly Schnell, and Hannes Schwandt, "Trauma at School: The Impacts of Shootings on Students' Human Capital and Economic Outcomes," working paper 28311, National Bureau of Economic Research, 2020. https://doi.org/10.3386/w28311.

Chapter 26

Mass Shootings Leave Behind Collective Despair, Anguish, and Trauma at Many Societal Levels

ARASH JAVANBAKHT

THE UNITED STATES HAS SUFFERED A LONG LIST of mass shootings, national tragedies that leave families and friends of the victims gripped with grief, anguish, and despair. In addition to those who experience loss directly, such events also take a toll on others, including those who witnessed the shooting, first responders, people who were nearby, and those who hear about it—yet again—through the media.

I am a trauma and anxiety researcher and clinician, and I know that the effects of such violence reach millions. While the immediate survivors are most affected, the rest of society suffers too.

First, the Immediate Survivors

It is important to understand that no two people experience such horrific exposure in the same way. The extent of the trauma, stress, or fear can vary. Survivors of a shooting may want to avoid the neighborhood where the shooting occurred or the context related to the shooting, such as grocery stores, if the shooting happened at one. In the worst case, a survivor may develop post-traumatic stress disorder.

PTSD is a debilitating condition that develops after exposure to a serious traumatic experience such as war, natural disaster, rape, assault, robbery, car accident, or, of course, gun violence. Nearly 8% of the US population deals with PTSD. Symptoms include high anxiety, avoidance of reminders of the trauma, emotional numbness, hypervigilance, frequent intrusive memories of the trauma, nightmares, and flashbacks. The brain switches to fight-or-flight mode, or survival mode, and the person is always waiting for something terrible to happen.

When the trauma is caused by people, as in a mass shooting, the impact can be profound. The rate of PTSD in mass shootings may be as high as 36% among survivors.[1] Depression, another debilitating psychiatric condition, occurs in as many as 80% of people with PTSD. Survivors of shootings may also experience survivor's guilt, the feeling that they failed others who died or did not do enough to help them or just carry guilt over having survived.

PTSD can improve by itself, but many people need treatment. There are effective treatments available in the

Grief-stricken community members attend a prayer vigil following the mass shooting at Robb Elementary School in Uvalde, Texas, on May 24, 2022. *Jordan Vonderhaar / Getty Images News via Getty Images*

form of psychotherapy and medications. The more chronic it gets, the more negative its impact on the brain, and the harder it becomes to treat.

Children and adolescents, who are developing their worldview and deciding how safe it is to live in this society, may suffer even more. Exposure to horrific experiences such as school shootings can fundamentally affect whether people perceive the world to be a safe or unsafe place and how much they can rely on adults and society in general to protect them. They can carry such a worldview for the rest of their lives and even transfer it to their own children. Research is also abundant on the long-term detrimental impact of such childhood trauma on a person's mental and physical health and their ability to function through their adult life.

The Effect on Those Nearby or Arriving Later

PTSD can develop not only through personal exposure to trauma but also from exposure to others' severe trauma. Humans have survived as a species because of the ability to fear as a group. That means we learn fear and experience terror through exposure to the trauma and fear of others. Even seeing a frightened face in black and white on a computer screen will make our amygdala, the fear area of our brain, light up in brain imaging studies.[2]

People in the vicinity of a mass shooting may see exposed, disfigured, burned, or dead bodies. They may see injured people in agony, hear extremely loud noises, and experience chaos and terror in the post-shooting environment. They must also face the unknown or a sense of lacking control over the situation. The fear of the unknown plays an important role in making people feel insecure, terrified, and traumatized.

A group whose chronic exposure to such trauma is usually overlooked is first responders. While victims and potential victims try to run away from an active school shooter, police, firefighters, and paramedics rush into the danger zone. These first responders might have children of their own at the school or nearby. They frequently face uncertainty; threats to themselves, their colleagues, and others; and terrible, bloody post-shooting scenes. This exposure happens to them too frequently. PTSD has been reported in up to 20% of first responders to mass violence.[3]

Widespread Panic and Pain

People who were not directly exposed to a disaster but who were exposed to the news about it also experience distress, anxiety, or even PTSD.[4] This happened after 9/11.[5] Fear of the unknown (Will there be another strike? Are other coconspirators involved?) and reduced faith in perceived safety may all play a role in this.

Every time there is a mass shooting in a new setting, people learn that kind of place is now on the not-so-safe list. People worry not only about themselves but also about the safety of their children and other loved ones.

Is There Any Good to Come of Such Tragedy?

We can channel the collective agony and frustration to encourage meaningful changes, such as opening constructive discussions, informing the public about risks, and calling on lawmakers to take real action. In times of hardship, humans often can raise the sense of community, support one another, and fight for their rights, including the right to be safe at schools, concerts, restaurants, and movie theaters.

One beautiful outcome of the tragic shooting at the Tree of Life synagogue in October 2018 was the solidarity of the Muslim community with the Jewish community. This is especially productive in the current political environment, with fear and division being so common. Sadness, anxiety, anger, and frustration can be channeled into actions such as becoming involved in activism and volunteering to help the victims.

It is also important not to spend too much time watching television coverage of tragic events; turn it off when it stresses you too much. Studies have shown that exposure to media coverage for several hours daily following a collective trauma can lead to high stress.[6] So check the news a couple of times a day to stay informed, but don't continually seek out coverage and exposure to graphic images and news. The constant news cycle tends to report the same stories repeatedly without much additional information.

Notes

1. Carol S. North, Elizabeth M. Smith, and Edward L. Spitznagel, "Post-traumatic Stress Disorder in Survivors of a Mass Shooting," *American Journal of Psychiatry* 151, no. 1 (January 1, 1994): 82–88. https://doi.org /10.1176/ajp.151.1.82.
2. Arash Javanbakht, Anthony P. King, Gary W. Evans, James E. Swain, Michael Angstadt, K. Luan Phan, and Israel Liberzon, "Childhood Poverty Predicts Adult Amygdala and Frontal Activity and Connectivity in Response to Emotional Faces," *Frontiers in Behavioral Neuroscience* 9 (June 12, 2015). https://doi.org/10.3389/fnbeh.2015.00154.
3. Laura C. Wilson, "A Systematic Review of Probable Posttraumatic Stress Disorder in First Responders following Man-Made Mass Violence," *Psychiatry Research* 229, nos. 1–2 (September 30, 2015): 21–26. https://doi.org/10.1016/j.psychres.2015.06.015.
4. Siri Thoresen, Helene Flood Aakvaag, Tore Wentzel-Larsen, Grete Dyb, and Ole Kristian Hjemdal, "The Day Norway Cried: Proximity and Distress in Norwegian Citizens following the 22nd July 2011 Terrorist Attacks in Oslo and on Utøya Island," *European Journal of Psycho-traumatology* 3, no. 1 (December 7, 2012). https://doi.org/10.3402 /ejpt.v3i0.19709.
5. William E. Schlenger, Juesta M. Caddell, Lori Ebert, B. Kathleen Jordan, Kathryn M. Rourke, David Wilson, Lisa Thalji, J. Michael Dennis, John A. Fairbank, and Richard A. Kulka, "Psychological Reactions to Terrorist Attacks: Findings from the National Study of Americans' Reactions to September 11," *Journal of the American Medical Association* 288, no. 5 (August 7, 2002). https://doi.org/10.1001/jama .288.5.581.
6. E. Alison Holman, Dana Rose Garfin, and Roxane Cohen Silver, "Media's Role in Broadcasting Acute Stress following the Boston Marathon Bombings," *Proceedings of the National Academy of Sciences* 111, no. 1 (December 9, 2013): 93–98. https://doi.org/10.1073 /pnas.1316265110.

Chapter 27

Gun Violence Has Fueled Enduring Trust Issues for Many Americans

CARY WU

AMERICA'S GUN VIOLENCE affects not only those killed, injured, or present during gunfire, but research suggests it can also sabotage the social and psychological well-being of all Americans.

Gun violence is widespread in the United States. More than half a million Americans have been murdered by those brandishing firearms over the last four decades. Many more are physically or psychologically injured by guns. A 2017 survey from the Pew Research Center reported that, overall, one in four Americans (23%) say that someone has used a gun to threaten or intimidate them or their families. This includes a third of Black Americans (32%). Over the course of their lifetime, Americans of all racial and ethnic groups are likely to know a victim of gun violence in their social network.[1]

Despite its commonplace occurrence, there has not been much scholarly attention paid to the social and psychological impacts of gun violence on Americans and American society. My research shows that such widespread gun violence, both fatal and nonfatal, has a detrimental effect on Americans' trust in one another. That erosion of trust is often long lasting and has a greater impact on Black Americans.[2] The likelihood that most Americans were either threatened or shot with a gun or else knew someone who was, from the 1960s to the 1990s, could be a plausible reason for the half-century decline in trust in public institutions in the United States.[3]

Generalized Trust and Why It Matters

People's trust in others they don't know personally, or generalized trust, reflects their expectation of good will and benign intent from most people.

Trust matters. Those who trust other people are better off financially, have a higher socioeconomic status, are more satisfied with their life, are generally happier, have better health, and even tend to live longer.[4] Trust can also explain why some societies function better, are richer, safer, more cohesive, and more democratic.

American society is currently facing a crisis of trust. While in neighboring Canada, more than 58% of Canadians say most people can be trusted, only about 33% of Americans in 2020 reported that they have trust in their fellow citizens.[5]

The proportion fell by almost half from 1960, when 59% of American citizens said that most people can be trusted.

Where does trust come from? Some scholars believe that people are trusting because that's how they're raised. Others suggest that trust is dependent on contemporary social experiences and contexts.

Gun Victimization and Trust

Research into how gun victimization affects trust provides a way to test this long-standing debate.

To do so, we need micro-level data from individuals on their personal experiences of gun violence, but it can rarely be found. This is partly due to what's known as the Dickey Amendment in the United States, which was enacted in 1996 to ban federal funding for gun violence research.

The only data I can find is from the US General Social Survey. This survey of a nationally representative sample of Americans included questions over 15 years, in its 1973–1994 surveys, about whether respondents had experienced gun victimization. Respondents were asked, "Have you ever been threatened with a gun, or shot at?" If so, the surveys then asked, When did it happen, when respondents were children or adults? Unfortunately, these questions were discontinued from 1996 onward, likely due to the Dickey Amendment. While the data is relatively old, research findings from it could be relevant today.

My analysis of the data from the General Social Surveys shows that those who had experienced being threatened with a gun or had suffered a gunshot wound were significantly less likely to say that most people can be trusted, that people are helpful, and that people are fair.

Gun victimization could have occurred in childhood, in adulthood, or repeatedly during both childhood and adulthood. It could affect trust differently when it occurred at different times in life. In terms of the size of the impact, for example, repeated gun victimization had the strongest effect, followed by adulthood victimization and then childhood victimization.

Individuals who later achieve higher socioeconomic status are better able to recover from the psychological impact of childhood gun victimization. This finding suggests that trust evolves according to new life experiences.

The Black–White Gap in Trust

Compared with whites, Black Americans are less likely to say they can trust in others.[6] Blacks are also much more likely to experience gun victimization. The General Social Survey data shows that Black Americans have about 60% higher odds of experiencing gun victimization than white Americans.

Long-standing systemic racism has also made Black Americans less likely to get ahead in terms of socioeconomic achievement. Considered together, these data could help explain why the trust gap between Black and white Americans has barely changed for decades.

Vicious Circle

The preponderance of personal gun victimization is often a neighborhood disadvantage. When communities have higher percentages of people who were victimized by guns, their withdrawal from community life, their greater sense of powerlessness, and their eroded trust in their fellow citizens can affect everyone living there. Harvard professor Robert

Putnam has long pointed out that places with low trust may become trapped in a "vicious circle in which low levels of trust and cohesion lead to higher levels of crime, which lead to even lower levels of trust and cohesion."[7]

My analysis shows that places with higher percentages of people who were victimized by guns correlate with lower levels of trust; over time trust erodes even further because they're living in neighborhoods with higher levels of gun violence.

But to fully understand how gun violence affects Americans' everyday life, more data needs to be collected and more research needs to be conducted, especially as the country continues to grapple with the ever-worsening scourge of violence involving firearms.

Notes

1. Bindu Kalesan, Janice Weinberg, and Sandro Galea, "Gun Violence in Americans' Social Network during Their Lifetime," *Preventive Medicine* 93 (September 22, 2016): 53–56. https://doi.org/10.1016/j.ypmed.2016.09.025.

2. Cary Wu, "How Does Gun Violence Affect Americans' Trust in Each Other?," *Social Science Research* 91 (September 2020). https://doi.org/10.1016/j.ssresearch.2020.102449.

3. Pamela Paxton, "Trust in Decline?," *Contexts* 4, no. 1 (2005): 40–46. https://doi.org/10.1525/ctx.2005.4.1.40.

4. Eric M. Uslaner, ed., *The Oxford Handbook of Social and Political Trust* (New York: Oxford University Press, 2017). https://doi.org/10.1093/oxfordhb/9780190274801.001.0001.

5. Cary Wu, "Does Migration Affect Trust? Internal Migration and the Stability of Trust among Americans," *Sociological Quarterly* 61, no. 3 (February 5, 2020): 523–43. https://doi.org/10.1080/00380253.2019.1711259.

6. Sandra Susan Smith, "Race and Trust," *Annual Review of Sociology* 36, no. 1 (August 11, 2010): 453–75. https://doi.org/10.1146/annurev.soc.012809.102526.

7. Robert D. Putnam, *Bowling Alone: The Collapse and Revival of American Community*, revised and updated (New York: Simon & Schuster, 2020), 317.

Chapter 28

Why Americans Bought More Guns Than Ever during the Pandemic

MICHELLE BARNHART and AIMEE DINNÍN HUFF

IN THE EARLY MONTHS OF THE COVID-19 PANDEMIC, amid protests for racial justice, the gun industry's trade association, the National Shooting Sports Foundation, estimated that gun sales from March through July of 2020 totaled 8.5 million dollars. That was 94% higher sales than in the same period in 2019. Firearms industry consultants estimated that July 2020 sales alone amounted to two million units, an increase of 136% over July 2019. These estimates were based on the number of background checks conducted by the National Instant Criminal Background Check System, or NICS. The FBI reported that eight of the weeks in this period were in the top 10 highest weeks for checks since the agency began collecting data in 1998.

Gun sales typically have seasonal cycles, with more guns being sold in winter months, and an increase in presidential election years and after high-profile mass shootings.

The pandemic, however, spurred a record-setting surge in demand for firearms that continued through 2020 and beyond. Gun sales first spiked in March 2020, when lockdown orders began in the United States. The figures jumped again in June following nationwide protests over the killing of George Floyd. The total number of background checks in 2020 ultimately exceeded 39.5 million—a 40% increase over 2019—and decreased only slightly in 2021 to 38.9 million.[1]

Our research examines American gun culture and offers insights into the complex relationship between Americans and guns. We believe there are generally three reasons why people purchased so many firearms during the pandemic.

1. Independence and Security

A study of ours published in 2019 showed that Americans feel that buying a gun is a way of asserting and maintaining independence.[2] Independence is threatened during a pandemic, when a concern for public health may curtail some individual freedoms, including the freedom to travel, operate some businesses, assemble in large groups, or visit the elderly. Gun ownership can be motivated by a belief that having guns helps to ensure the freedom to do and live as one chooses, particularly for individuals concerned with protection and defense.

The National Shooting Sports Foundation estimated that 40% of those who purchased guns during the early months of the pandemic were doing so for the first time, partly driven by

Gun sales surged during the pandemic, driven by fears of personal safety. *George Frey / AFP via Getty Images*

their perceived need to protect themselves in a period of uncertainty and civil unrest, as well as by calls to defund the police. This idea is supported by data showing that more than 99% of sales during that period were of handguns, which are typically used for self-defense, and by research showing that buying a gun for self-defense can be motivated by feeling that the world is generally dangerous.[3]

Gun owners also find comfort and security in routines. This means that existing gun owners may purchase additional guns in an effort to maintain a sense of normalcy.

2. Market Signals and Forces

Another reason relates to market conditions. Governors chose to include gun retailers as "essential businesses," allowing them to remain open during many statewide closures in March and April of 2020. This reinforced the legitimacy of guns and gun retailers in the United States by strengthening perceptions of gun purchases as appropriate and necessary.

Meanwhile, gun retailers struggled to keep firearms, ammunition, and accessories in stock. When consumers face scarcity, they may experience a sense of urgency to purchase, and they may be willing to travel farther, pay more, or purchase an item different from what they initially sought.

3. Social Connection and Recreation

Finally, guns can provide a tangible basis for social connection. Social bonding through consumption is a well-established phenomenon in consumer research. Retailers facilitate this by serving as a social hub and by providing expertise on desired products. Visiting a firearms retailer and buying a gun can make consumers feel socially connected to like-minded others.

According to our research, going to shooting ranges and hunting are lower-risk activities in terms of accidental shootings.[4]

Americans who didn't join in the buying frenzy may question the motive for acquiring a gun in reaction to a microbe or rioters in faraway cities. During a time of crisis, citizens want to feel connected, secure, and independent. For some Americans, buying guns may help them do so.

Notes

1. *2020–2021 NICS Operations Report* (Washington, DC: US Department of Justice, Federal Bureau of Investigation, April 2022). https://www.fbi.gov/file-repository/nics-2020-2021-operations -report.pdf/view.

2. Michelle Barnhart, *Aimee Dinnin Huff, and Inara Scott, "Relating Americans' Responses to the Marketization of Armed Self-Defense to Their Understandings of the Second Amendment," Advances in Consumer Research 47 (2019): 135–41. https://www.acrwebsite.org /volumes/2552033/volumes/v47/NA-47.*
3. Wolfgang Stroebe, N. Pontus Leander, and Arie W. Kruglanski, "Is It a Dangerous World Out There? The Motivational Bases of American Gun Ownership," *Personality and Social Psychology Bulletin* 43, no. 8 (June 8, 2017): 1071–85. https://doi.org/10.1177/0146167217703952.
4. Michelle Barnhart, Aimee Dinnin Huff, Brandon McAlexander, and James H. McAlexander, "Preparing for the Attack: Mitigating Risk through Routines in Armed Self-Defense," *Journal of the Association for Consumer Research* 3, no. 1 (January 2018): 27–45. https://doi.org /10.1086/695762.

Chapter 29

Are Looser Gun Laws Changing the Social Fabric of Missouri?

JONATHAN M. METZL

IN 2014 MISSOURI TOOK A STEP TO ARM TEACHERS after lawmakers passed a bill that allowed school districts to recast teachers and administrators as "school protection officers." In 2022 the Missouri House endorsed legislation that expanded the designation to all school personnel, such as cooks and custodians.

The specter of loaded firearms in classrooms raises concerns in no small part because the dynamics of learning often depend on instructors challenging students to step outside their comfort zone. But beneath these concerns lies a broader question: Do guns change the ways that people engage with one another?

Scholars who research guns and gun violence, myself included, often track the impact of guns through homicide and injury rates.[1] But the impact of guns on everyday interactions, and in instances when guns are neither drawn nor discharged, remains a largely unstudied topic.

So I decided to talk to people about it. I'm a native Missourian, and I went back home for research as part of a book project about guns in everyday life. In the mid-2010s, I interviewed 100 people, including ordinary citizens, religious and political leaders, and gun-violence prevention advocates in Kansas City, Columbia, and St. Louis, about the impact that increasingly permissive gun laws are having on social interactions in the state.

Again and again, people with whom I spoke raised concerns, not just about the lethal potential of firearms, but about the ways that allowing guns into previously gun-free public spaces might impact a host of commonplace civic encounters as well.

Missouri Used to Have Some of the Strictest Gun Laws in the Country

Missouri used to have among the strictest gun laws in the nation, including a requirement that handgun buyers undergo a background check in person at a sheriff's office before obtaining a gun permit. But over the past decade and a half, an increasingly conservative legislature and citizenry relaxed limitations governing practically every aspect of buying, owning, and carrying guns. The legislature relaxed prohibitions on the concealed and open carry of firearms in public spaces, lowered the legal age to carry a concealed gun from 21 to 19, and repealed many of the requirements for comprehensive background checks and purchase permits.

And in 2014 voters approved Amendment 5, which effectively negated the rights of cities or towns to pass or enforce practically any form of gun control.

A Natural Experiment

What followed was a state of affairs that the *New York Times* described as a "natural experiment" for testing whether more guns would lead to more safety and less crime.[2]

Instead, according to research, the opposite occurred, inasmuch as gun deaths soared when it became easier for people to buy and carry firearms. A team of researchers led by Daniel Webster, director of the Johns Hopkins Center for Gun Policy and Research, analyzed extensive crime data from Missouri and found that the state's 2007 repeal of its permit-to-purchase handgun law correlated with an increase of 25% in the rate of firearm homicides. Between 2008 and 2014 the gun homicide rate in Missouri rose to 47% above the national average.[3]

Missouri's startling rate of gun death made national news. At the same time, many people with whom I spoke— particularly people who did not support the legislative developments—suggested that loosening gun laws had forced nonarmed citizens to adapt in ways that ranged from acceptance to anxiety to avoidance.

Heightening Racial Tensions

A number of African Americans I interviewed worried that guns had heightened racial tensions. I met a man named John

Steen, who now thinks twice about shopping at Sam's Club. Steen, a Vietnam veteran who works in Kansas City, used to stop by the wholesale megastore on his way home from his job as an in-home health care provider. But that was before he saw armed white men strolling through the aisles exercising what gun proponents describe as their "unalienable" right to carry firearms in public spaces such as a retail store.

For Steen and other African Americans in Kansas City, the result was intimidation. "I see white guys and their sons walking around Sam's Club, Walmart, and other places where we shop, strolling with guns on their hips like it's the wild west," he told me. "They're trying to be all macho, like they have power because of their guns, walking down the aisles. It just makes me . . . stay away."

Subverting the traditional narrative of racial anxiety, African Americans often cited the charged implications of white citizens brandishing guns in mixed-race settings—a narrative that played out in downtown St. Louis after the passage of Amendment 5 and just months before protests began in nearby Ferguson, when white Missouri advocates of open carry paraded through the streets waving handguns, long guns, and assault rifles.

For Reverend Dr. Cassandra Gould, events such as these illustrate a double standard by which society codes white gun owners as "protectors" and black gun owners as "threats." As Pastor of Quinn Chapel AME Church in Jefferson City, Gould led an intense debate among her congregants after the shooting in Charleston, South Carolina, in June 2015 that yielded a decision to ban guns in their house of worship. For Gould, "even though I want us to be protected, I can't escape the fact that these are the same guns that are oppressing communities of color in our state."

Accidental Shootings Are Up

The complexities of parenting in a milieu filled with firearms emerged as another theme.

In Missouri there are now virtually no remaining laws governing gun safety or storage. When I conducted my research, up until 2018, Missouri led the nation in accidental shootings by toddlers: instances where young children found unlocked guns and accidentally discharged them. In response, the Missouri chapter of Moms Demand Action signed onto a BeSmart campaign promoting safety steps; these included training parents to secure guns in their home and asking about proper firearm storage before dropping their children off at a friend's house. As Becky Morgan, the Missouri chapter lead for Moms put it when we spoke, "this is a new step parents are taking to look out for our children's safety. We already ask about food allergies, pet allergies, and pools. Now we ask if firearms are in the home, are they stored properly out of children's reach?"

Caution surrounds a host of everyday interactions as well. Consultant Jeff Fromm thinks about armed motorists when he drives to and from work in downtown Kansas City. "I try not to drive too close to other cars on the highway or pass in front of anyone at a stoplight. Road rage takes on a whole new meaning when you don't know who's going to be armed." "I've seen people with guns in their belts at the supermarket," a Columbia parent named Megan White added. "It makes me reconsider bringing my kid on shopping trips."

Changing the Fabric of Social Interactions?

Thoughts about gun proliferation even impact exchanges in the halls of power where gun legislation was passed in the first place.

Former Missouri Democratic state representative Stacey Newman told me she worried that many legislators and their staff carry concealed weapons during heated debates on the Missouri House floor. "With new laws, capital security can no longer ask lawmakers to check their firearms at the door," she explained. "And I often find it quite unnerving that the people I'm working with or arguing against might well be carrying secret guns during our legislative sessions."

To be sure, an armed society is precisely what many Missourians and legislators who support gun rights envision and support. John L., an advertising consultant who asked that his last name not be used, told me that he appreciates being able to carry a concealed firearm when he visits printing factories and other work sites. "I've been robbed before," he explained. "The thought that I can carry a gun just makes me feel safer." Linda Hopkins, owner of Smokin' Guns BBQ in North Kansas City, told me that she welcomes customers who carry concealed weapons and feels far more angered by "food prices and intrusive government regulations."

For these and other reasons, *Guns & Ammo* magazine in 2014 cited Missouri as "ahead of the curve when it comes to gun rights" and a "top state for gun owners," thanks in large part to legislation allowing concealed carry.[4]

But a number of Missourians with whom I spoke felt otherwise. Their concerns seemed to provide a broader context for matters of civic engagement, power relations, and conflict resolution that lie at the core of debates about allowing guns in college classrooms. The experiences of Missourians suggest a need for more research into ways that allowing guns in the public sphere might impact quotidian social interactions.

Newman, the former state representative introduced above, particularly worried about the effect that guns will have on the "psyches of our children," who go to college with a desire to learn and grow in a safe environment and who instead may soon enter classrooms where bearing arms and armed confrontation remain "constant possibilities." For Newman, the issue hit home when her daughter enrolled in graduate school at the University of Missouri in Kansas City. "As a parent this is my worst nightmare."

Steen, the in-home health care provider, had seen enough of guns in his lifetime. "I was in Vietnam with the US military; I saw what it means to draw a gun and shoot another person; it's devastating. Trust me . . . most of these people have no idea."

Notes

1. Jonathan M. Metzl and Kenneth T. MacLeish, "Mental Illness, Mass Shootings, and the Politics of American Firearms," *American Journal of Public Health* 105, no. 2 (February 2015): 240–49. https://doi.org /10.2105/ajph.2014.302242.
2. Sabrina Tavernise, "In Missouri, Fewer Gun Restrictions and More Gun Killings," *New York Times*, December 21, 2015. https://www.nytimes .com/2015/12/22/health/in-missouri-fewer-gun-restrictions-and -more-gun-killings.html.
3. Daniel Webster, Cassandra Kercher Crifasi, and Jon S. Vernick, "Effects of the Repeal of Missouri's Handgun Purchaser Licensing Law on Homicides," *Journal of Urban Health* 91, no. 2 (March 7, 2014): 293–302. https://doi.org/10.1007/s11524-014-9865-8.
4. Keith Wood, "Best States for Gun Owners (2015)," Guns & Ammo (website), July 21, 2015. https://www.gunsandammo.com/editorial /best-states-for-gun-owners-2015/249293.

Part V

The Politics and Policies of Gun Control

America is nothing if not a "confusing patchwork" of gun leg-islation.[1] The 1934 National Firearms Act—the first major federal gun law—and the 1938 Federal Firearms Act together created a licensing system for gun dealers and imposed tax and registration requirements on "gangster guns" (for example, machine guns and sawed-off shotguns) used by Prohibition-era organized criminals. The 1968 Federal Gun Control Act, enacted after the assassina-tions of Robert F. Kennedy and Martin Luther King Jr., restricted the importation of military-surplus firearms and prohibited gun deal-ers from selling to "dangerous" categories of persons, such as ju-veniles, convicted felons, fugitives, drug users, and former mental patients. Under the common-law concept of "negligent entrust-ment," a firearm also cannot be sold to a person if the seller knows, or reasonably should know, that the buyer poses an unusually high risk of misusing it.

The challenge is that purchases from Federal Firearms Licens-ees account for only about 60% of all gun sales. The remaining 40% of gun transactions occur in the "secondary market," where federal law does not require transaction records or criminal back-ground checks for prospective gun buyers.[2] The secondary market includes gun brokers who (a) sell guns directly; (b) find customers for gun dealers who sell off the books; and (c) match sellers with gun buyers in gun shows, which include both licensed and unli-censed gun dealers. And then there are illegal transactions. Thou-sands of guns stolen from manufacturers, importers, distributors, licensed dealers, and private citizens each year make their way into the hands of prohibited persons.

Prohibited persons also acquire firearms from licensees with-out theft through straw purchases (when the actual buyer uses another person to complete the purchase and fill out the paper-work), "lying and buying" (that is, a buyer showing false identifica-tion and lying about their status), or buying from a dealer willing to disguise the illegal transaction by falsifying the record of sale or reporting the gun as stolen.[3] Corrupt gun dealers account for less than 10% of gun-trafficking investigations conducted by police but for more than half of all guns diverted to prohibited users.[4]

Roughly half of Americans (53%) favor stricter gun laws to address some of these issues, down from about 60% in 2019. There is even broad bipartisan agreement on some gun policy proposals. Majorities in both parties oppose allowing people to carry concealed firearms without a permit, while 70% of Republicans and 92% of Democrats favor background checks for private gun sales and gun show sales.[5] Other proposals bring out stark partisan rifts, however. While 80% or more of Democrats favor banning assault-style weapons and high-capacity ammunition magazines that hold more than 10 rounds, most Republicans oppose this and would instead prefer to allow people to carry concealed guns in more places or to arm teachers and school officials in K–12 schools—ideas widely rejected by Democrats.

Yet, even in areas of relative consensus, Congress has repeatedly failed to pass major gun-control legislation. For example, it tried to pass a compromise bill to expand background checks in 2013, months after the horrific mass shooting at Sandy Hook Elementary School in Newtown, Connecticut, but the bill failed to overcome a Senate filibuster because most Republicans and a handful of Democrats opposed the legislation.

As the chapters in part V highlight, the hurdles to enacting stricter gun laws in the United States are numerous and significant. Still, federal law is the floor, not the ceiling, on gun safety. As Conservative Justice Antonin Scalia's majority opinion in *District of Columbia v. Heller, 554 U.S. 570* (2008) made clear: "Like most rights, the right secured by the Second Amendment is not unlimited. . . . It is not a right to keep and carry any weapon whatsoever in any manner whatsoever and for whatever purpose. . . . Nothing in our opinion should be taken to cast doubt on long-standing prohibitions on the possession of firearms by felons and the mentally ill, or laws forbidding the carrying of firearms in sensitive places such as schools and government buildings, or laws imposing conditions and qualifications on the commercial sale of arms." In other words, states have the right to pass their own gun control measures, but they can't deny firearms outright. In 2019, the average number of firearm law provisions per state was 29 but ranged from 1 provision in Idaho to more than 100 in California.[6]

As an example, several states regulate concealed-carry permits, at least they did until *New York State Rifle & Pistol Association, Inc. v. Bruen, 597 U.S.* (2022), when the US Supreme Court struck down a 100-year-old New York law requiring that permit applicants show "proper cause," or a particular need, to carry a firearm for self-defense. This ruling could make it easier for citizens to carry concealed weapons, and when more people carry guns, violent crime increases.[7] Gun rights advocates counter that concealed carry deters criminals, but an analysis of 433 "active shooter" attacks from 2000 to 2021, in which one or more shooters killed or attempted to kill multiple unrelated people in a populated place, found that armed bystanders shot attackers in just 22 cases (5%); and in 10 of those, the "good guy with a gun," to use the phrase du jour, was a security guard or an off-duty police officer.[8]

The chapters in this part explain how the United States has arrived at its current state with regard to the rights of gun owners and gun control policy. They evaluate the effectiveness of specific policies, including red flag laws and an assault weapons ban, both in the United States and in other countries. Chapters also explore special protections afforded gun-makers in the United States and the politics of gun control, plus innovative public health and community-led initiatives to curb gun violence. These chapters argue that change is possible in what often appears to be an intractable debate over gun rights and gun safety.

Recommended Further Reading

- *Private Guns, Public Health* by David Hemenway
- *Gunfight: The Battle over the Right to Bear Arms in America* by Adam Winkler
- *Misfire: Inside the Downfall of the NRA* by Tim Mak
- *The Positive Second Amendment* by Joseph Blocher and Darrell A. H. Miller

Notes

1. Brian Resnick, "How to Make Sense of America's Wildly Different, Confusing Patchwork of Gun Control Laws," *Atlantic*, December 17, 2012. https://www.theatlantic.com/politics/archive/2012/12/how-to-make-sense-of-americas-wildly-different-confusing-patchwork-of-gun-control-laws/454299/.
2. Philip J. Cook and Jens Ludwig, *Gun Violence: The Real Costs* (New York: Oxford University Press, 2000).
3. Anthony A. Braga, Philip J. Cook, David M. Kennedy, and Mark H. Moore, "The Illegal Supply of Firearms," *Crime and Justice* 29 (January 2002): 319–52. https://doi.org/10.1086/652223.
4. Charles F. Wellford, John Pepper, and Carol Petrie, eds., *Firearms and Violence: A Critical Review* (Washington, DC: National Academies Press, 2005).
5. Katherine Schaeffer, "Key Facts about Americans and Guns," Pew Research Center, September 13, 2021. https://www.pewresearch.org/fact-tank/2021/09/13/key-facts-about-americans-and-guns/.
6. Michael Siegel, State Firearms Laws Database, 1991–2020. https://www.statefirearmlaws.org/state-state-firearm-law-data.
7. "The Effects of Concealed-Carry Laws," RAND, updated January 10, 2023. https://www.rand.org/research/gun-policy/analysis/concealed-carry.html.
8. Larry Buchanan and Lauren Leatherby, "Who Stops a 'Bad Guy with a Gun'?," *New York Times*, June 22, 2022. https://www.nytimes.com/interactive/2022/06/22/us/shootings-police-response-uvalde-buffalo.html.

Chapter 30

How US Gun Control Compares to the Rest of the World

JOHN J. DONOHUE III

WHILE DEATHS FROM MASS SHOOTINGS are a relatively small part of overall homicidal violence in America, they are particularly heart wrenching. The problem is worse in the United States than in most other industrialized nations. And it is getting worse.

I've been researching gun violence—and what can be done to prevent it—in the United States for more than 25 years. The fact is that if the claim of the National Rifle Association (NRA) were true, namely, that guns help to reduce crime, the United States would have the lowest

Handgun in a holster, baby in a stroller at
the 2016 convention of the National Rifle
Association in Louisville, Kentucky.
AP Photo / Mark Humphrey

homicide rate among industrialized nations instead of the
highest one—and by a wide margin.

The United States is by far the world leader in the
number of guns in civilian hands. The stricter gun laws of
many other developed countries have restrained homicidal
violence, suicides, and gun accidents, even when, in some
cases, laws were introduced over massive protests from their
armed citizens.

The Danger of Guns in the Home

Many states in the United States and a number of cities
including Chicago, New York, and San Francisco have tried to

reduce the unlawful use of guns and gun accidents by adopting laws requiring that guns be safely stored when they are not in use. Safe storage is a common form of gun regulation in nations with stricter gun regulations.

The NRA has been battling such laws for years. But that effort was dealt a blow in June 2015 when the US Supreme Court—over strident dissent by Justices Thomas and Scalia—refused to consider the San Francisco law requiring that guns not in use be stored safely. This was a positive step because hundreds of thousands of guns are stolen every year, and good public policy must try to keep guns out of the hands of criminals and children.

The dissenters were alarmed by the thought that a gun stored in a safe would not be immediately available for use, but they seemed to be unaware of how unusual it is that a gun proves helpful when someone is under attack. Statistics show that only the tiniest fraction of victims of violent crime are able to use a gun in their defense. Over the period from 2007 to 2011, roughly six million nonfatal violent crimes occurred each year. Yet data from the National Crime Victimization Survey show that 99.2% of victims in these incidents did not protect themselves with a gun—this in a country with roughly 400 million guns in civilian hands today.

In fact, a classic study of 198 cases of unwanted entry into occupied single-family dwellings in Atlanta found that the invader was twice as likely to obtain the victim's gun than to have the victim use a firearm in self-defense. The authors of the study concluded with a statement that those who oppose safe storage of guns should heed: "On average, the gun that represents the greatest threat is the one that is kept loaded and readily available in a bedside drawer."[1]

A loaded, unsecured gun in the home is like an insurance policy that fails to deliver at least 95% of the time but that has the constant potential—particularly in the case of handguns, which are more easily manipulated by children and more attractive for use in crime—to harm someone in the home or be stolen and harm someone else.

Unfortunately, a more pro-gun majority of justices is now in place on the Supreme Court, which stumbled badly in June 2022 in striking down a 109-year-old law limiting the carrying of guns. Public safety will doubtless be harmed by the unwise and inexplicable extension of the Second Amendment.

More Guns Won't Stop Gun Violence

For years, the NRA's mantra has been that allowing citizens to carry concealed handguns would reduce crime, as they would fight off or scare off the criminals. Some early studies even purported to show that so-called right-to-carry (RTC) laws did just that, but a 2004 report from the National Research Council refuted that claim, saying it was not supported by "the scientific evidence," while remaining uncertain about what the true impact of RTC laws was.[2]

The research on this issue from my team at Stanford University has provided compelling evidence that RTC laws are associated with significant increases in violent crime. Looking at Uniform Crime Reports data from 1979 to 2014, we found that, on average, the 33 states that had adopted RTC laws over this period experienced violent crime rates roughly 14% higher after 10 years than if they had not adopted them. This research has now been widely endorsed as reflecting the true effect of increased gun carrying, which is worrisome in light of the 2022 Supreme Court decision.[3]

Gun Control around the World

As an academic exercise, one might speculate whether law could play a constructive role in reducing the number or the deadliness of mass shootings.

Most other advanced nations apparently think so, since they make it far harder for someone like the typical American mass killer to get his hands on particularly lethal weapons. Universal background checks are common features of gun regulation in other developed countries:

- In Germany, to buy a gun, anyone under the age of 25 has to pass a psychiatric evaluation. Presumably, 21-year-old Charleston shooter Dylann Roof would have failed.
- In Finland, handgun license applicants are allowed to purchase firearms only if they can prove they are an active member of a regulated shooting club. Before they can get a gun, applicants must pass an aptitude test, submit to a police interview, and show they have a proper gun storage unit.
- In Italy, to secure a gun permit, one must establish a genuine reason to possess a firearm and pass a back-ground check that considers both criminal and mental health records.
- In France, applicants for acquiring a firearm must have no criminal record and pass a background check that considers the reason for the gun purchase and evaluates the criminal, psychological, and health records of the applicant.
- In the United Kingdom and Japan, handguns are illegal for private citizens.

Mass shootings, as well as gun homicides and suicides, are not unknown in these countries, yet their rates of occurrence are substantially lower than in the United States. NRA supporters frequently challenge me on these statistics, saying the elevated US rates are due to Black Americans' violence while pointing to wildly incorrect claims, such as those spouted by Dylann Roof or tweeted by Donald Trump, about the percentage of white Americans killed by Blacks. This overlooks the fact that the rate of murder committed by white criminals in the United States is well over twice that of the murder rates in any other affluent nation.

Australia Hasn't Had a Mass Shooting since 1996

The story of Australia, which had 13 mass shootings in the 18-year period from 1979 to 1996 but only 1 in the succeeding 26 years, is worth examining.[4]

The turning point was the 1996 Port Arthur massacre in Tasmania, in which a gunman killed 35 individuals using semiautomatic weapons. In the wake of the massacre, the conservative federal government succeeded in implementing tough new gun-control laws throughout the country. A large array of weapons was banned, including the Glock semiautomatic handgun used in the Charleston shootings. The government also imposed a mandatory gun buy-back that substantially reduced gun possession in Australia.

The effect was that both gun suicides and homicides fell. In addition, the 1996 legislation disallowed self-defense as a legitimate reason for purchasing a firearm.

When I mention this to disbelieving NRA supporters, they insist that crime must now be rampant in Australia. In fact, the murder rate in Australia has fallen to 1 per 100,000, while the

US rate is more than five times higher. Moreover, robberies in Australia are substantially lower than in the United States: 36 in Australia versus 60.9 per 100,000 persons in the United States in 2021.

How did Australia do it? Politically it took a brave prime minister to face down the anger of Australian gun interests. Prime Minister John Howard wore a bulletproof vest when he announced the proposed gun restrictions in June 1996, and the deputy prime minister was hung in effigy. Notably, Australia did not have a domestic gun industry to oppose the new measures, so the will of the people was allowed to emerge. And today, support for the safer, gun-restricted Australia is so strong that going back would not be tolerated by the public.

Australia's success in dramatically curtailing mass shootings is likely more than merely a result of the considerable reduction in the number of guns; it's certainly not the case that guns have disappeared altogether. I suspect the country has also experienced a cultural shift after the shock of the Port Arthur massacre and the removal of guns from everyday life, as guns are no longer available for self-defense and are simply less present in the country. Troubled individuals are not constantly reminded that guns are a means of acting on their alleged grievances to the extent they had been in the past, or continue to be in the United States.

Lax Gun Control in One Nation Can Create Problems in Another

Of course, strict gun regulations cannot ensure that the danger of mass shootings has been eliminated.

Norway has strong gun control and committed humane values. But that didn't prevent Anders Breivik from opening fire on a youth camp on the island of Utøya in 2011. His clean criminal record and hunting license had allowed him to secure semiautomatic rifles, but Norway had restricted his ability to get high-capacity clips for them. In his manifesto, Breivik wrote about his attempts to buy weapons legally, stating, "I envy our European American brothers as the gun laws in Europe sucks ass in comparison." In the same manifesto, Breivik wrote that it was from a US supplier that he had purchased, and received by mail, 10 magazines of 30 rounds of ammunition for the rifle he used in his attack.

In other words, even if one nation or one state makes it harder for some would-be killers to get their weapons, these controls may be undercut by other jurisdictions that hold out. In the United States, of course, gun-control measures enacted by some states are thwarted by lax laws for gun acquisition in others.

Notes

1. Arthur L. Kellermann, Lori Westphal, Laurie Fischer, and Beverly Harvard, "Weapon Involvement in Home Invasion Crimes," *Journal of the American Medical Association* 273, no. 22 (June 14, 1995). https://doi.org/10.1001/jama.1995.03520460041032.
2. Charles F. Wellford, John V. Pepper, and Carol V. Petrie, eds., *Firearms and Violence: A Critical Review* (Washington, DC: National Academies Press, 2005).
3. "Effects of Concealed-Carry Laws on Violent Crime," RAND, January 10, 2023. https://www.rand.org/research/gun-policy/analysis /concealed-carry/violent-crime.html.
4. S. Chapman, P. Alpers, K. Agho, and M. Jones, "Australia's 1996 Gun Law Reforms: Faster Falls in Firearm Deaths, Firearm Suicides, and a Decade without Mass Shootings," *Injury Prevention* 12, no. 6 (December 2006): 365–72. https://doi.org/10.1136/ip.2006.013714.

Chapter 31

Public Database Reveals Striking Differences in How Guns Are Regulated from State to State

MICHAEL SIEGEL and MOLLY PAHN

IN THE WAKE OF TWO MASS SHOOTINGS, the federal government passed a gun reform law in June 2022. But that was a rarity. Because of years of inaction on the part of the federal government, individual states have passed their own laws to reduce gun violence. To evaluate the effectiveness of these laws, researchers and policy makers need a way to track differences in states' firearm legislation over an extended time period. Previously, there was no such resource.

In 2017 we launched a public database that tracks a wide range of firearm laws across all 50 states for the past 27 years.[1] With it, long-term trends in the enactment of gun safety laws can be compared across states. We have found striking disparities among states both in the number of firearm laws on the books and in the rate of adoption of these laws over time.[2]

Fewer Limits for Gun Owners

Our database includes 133 different measures intended to reduce gun violence, noting the presence or absence of each in all 50 states beginning in 1991.

As of 2020, five states had fewer than five of these 133 possible firearm law provisions in place, while two states had 100 or more. Between 1991 and 2016, one state enacted 62 of the firearm law provisions, while 16 states actually repealed more provisions than they enacted.

States have enacted laws that allow people to shoot other people as a first resort when threatened in public instead of having to retreat. If someone perceives a threat of serious bodily harm, so-called stand-your-ground laws allow them to fire their gun with immunity from prosecution, as long as they are in a place where they have a legal right to be.[3] Between 2004 and 2020, 27 states enacted a stand-your-ground law. States are also increasingly loosening the requirements for carrying concealed weapons. As of early 2023, there were 24 states that allowed people to carry a concealed weapon without a permit.[4]

More Laws Are Being Enacted to Protect
the Gun Industry

States are increasingly enacting laws that protect the gun industry from potential liability.[5] These laws prevent citizens who are injured by a firearm from suing its manufacturer for damages resulting from a misuse of the product. They also stop local governments from filing lawsuits against gun manufacturers. While only 7 states had a gun industry immunity law in 1991, 33 states had such a law as of 2020.

No other manufacturer of a consumer product enjoys such broad immunity. A similar law at the federal level resulted in the dismissal of a lawsuit against gun manufacturers brought by the families of children killed in the 2012 Newtown tragedy in Connecticut.

In 1998 the Federal Bureau of Investigation implemented a federal system for background checks for gun purchases from licensed dealers. This left a "gun show loophole" that allows any adult to purchase a gun without undergoing a background check merely by purchasing it from a private seller, rather than a licensed dealer. As of 2020, adults in 34 states could legally purchase a firearm from a private seller without being subject to a background check.

There is, however, one area of gun regulation that most of the states, even those with few other gun safety laws, are progressively pursuing: laws that prohibit domestic violence offenders from possessing firearms. In 1991 only three states had enacted laws that prohibit gun possession by people convicted of misdemeanor crimes of domestic violence. As of 2020, 31 states had such laws in place.

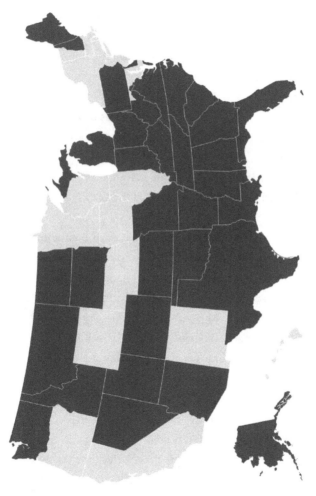

Legal immunity for the gun industry. Laws in 33 states (*darker gray*) protect the gun industry from potential liability as of 2020. These laws prevent citizens who are injured by firearms from suing gun manufacturers for damages resulting from the misuse of their products. They also prevent local governments from filing lawsuits against gun manufacturers. *The Conversation, CC BY-ND. Data from State Firearm Laws*

Moreover, the federal gun legislation compromise in 2022 resulted in the removal of the "boyfriend loophole" in federal gun law, which previously had allowed domestic violence offenders to retain their guns if their victim was a dating partner rather than a spouse, ex-spouse, or cohabiting partner.

Why Our Database Matters

By examining trends in firearm legislation, rather than just looking at a single snapshot in time, we can discover patterns in firearm law adoption. These patterns may reflect changes in social norms or specific lobbying campaigns by special interest groups.

For example, the surge in stand-your-ground laws was not a coincidence but rather was the result of a concerted lobbying campaign by the National Rifle Association. Florida's 2005 law—the second such to be adopted, after Utah's in 1994—was crafted by former NRA president Marion Hammer. These laws were pushed by the American Legislative Exchange Council (ALEC), of which the NRA was a member. An NRA official cochaired an ALEC committee that drafted a model law, which was then introduced in states throughout the country.

More than anything else, our database is intended to help researchers evaluate the effectiveness of different state-level approaches to reducing gun violence. By examining the relationship between changes in these laws over time and changes in firearm mortality, researchers may be able to identify which policies are effective and which are not.

In our view, legislators must balance the protection of the constitutional right to possess a firearm for self-defense with the responsibility to reduce firearm-related injury and death. To do this, they need to distinguish policies that effectively reduce firearm violence from those that are ineffective and therefore unnecessary. Reliable longitudinal data can help them find ways to mitigate the impact that gun violence has on the lives of thousands of Americans each year.

Notes

1. "State-by-State Firearm Law Data," State Firearm Laws, accessed October 5, 2022. http://www.statefirearmlaws.org/.
2. Michael Siegel, Molly Pahn, Ziming Xuan, Craig S. Ross, Sandro Galea, Bindu Kalesan, Eric Fleegler, and Kristin A. Goss, "Firearm-Related Laws in All 50 US States, 1991–2016," *American Journal of Public Health* 107, no. 7 (2017): 1122–29. https://doi.org/10.2105/ajph.2017.303701.
3. Cynthia V. Ward, "'Stand Your Ground' and Self Defense," *American Journal of Criminal Law* 42, no. 1 (2014): 89–138. https://scholarship.law.wm.edu/facpubs/1800.
4. "Constitutional Carry / Unrestricted / Permitless Carry," U.S. Concealed Carry Association, accessed January 2023. https://www.usconcealedcarry.com/resources/terminology/types-of-concealed-carry-licensurepermitting-policies/unrestricted/
5. Jon S. Vernick and Julia Samia Mair, "State Laws Forbidding Municipalities from Suing the Firearm Industry: Will Firearm Immunity Laws Close the Courthouse Door?," *Journal of Health Care Law and Policy* 4, no. 1 (2000): 126–46. https://digitalcommons.law.umaryland.edu/jhclp/vol4/iss1/8/.

Chapter 32

US Tragedies from Guns Have Often—but Not Always—Spurred Political Responses

ROBERT SPITZER

THE NATIONWIDE CALL FOR STRONGER GUN LAWS in the aftermath of mass shootings is understandable. It's also predictable. Whether legislative efforts to raise the minimum age for buying semiautomatic rifles or to expand background checks and similar measures succeed or fail, they tend to follow a pattern in American politics that traces back more than a century.

As I explain in my book *The Politics of Gun Control*, efforts to restrict and regulate firearms have followed the assassinations of political leaders, crime waves, and mass shootings since before World War I.[1]

A Spate of Shootings in 1910–1911

In 1910, New York City mayor William J. Gaynor boarded the steamship *Kaiser Wilhelm der Grosse*, docked in Hoboken, New Jersey. He was embarking on a monthlong European vacation. The trip was interrupted when a disgruntled former city employee shot him in the neck with a concealed pistol. Gaynor, seriously wounded in the assassination attempt, died in 1913. The incident heightened already-growing calls for a new handgun law in New York State amid rising gun violence, especially in New York City.

In 1911, the noted novelist David Graham Phillips was shot in Manhattan by a man who then turned his gun on himself. Both died.

With the city coroner's office reporting a sharp increase in gun homicides, state lawmakers in New York responded by enacting a law requiring permits to buy, own, and carry handguns. Other states enacted similar pistol permit laws.

The US Supreme Court ruled on June 23, 2022, that the 1911 measure violated the Second Amendment, thus striking down strict limits on who can carry guns in New York.

Prohibition-Era Tumult

Gangland violence tied to alcohol trafficking during Prohibition flared throughout the 1920s and early 1930s. This mayhem led to many new laws restricting gun ownership.[2] Most states banned the fully automatic weapons that gangsters favored. At least eight enacted laws restricting or barring semiautomatic firearms too.

In 1933, shortly before his first presidential inauguration, Franklin D. Roosevelt narrowly escaped an assassin's bullet. A year later, Congress passed the National Firearms Act of 1934. This first significant federal gun law required that those wanting to own the listed weapons be registered with the Treasury Department, fingerprinted, and subject to a background check; plus, would-be gun owners had to pay a substantial fee to own fully automatic firearms, sawed-off shotguns, silencers, and similar equipment.

One month before Roosevelt signed the measure into law, Texas police gunned down the infamous gangster duo Bonnie Parker and Clyde Champion Barrow. A month later, the Federal Bureau of Investigation killed John Dillinger, another notorious outlaw.

Assassinations and Upheaval in the 1960s

President John F. Kennedy's assassination in 1963 led Congress to consider new gun measures. Lawmakers held hearings, but those efforts languished until the assassinations of the Reverend Dr. Martin Luther King Jr. and Senator Robert F. Kennedy in 1968. Rising crime rates and unrest in the cities of Detroit, Los Angeles, Chicago, and Washington, DC, also increased the public's concerns over safety.

Congress responded by passing the Gun Control Act of 1968, which President Lyndon B. Johnson signed into law. The act restricted interstate gun shipment; barred gun sales to minors, felons, and people deemed "mentally defective"; and strengthened licensing and record-keeping, among other measures.

The first modern gun control groups devoted exclusively to advocating for stronger regulations arose in the 1970s.

President Lyndon B. Johnson signed a major gun control law after the assassinations of President John F. Kennedy and his brother Robert, and Martin Luther King Jr. *AP Photo*

Chief among them were Handgun Control, Inc., and the National Coalition to Ban Handguns, later renamed the Coalition to Stop Gun Violence. Both were formed in 1974.

Aftermath of Reagan Assassination Attempt

The foiled 1981 assassination attempt against Ronald Reagan left James Brady, his press secretary, disabled. Brady and his wife, Sarah, joined Handgun Control, Inc., later renamed the Brady Campaign. The organization spearheaded a successful effort to enact a new federal law named after Brady that required background checks before most purchases of new guns.

In 1989, a man using an AK-47 assault rifle shot and killed five children and wounded 29 others at an elementary school in Stockton, California. That same year, California became the first state to ban semiautomatic assault weapons: military-style weapons designed to fire a round with each pull of the trigger.

After a multiyear effort, Congress finally enacted a 10-year federal ban on assault weapons in 1994. The law also limited ammunition magazines to those holding no more than 10 rounds, excluding those previously manufactured.

The law expired in 2004, after which mass shootings became more frequent, with assault weapons being increasingly used by mass shooters. Repeated efforts to renew the federal ban have failed.

The gun control movement pressed to strengthen gun regulations further. Those efforts culminated in the passage of the Brady Handgun Violence Prevention Act in 1993, which amended the 1968 gun-control law by establishing a national system of background checks and a five-day waiting period for handgun purchases. The law called for eliminating that waiting period in 1998, replacing it with an instant background check system.

Congress Balks

In the aftermath of the April 1999 Columbine High School shooting, where two heavily armed students killed 12 of their peers and 1 teacher and wounded 23 others in Littleton, Colorado, Congress considered several new gun measures.

The Senate narrowly passed a bill in 1999 to establish uniform background checks for all gun purchases, to have tougher penalties for juvenile gun offenders, and to require

For Our Lives" demonstrations mobilized thousands of students across the country, as did the organization Students Demand Action, which went nationwide in 2018 and is affiliated with Everytown.

That year, 27 states, including Florida, enacted over 60 new gun regulations.

Still, Congress failed to act, with the exception of passing the modest Fix NICS Act. Passed with bipartisan support in 2018, the law improves data-gathering and reporting to the National Instant Criminal Background Check System for those seeking to buy guns. The NRA didn't oppose the measure.

As this history attests, predicting the likelihood of congressional action is difficult to do. Yet in a defiance of recent history, Congress managed to enact a new set of modest gun measures that President Joe Biden signed into law on June 25, 2022, after a mass shooting in Buffalo, New York, followed shortly by another in a school in Uvalde, Texas.

Notes

1. Robert J. Spitzer, *The Politics of Gun Control* (New York: Routledge, 2021).
2. Robert J. Spitzer, "Gun Law History in the United States and Second Amendment Rights," *Law and Contemporary Problems* 80 (2017): 55–83. https://scholarship.law.duke.edu/lcp/vol80/iss2/3.

Chapter 33

Supreme Court Swept Aside New York's Limits on Carrying a Gun, Raising Second Amendment Rights to New Heights

MORGAN MARIETTA

WITH ITS DECISION in *New York State Rifle & Pistol v. Bruen* on June 23, 2022, the US Supreme Court announced that the Second Amendment is not a second-class right. The core argument of the decision is that gun rights are to be treated the same as other hallowed rights like the freedom of speech or freedom of religion recognized in the First Amendment.

For most of the history of the court, Second Amendment rights have been seen as distinct, more dangerous and thus more open to regulation. Then in 2022, the court's majority of justices announced a major change, with implications for many rights and regulations in American society.

The Case

To get a license to carry a concealed firearm in New York State, a citizen had to show a "proper cause." In practice, this meant that a local licensing official had to agree that the person had a "special need," such as facing a current threat or recurring danger.

California, Hawaii, Maryland, Massachusetts, and New Jersey employed similar standards, known as "may issue" laws. Many other states instead have a "shall issue" regime where local officials must issue a license to carry a concealed firearm as long as the person does not have a disqualifying characteristic, including a felony conviction, mental illness, or restraining order against them.[1]

In the case heard by the Supreme Court, two applicants living in upstate New York, Robert Nash and Brandon Koch, were denied unrestricted concealed carry licenses because they had no special need other than personal protection. They insisted that New York law denied their constitutional rights.

The History of Second Amendment Rulings

For most of American history, the court ignored the Second Amendment. The first major ruling on its meaning did not come until the 1930s,[2] and the court did not address whether the amendment recognized a fundamental individual right until 2008 in the landmark *D.C. v. Heller*.

That ruling, written by the famously conservative Justice Antonin Scalia, recognized a right to keep a firearm in the

Gun rights activists outside the New York State
Capitol in 2018. *AP Photo/Hans Pennink*

home. How far the right extended into public spaces was not
clear. Scalia wrote that "like most rights, the right secured by
the Second Amendment is not unlimited." That meant
"longstanding prohibitions on the possession of firearms by
felons and the mentally ill" or "prohibitions on carrying
concealed weapons" were "presumptively lawful."[3]

A Fundamental Right

The 2022 ruling establishes that the gun right recognized
by the Second Amendment is a fundamental right like any
other and must be accorded the highest level of protection.
Its inherently dangerous nature does not mean that the right
is interpreted or limited differently.

Justice Clarence Thomas—perhaps the most conservative justice on the court—wrote the majority opinion. In Thomas's view, we do not need to ask prior permission of a government official to exercise a constitutional right: "We know of no other constitutional right that an individual may exercise only after demonstrating to government officials some special need." Thomas concludes that the Bill of Rights, including the Second Amendment, "demands our unqualified deference."[4]

This means that a local government may regulate but not eradicate the core right, including the ability to carry a concealed firearm. Any allowable regulation demands a compelling state interest, with convincing evidence of the need and effectiveness of the regulation.

The Constitutional Case for Stronger Regulation

The dissenters were led by Justice Stephen Breyer, who opened his dissent with the number of Americans killed with firearms in 2020: 45,222. His long-standing view is that the Second Amendment deals with a more dangerous right, and thus it is more open to being regulated.

In Breyer's view, the majority's ruling "refuses to consider the government interests that justify a challenged gun regulation." Breyer concludes that "the primary difference between the Court's view and mine is that I believe the Amendment allows States to take account of the serious problems posed by gun violence. . . . I fear that the Court's interpretation ignores these significant dangers and leaves States without the ability to address them."[5]

New Reading of the Constitution

The majority's view of the Second Amendment is part of a dramatic shift in the court's understanding of the Constitution. That shift reflects the arrival in 2020 of a conservative justice, Amy Coney Barrett, increasing the previous majority of five to a supermajority of six justices. That supermajority, all nominated by Republican presidents, insists that the Constitution is not a living document that evolves as the beliefs and values of society shift.[6] That was the longtime perspective more influential on the court since the rights revolution of the 1960s and 1970s, but it is now held by only a minority of justices.

The conservative majority believes the Constitution should be read in the original fashion of how the text itself would have been understood by those who wrote and ratified it. This is often called "originalism." The ramifications of this shift are just becoming clear. Beyond this gun ruling, the effects will continue to be seen in decisions on abortion, religion, criminal justice, environmental regulation, and many other issues.

I believe the briefest way to describe the change in the court's understanding of rights is to say that the explicit protections in the Bill of Rights (enumerated in the first 10 constitutional amendments)—such as free exercise of religion, freedom of speech, freedom of the press—will be given greater weight and deference. The originalist reading means that the enumerated rights of the amendments, including the Second Amendment, are not up for majority rule. They are core, established rights.

By contrast, additional protections apart from the Bill of Rights, which have been recognized by the court over time—abortion, privacy, same-sex marriage—will not be accorded the same protection and respect. Public debates on issues outside the scope of the Bill of Rights, including abortion, are matters better left to the decisions of state legislatures. This is a dramatic shift in the meaning and application of the US Constitution.

The State of Gun Regulation

The ruling by the majority does not insist that states adopt the most unrestricted standards for concealed carry that the states of Maine or Texas have. Only the states with the most restrictive gun laws, including California and New York, will be forced to change their policies.

Justice Brett Kavanaugh wrote a separate opinion to highlight that "the Court's decision does not prohibit States from imposing licensing requirements for carrying a handgun for self-defense." He emphasized that "properly interpreted, the Second Amendment allows a 'variety' of gun regulations."

The majority opinion specifically states that the concealed carry of firearms in sensitive places can be regulated: "We can assume it settled" that prohibitions on concealed carry in sensitive locations, including historically prohibited ones such as "legislative assemblies, polling places, and courthouses" as well as other "new and analogous sensitive places," shall be "constitutionally permissible." This likely includes government buildings, stadiums, churches and schools.

Altering American Law

This landmark ruling on the meaning and application of the Second Amendment changes the law in several states that would prefer to impose greater restrictions on the concealed carry of firearms. More broadly, it announces a major shift in how the court will understand the nature of rights under the Constitution.

The liberal justices in the waning minority believe that the new approach is changing American constitutional law "without considering the potentially deadly consequences," in Breyer's words. The majority sees the Constitution and Bill of Rights in a more uncompromising light that will alter American law in the coming years.

Notes

1. "State-by-State Concealed Carry Permit Laws," Britannica ProCon, April 22, 2022. https://concealedguns.procon.org/state-by-state-concealed-carry-permit-laws/.
2. United States v. Miller, 307 U.S. 174 (1939). Oyez (online archive of Supreme Court opinions). https://www.oyez.org/cases/1900-1940/307us174.
3. District of Columbia v. Heller, 554 U.S. 570 (2008). Oyez (online archive of Supreme Court opinions). https://www.oyez.org/cases/2007/07-290. Scalia's opinion of the court: https://supreme.justia.com/cases/federal/us/554/570/#tab-opinion-1962738.
4. New York State Rifle & Pistol Association, Inc. v. Bruen, 597 U.S. ___ (2022). Cornell Law School, Legal Information Institute. https://www.law.cornell.edu/supremecourt/text/20-843. Thomas's opinion of the court: https://www.law.cornell.edu/supremecourt/text/20-843#writing-20-843_OPINION_4.
5. Breyer's dissent: https://www.law.cornell.edu/supremecourt/text/20-843#writing-20-843_DISSENT_8.
6. David A. Strauss, "The Living Constitution," University of Chicago Law School, September 27, 2010. https://www.law.uchicago.edu/news/living-constitution.

Chapter 34

Red Flag Laws Saved 7,300 Americans from Gun Deaths in 2020 Alone and Could Have Saved 11,400 More

JOHN A. TURES

IN 2022, lawmakers in Congress passed the first gun control legislation in three decades. Among the elements in that legislation is support for states to pass what are called "red flag laws." These laws, already in place in many states, let police take guns from people deemed a threat to themselves or others. The laws also seek to bar those people from buying guns.

The contrast between states that have them and states that don't provides a useful opportunity for a scholar like me, who uses data for understanding politics, to examine whether the laws may help to reduce gun-related deaths.

Red Flag Laws Spread after the Parkland Shooting

The nation's first red flag law was passed in Connecticut in 1999, allowing police, but not medical professionals or family members, to ask a judge for permission to seize the guns of a person believed to be imminently dangerous to themselves or others. In the subsequent two decades, a handful of other states passed similar laws.

In 2018, the mass shooting at Marjory Stoneman Douglas High School in Parkland, Florida, sowed a new crop of the laws. That year, Florida passed a red flag law, and many other states followed suit. By the end of 2021, 19 states and the District of Columbia had done so. Not every state is on board: in 2020 Oklahoma banned its counties and municipalities from passing red flag laws.

While differing slightly from state to state where they do exist, these laws generally allow a judge to declare a person legally ineligible to own or purchase guns for a maximum of one year. The request has to come from the police or, in some states, a doctor or relative. The person can usually challenge the ruling in court, and police can seek an extension of the decision, which is often called a "risk protection order," if they deem it appropriate.

In Florida, where the request must come from police, an average of five of these orders are granted every day.

Do They Reduce Gun Deaths?

Research has shown that Connecticut's red flag law reduced suicides,[1] which involve firearms more than half the time.[2] To

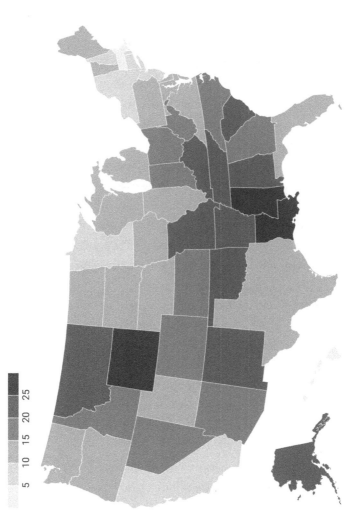

States with red flag laws had fewer firearm deaths in 2020. On average, states with red flag laws had 11.25 firearm deaths per 100,000 residents in 2020. States without red flag laws averaged 17.5 firearm deaths per 100,000 residents in the same year. New Mexico's red flag law took effect halfway through 2020. *The Conversation, CC BY-ND. Data from the Centers for Disease Control and Prevention*

determine whether red flag laws have reduced gun deaths overall, I examined states' firearm death rates in light of whether they had a red flag law or not, in each of three years: 2018, 2019, and 2020.[3]

The seven states with the lowest rates of firearm death for 2020 all had red flag laws. And 14 of the 15 states with the highest rates of firearm death that year did not have a red flag law. The exception was New Mexico, where a red flag law took effect halfway through the year. On average, states with red flag laws in 2019 and 2020 had significantly lower firearm death rates than states without them. In 2018, the average death rates for both groups were closer, but states with red flag laws still had a meaningfully lower rate.

Then I imagined those average rates applied to the whole country—that is, I recalculated firearm death rates for the country as if it had nationwide red flag laws versus having none at all.

In 2020, if there were no red flag laws, I estimated that 52,530 Americans would have died in gun deaths. The number actually recorded was 45,222, indicating that red flag laws saved 7,308 American lives that year. If red flag laws had existed either state by state or at the federal level, my estimate is that 33,780 people would have died by firearms in 2020, thereby sparing an additional 11,442 lives.

Notes

1. Jeffrey W. Swanson, Michael A. Norko, Hsiu-Ju Lin, Kelly Alanis-Hirsch, Linda K. Frisman, Madelon V. Baranoski, Michele M. Easter, Allison G. Robertson, Marvin S. Swartz, and Richard J. Bonnie, "Implementation and Effectiveness of Connecticut's Risk-Based Gun Removal Law: Does It Prevent Suicides?," *Law and Contemporary Problems* 8, no. 2 (2017): 179–208. https://doi.org/https://scholarship.law.duke.edu/lcp/vol80/iss2/8/.

2. Scott R. Kegler, Thomas R. Simon, Marissa L. Zwald, May S. Chen, James A. Mercy, Christopher M. Jones, Melissa C. Mercado-Crespo, et al. "Vital Signs: Changes in Firearm Homicide and Suicide Rates—United States, 2019–2020," *Morbidity and Mortality Weekly Report* 71, no. 19 (May 13, 2022). https://doi.org/10.15585/mmwr.mm7119e1.
3. "Stats of the States—Firearm Mortality," Centers for Disease Control and Prevention, March 1, 2022. https://www.cdc.gov/nchs/pressroom/sosmap/firearm_mortality/firearm.htm.

Chapter 35

Would Closing the "Boyfriend Loophole" in Gun Legislation Save Lives?

Here's What the Research Says

APRIL M. ZEOLI

IN JUNE 2022, the US Congress passed the Bipartisan Safer Communities Act, the first federal gun safety legislation to be passed in a generation. The legislation is limited in scope, but among its provisions is the closing of the so-called boyfriend loophole, which had allowed some people convicted of a domestic violence crime to continue buying and owning firearms.

What Is the Boyfriend Loophole?

Under federal legislation passed in the 1990s, intimate partner relationships were defined as those in which two people are or were married, live or lived together as a couple, or have a child together. People who are or were in a dating relationship were largely excluded from this definition.

As a result, dating partners were exempt from federal laws that prohibited those convicted of domestic violence misdemeanors, or those who were under domestic violence restraining orders, from buying or possessing a firearm. This is what is referred to as the "boyfriend loophole."

To put it another way, if you have two domestic abusers who both have committed the same unlawful violence against their partners, but one of them is married to their intimate partner while the other isn't, then only the domestic abuser who is married would be prohibited from having guns. The dating partner would get to keep their guns and be able to buy more.

What Does the Data Tell Us about Domestic Violence and Guns?

Intimate partner homicide rates have been rising since about 2015, and this increase is due almost entirely to intimate partner homicides committed with guns. Indeed, guns are the most common weapon used in intimate partner homicide.[1] In contrast, the rates of intimate partner homicide not committed with a gun have stayed roughly the same since 2015.

Research suggests that when a violent male partner has access to a gun, the risk of murder to the female partner increases fivefold.[2] We also know that guns are used to coerce, intimidate, and threaten intimate partners[3] and that gun-involved intimate partner violence can result in more symptoms of post-traumatic stress disorder than intimate partner violence that doesn't involve a gun.[4] Because a nationally representative survey suggests that 3.4% of domestic violence victimizations have involved nonfatal gun use,[5] on top of the high number of intimate partner murders committed with guns, this constitutes a large public health threat.

Why Did Congress Address the Boyfriend Loophole?

The conversation over extending domestic violence firearm restrictions to dating partners has arisen every few years. The federal law enacted in 2022 closes, or at least narrows, the loophole for individuals convicted of misdemeanor crimes of domestic violence. The wording of the legislation extends the ban to include those who "have or have recently had a continuing serious relationship of a romantic or intimate nature."

There are a few issues to note here. First, the motivation to pass new gun safety legislation came from recent mass shooting events and the hope of preventing future mass shootings. We know that many mass shootings involve killing intimate partners or family members and that some of the shooters have a criminal history of domestic violence predating the mass shooting.[6] But mass shootings are only a small percentage of shootings in the United States. Intimate partner homicide is a more frequent occurrence.

Second, my research shows that when states extend firearm restrictions for individuals under a domestic violence restraining order to cover dating partners as well, there is an associated reduction in intimate partner homicide.[7] The

Bipartisan Safer Communities Act does not do this, however. The law closes the loophole only for those convicted of a domestic violence misdemeanor and does not cover individuals under a restraining order for domestic violence.

What Is the Current Situation at the State Level?

Some states, such as Minnesota and West Virginia, had already extended firearm restrictions for misdemeanor domestic violence to include dating partners. Others, including Tennessee, had not. As of July 2022, when the Bipartisan Safer Communities Act was enacted, fewer than half of states had extended the misdemeanor domestic violence firearm restriction to cover dating partners.

This created a situation in which having legal safety from gun violence by a dating partner depended on the state in which you lived. The 2022 federal legislation helps to create a more consistent picture across the country when it comes to firearm restrictions for dating partners who commit violence.

What Effect Will Closing the Boyfriend Loophole Have at a National Level?

My research suggests that the federal firearm restriction for individuals convicted of domestic violence misdemeanors is associated with reductions in intimate partner homicide committed with firearms. As such, one could hypothesize that restricting access to guns for a greater number of dangerous intimate partners will further reduce firearm homicides within violent relationships. By the same thinking, closing the boyfriend loophole for individuals under domestic violence restraining orders would also probably save lives.

Notes

1. Emma E. Fridel and James Alan Fox, "Gender Differences in Patterns and Trends in U.S. Homicide, 1976–2017," *Violence and Gender* 6, no. 1 (March 11, 2019): 27–36. https://doi.org/10.1089/vio.2019.0005.
2. Jacquelyn C. Campbell, Daniel Webster, Jane Koziol-McLain, Carolyn Block, Doris Campbell, Mary Ann Curry, Faye Gary, et al., "Risk Factors for Femicide in Abusive Relationships: Results from a Multisite Case Control Study," *American Journal of Public Health* 93, no. 7 (July 2003): 1089–97. https://doi.org/10.2105/ajph.93.7.1089.
3. Susan B. Sorenson and Rebecca A. Schut, "Nonfatal Gun Use in Intimate Partner Violence: A Systematic Review of the Literature," *Trauma, Violence & Abuse* 19, no. 4 (September 14, 2016): 431–42. https://doi.org/10.1177/1524838016668589.
4. Tami P. Sullivan and Nicole H. Weiss, "Is Firearm Threat in Intimate Relationships Associated with Posttraumatic Stress Disorder Symptoms among Women?," *Violence and Gender* 4, no. 2 (June 1, 2017): 31–36. https://doi.org/10.1089/vio.2016.0024.
5. Jennifer L. Truman and Rachel E. Morgan, "Nonfatal Domestic Violence, 2003–2012," Bureau of Justice Statistics, Special Report NCJ 244697 (April 2014). https://bjs.ojp.gov/library/publications/nonfatal-domestic-violence-2003-2012.
6. April M. Zeoli and Jennifer K. Paruk, "Potential to Prevent Mass Shootings through Domestic Violence Firearm Restrictions," *Criminology & Public Policy* 19, no. 1 (December 16, 2019): 129–45. https://doi.org/10.1111/1745-9133.12475.
7. April M. Zeoli, Alexander McCourt, Shani Buggs, Shannon Frattaroli, David Lilley, and Daniel W. Webster, "Analysis of the Strength of Legal Firearms Restrictions for Perpetrators of Domestic Violence and Their Associations with Intimate Partner Homicide," *American Journal of Epidemiology* 187, no. 11 (November 1, 2018): 2365–71. https://doi.org/10.1093/aje/kwy174.

Chapter 36

Why the Legal Age for Purchasing Assault Weapons Does Not Make Sense

ASHWINI TAMBE

THE UVALDE AND BUFFALO MASS SHOOTINGS in May 2022 had at least two things in common: the shooters were 18 years old, and they both had legally purchased their own assault rifles.

The shooters' young age was not an aberration. The average age of school shooters has been 18 in incidents since 1966.[1] The relatively young age of most mass shooters has ignited conversations about the minimum legal age for purchasing firearms.

In this context, it's useful to recall that societies have determined the age of adulthood in shifting ways through history. As I've examined in my work on the age of marriage and sexual consent, considering someone an adult once they turn 18 is a relatively recent trend.[2] It's not clear that it can stand up to public scrutiny as a meaningful threshold for legally purchasing firearms.

A Push for Higher Age Limits

In the Parkland, Florida, school shooting in 2018, the shooter was 19. The Sandy Hook Elementary School shooter in Newtown, Connecticut, was 20 years old. And the shooters at the Columbine High School massacre in Littleton, Colorado, in 1999 were 18 and 17.

Following the Uvalde massacre, Democratic Texas state senators called for an emergency legislative session to raise the minimum age for purchasing firearms in the state from 18 to 21, a move that Governor Greg Abbott has resisted. The day after the Buffalo massacre, on May 15, 2022, New York governor Kathy Hochul called for raising the minimum age to purchase assault rifles from 18 to 21. The New York State legislature then voted on June 2 to ban anyone under the age of 21 from buying assault weapons. On June 2, President Joe Biden also called for a ban on assault rifles or for raising the age when someone is allowed to purchase one.

Counterposed to these measures is the National Rifle Association, which has challenged state laws in Florida and California that restrict people under 21 from buying rifles. When it comes to gun laws, there are clearly deep political differences over how to define adulthood.

When Adulthood Begins

Several news outlets, including the Associated Press and the *New York Times*, called the mass shooters in Buffalo and Uvalde "men" and "gunmen" in their coverage. Some observers argued that these terms were accurate because the age of the shooters was 18. But there is no single, cohesive legal answer to whether 18-year-olds are actually adults, in every respect.

In most US states, 18 is the legal age of majority; this is the age when people are no longer entitled to parental support and can be emancipated from their parents or foster care, tried as adults for crimes, and enlist for military service. But not all states follow this age standard; in a few states, the age of majority is 19 or 21.

Adulthood wasn't always set at 18 in the United States. The legal age of adulthood in the United States was 21 for most of its early history, a holdover from colonial rule reflecting a British feudal custom for when knighthood was possible.[3]

In the early 1970s, following a congressional push to make the voting age consistent with the age of compulsory enlistment in the army, the Twenty-Sixth Amendment lowered the voting age from 21 to 18. In the following years, most states classified someone as an adult at the age of 18, aligning with the voting age.[4] This age does not rigidly define adulthood across every legal context, though. Generally, at 18, a person can participate in activities that require a certain amount of cognitive independence, such as voting, consenting to medical treatment, and suing someone in court.

Most states set the age of sexual consent between 16 and 18 years. The federal age of marriage is 18, but most states set a lower age for marriage with parental consent.

A Higher Limit

Activities that can directly harm others or oneself, on the other hand, are subject to a higher age threshold than 18.

The federal minimum legal age for drinking alcohol is 21 because, after being dropped to 18 in the 1970s, an increase in drunken-driving accidents pushed states to raise it again to age 21 in the 1980s. Government studies showed that states with a minimum drinking age of 18 had higher fatalities from motor vehicle accidents.[5] Drivers below the age of 25 find it either difficult or more expensive to rent a car, given the higher risk of accidents for the car, the driver, and others on the road.

The age threshold is also higher for activities involving financial risk. For example, someone under the age of 21 needs a cosigner to get a credit card in their own name because of the Credit Card Accountability Responsibility and Disclosure Act, passed in 2009.

Phased-In Adulthood

Researchers who study adolescent brain development argue that different types of maturity develop along distinct time lines. They offer nuanced distinctions between the ability to reason in a systematic way, which typically happens around age 16, and decision-making that involves emotion and risk assessment.[6] This can take many more years to develop. Such cognitive growth continues, in fact, until around age 25. For these reasons, some legal scholars argue strongly against an absolute single standard for adulthood: one that holds across all activities.

The frequency of mass shootings by teenagers poses a challenge to existing legal standards for access to firearms.

Emotional maturity—the ability to recognize and process one's fear and to control impulses—should be weighed when setting a minimum age for gun ownership, if civilians are to have access to guns at all. The decision to pull a trigger requires exactly the kind of forethought that neuroscientists argue develops slowly.

In most legal contexts, activities that can put others at risk are not permissible at age 18. Adult status is actually granted in phases, depending on the activity in question. There is thus a strong case to be made on both historical and scientific grounds that 18-year-olds should not be allowed to purchase firearms.

Notes

1. James Densley and Jillian Patterson, "What We Know about Mass Shootings—and the Gunmen Who Carry Them Out," The Conversation, June 6, 2022, https://theconversation.com/what-we-know-about -mass-school-shootings-in-the-us-and-the-gunmen-who-carry -them-out-183812.
2. Ashwini Tambe, *Defining Girlhood in India: A Transnational History of Sexual Maturity Laws* (Urbana: University of Illinois Press, 2020).
3. T. E. James, "The Age of Majority," *American Journal of Legal History* 4, no. 1 (1960): 22–33. https://doi.org/10.2307/844549.
4. Vivian E. Hamilton, "Adulthood in Law and Culture," *Tulane Law Review* 19, no. 1 (2016): 55–97. https://scholarship.law.wm.edu/facpubs/1824/.
5. "Decline In Youth Alcohol-Related Fatalities Attributed to Four Factors," *Traffic Tech* 261 (October 2001). https://one.nhtsa.gov /people/outreach/traftech/tt261.htm.
6. Alexandra O. Cohen, Kaitlyn Breiner, Laurence Steinberg, Richard J. Bonnie, Elizabeth S. Scott, Kim Taylor-Thompson, Marc D. Rudolph, et al., "When Is an Adolescent an Adult? Assessing Cognitive Control in Emotional and Nonemotional Contexts," *Psychological Science* 27, no. 4 (2016): 549–62. https://doi.org/10.1177/0956797615627625.

Chapter 37

Did the Assault Weapons Ban of 1994 Bring Down Mass Shootings?

Here's What the Data Tells Us

MICHAEL J. KLEIN

A SPATE OF HIGH-PROFILE MASS SHOOTINGS in the United States in 2022 sparked calls for Congress to look at imposing a ban on so-called assault weapons, covering the types of guns used in both the May 14, 2022, Buffalo grocery store attack and that on an elementary school in Uvalde, Texas, 10 days later.

Such a prohibition has been in place before. As President Joe Biden noted in his June 2, 2022, speech addressing gun violence, almost three decades ago bipartisan support in Congress helped push through a federal ban on assault weapons in 1994, as part of the Violent Crime Control and Law Enforcement Act.

That ban was limited: it covered only certain categories of semiautomatic weapons, such as AR-15s, and banned sales only after the act was signed into law, allowing people to keep hold of weapons purchased before that date. It also had in it a so-called sunset provision, which allowed the ban to expire in 2004.

Nonetheless, the 10-year life span of that ban—with a clear beginning and end date—gives researchers the opportunity to compare what happened with mass shooting deaths before, during, and after the prohibition was in place. Our group of injury epidemiologists and trauma surgeons did just that. In a 2019 population-based study, we analyzed the data to evaluate the effect that the federal ban on assault weapons had on mass shootings,[1] defined by the FBI as a shooting with four or more fatalities, not including the shooter. Here's what the data show.

Before the 1994 Ban

From 1981, the earliest year in our analysis, to the rollout of the assault weapons ban in 1994, the proportion of deaths in mass shootings in which an assault rifle was used was lower than it is today. Yet in this period, mass shooting deaths were steadily rising. Indeed, high-profile mass shootings involving assault rifles—such as the killing of five children in Stockton, California, in 1989 and a 1993 San Francisco office attack that left eight victims dead—provided the impetus for a prohibition on some types of gun.

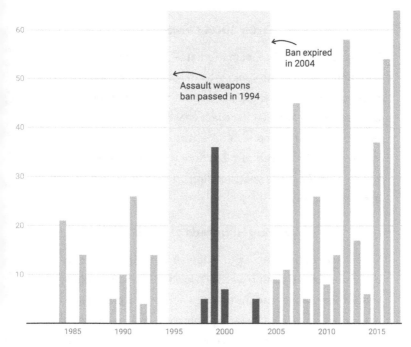

Mass shooting deaths in the United States
from 1981 to 2017. *The Conversation,*
CC BY-ND. Data from DiMaggio et al. (2019)

During the 1994–2004 Ban

In the years after the assault weapons ban went into effect,
the number of deaths from mass shootings fell, and the
increase in the annual number of incidents slowed down. Even
including 1999's Columbine High School massacre—the
deadliest mass shooting during the period of the ban—the
1994 to 2004 period saw lower average annual rates of both
mass shootings and their resulting deaths than what had
occurred before the ban's inception.

From 2004 Onward

The data shows an almost immediate—and steep—rise in mass shooting deaths in the years after the assault weapons ban expired in 2004. Breaking the data into absolute numbers, between 2004 and 2017, the last year of our analysis, the average number of yearly deaths attributed to mass shootings was 25, compared with 5.3 during the 10-year tenure of the ban and 7.2 in the years leading up to the prohibition on assault weapons.

Saving Hundreds of Lives

We calculated that the risk of a person in the United States dying in a mass shooting was 70% lower during the period in which the assault weapons ban was active. The proportion of overall gun homicides resulting from mass shootings was also down, with nine fewer mass-shooting-related fatalities per 10,000 shooting deaths.

Taking population trends into account, a model we created based on this data suggests that had the federal ban on assault weapons been in place throughout the whole period of our study—that is, from 1981 through 2017—it might have prevented 314 of the 448 mass shooting deaths that occurred during the years in which there was no ban.

This calculation almost certainly underestimates the total number of lives that could have been saved. For our study, we chose to include only mass shooting incidents that were reported and agreed on by all three of our selected data sources: the *Los Angeles Times*, Stanford University, and *Mother Jones* magazine. Furthermore, for uniformity, we chose to use the strict federal definition of an assault weapon, which may not include the entire spectrum of what many people now consider to be assault weapons.

Cause or Correlation?

Our study cannot definitively say that the assault weapons ban of 1994 caused a decrease in mass shootings or that its expiration in 2004 resulted in the growth of deadly incidents in the years since. Many additional factors may contribute to the increased frequency of these shootings, such as changes in domestic violence rates, political extremism, psychiatric illnesses, as well as a surge in firearm sales and the recent rise in hate groups.

Nonetheless, according to our study, President Biden's claim that the rate of mass shootings during the period of the assault weapons ban "went down," only to rise again after the law was allowed to expire in 2004, is true.[2]

As the United States looks toward a solution to the country's epidemic of mass shootings, it is difficult to conclude that reinstating the ban on assault weapons would have a profound impact, especially given the growth in sales in the 18 years over which Americans have been allowed to purchase and stockpile such weapons. But because many of the high-profile mass shooters in recent years purchased their weapons less than one year before committing their acts, the evidence we found suggests that a new ban might make a difference.

Notes

1. Charles DiMaggio, Jacob Avraham, Cherisse Berry, Marko Bukur, Justin Feldman, Michael Klein, Noor Shah, Manish Tandon, and Spiros Frangos, "Changes in US Mass Shooting Deaths Associated with the

1994–2004 Federal Assault Weapons Ban: Analysis of Open-Source Data," *Journal of Trauma and Acute Care Surgery* 86, no. 1 (January 2019): 11–19. https://doi.org/10.1097/ta.0000000000002060.

2. "Remarks by President Biden on Gun Violence in America," White House, June 2, 2022. https://www.whitehouse.gov/briefing-room/speeches-remarks/2022/06/02/remarks-by-president-biden-on-gun-violence-in-america/.

Chapter 38

Why Is There So Little Research on Guns in the US?

LACEY WALLACE

ON VALENTINE'S DAY 2018, 19-year-old Nikolas Cruz opened fire at Marjory Stoneman Douglas High School in Parkland, Florida. He killed 17 students and teachers and injured at least a dozen others.

Like other mass shootings, the event in Parkland was quickly followed by a public outcry for increased gun control. Teens for Gun Reform hosted a "lie-in" in front of the White House to demand tougher gun laws. Others gathered in protest outside the National Rifle Association's headquarters. Speaking at that event, Representative Gerald Connolly

(D-Va.) argued for an assault weapons ban, universal background checks, and closing gun-show-purchasing loopholes. Then-president Trump called for regulations on so-called bump stocks that convert semiautomatic weapons into fully automatic machine guns, like that used in the 2017 shooting in Las Vegas.

But will these laws prevent another mass shooting? Is there a better policy option?

Unfortunately, the research we need to answer these questions doesn't exist, and part of the problem is that the federal government largely doesn't support it.

Why Do We Need Research on Guns?

Gun violence is a public health issue. It's a leading cause of premature death in the United States, killing more people each year than diseases such as AIDS, hypertension, or viral hepatitis.

While violent crime has generally been on the decline since the mid-1990s,[1] gun crime has remained a persistent problem. According to the Centers for Disease Control and Prevention, 33,594 individuals were killed by firearms in 2014 alone. That's only about 200 less than the number of people killed in motor vehicle accidents. In 2015, roughly 85,000 people were injured by firearms, including nearly 10,000 children.

To prevent gun injuries and deaths, we need accurate information about how they occur and why. While police reports and FBI data can provide some detail, they don't include the thousands of cases that go unreported each year. Between 2006 and 2010, the Bureau of Justice Statistics estimated that more than a third of victims of crimes involving a firearm did not report the crime to police. The National

Crime Victimization Survey, which collects victimization data from about 90,000 households each year, helps to fill this gap. Even this survey, though, has its drawbacks. It doesn't collect data from youth under 12 years of age, it doesn't include murder, and it doesn't help us fully understand the offender's motivations and beliefs.

Social scientists need more research to get the level of detail we need about gun crime. There's just one major roadblock: the federal government won't fund it.

How Much Federal Money Is There?

In 1996, Congress passed the Dickey Amendment.[2] The legislation stated that "none of the funds made available for injury prevention and control at the Centers for Disease Control and Prevention may be used to advocate or promote gun control." While that wording did not ban CDC gun research outright, the legislation was accompanied by a US$2.6 million budget cut. That amount happened to match the amount the CDC had spent on firearms research the previous year. The message was clear. From 1996 to 2013, CDC funding for gun research dropped by 96%.

The CDC wasn't the only federal agency affected. In 2011, Congress added a similar clause to legislation that regulated funding for the National Institutes of Health. However, due to a directive from the Obama administration, the NIH continued to provide funding for gun research. That push faded as the Obama administration left office. In 2017, the NIH discontinued its funding program that focused specifically on firearm violence. While firearms researchers can still apply for funding through more general NIH funding opportunities, critics say that makes funding for gun research less likely.

What Prompted These Funding Restrictions?

The Dickey Amendment was passed after a CDC-funded study, led by physician and epidemiologist Arthur Kellerman, found that having a gun in the home increased homicide risk.[3] After the results were published, the National Rifle Association pressured lawmakers, arguing that the CDC was inappropriately using its funds to advocate for gun control.

Opposition from the NRA is serious business for lawmakers. The NRA is one of the most powerful special-interest lobbying organizations in the United States. The NRA spends millions of dollars on lobbying activities: things like meeting with politicians, drafting model legislation, and advertising. The NRA spends additional millions to back or oppose political candidates. In 2016, the NRA spent nearly $20 million on efforts opposing Hillary Clinton and nearly $10 million on efforts supporting Donald Trump.

Not surprisingly, the NRA has successfully blocked gun control legislation in the past, including the renewal of the 2004 assault weapons ban.

Can Private-Sector or State Dollars Fill the Gap?

Another potential option for researchers is to seek out funding from private agencies or philanthropists. But few such opportunities are available.

According to Garen Wintemute, director of the Violence Prevention Research Program at the University of California–Davis Medical Center, fewer than five private organizations are willing to provide gun research funding. Private funding is also somewhat risky for researchers. If a funder has a political leaning on gun-related issues, the researcher may be under pressure to produce the "right" results. Even just the implication that a researcher could have a conflict of interest can undermine a study's perceived legitimacy.

State funding may be another option. In 2016, California announced its intent to fund the University of California Firearm Violence Research Center. This is the first time a state has stepped forward to fund a research center focused on guns.

Has Gun Research Stopped?

The lack of funding has discouraged firearms research. Many researchers are employed in academia. In this publish-or-perish environment, researchers are pressured to publish their work in academic journals and fund it through sources outside their home institution. Without outside funding, their research often isn't possible. Leading firearms researcher Wintemute said "no more than a dozen active, experienced investigators in the United States have focused their careers primarily on firearm violence."[4]

A lack of funding leaves some researchers limited to small-scale studies with a low budget. The problem with studies like these is that they are often based on samples that are not nationally representative. That means researchers can't generalize from the findings or address all the questions they might have.

Without increased funding for gun research, it will be extremely difficult for researchers to provide accurate answers to the gun policy questions currently under debate.

Notes

1. John Gramlich, "What the Data Says (and Doesn't Say) about Crime in the United States," Pew Research Center, November 20, 2020.

https://www.pewresearch.org/fact-tank/2020/11/20/facts-about
-crime-in-the-u-s/.
2. "Ex-Rep. Dickey Regrets Restrictive Law on Gun Violence Research,"
National Public Radio, October 9, 2015. https://www.npr.org/2015/10
/09/447098666/ex-rep-dickey-regrets-restrictive-law-on-gun
-violence-research.
3. Arthur L. Kellermann, Frederick P. Rivara, Norman B. Rushforth,
Joyce G. Banton, Donald T. Reay, Jerry T. Francisco, Ana B. Locci,
Janice Prodzinski, Bela B. Hackman, and Grant Somes, "Gun
Ownership as a Risk Factor for Homicide in the Home," *New England
Journal of Medicine* 329, no. 15 (1993): 1084–91. https://doi.org/10
.1056/nejm199310073291506.
4. Garen J. Wintemute, "Responding to the Crisis of Firearm Violence in
the United States: Comment on 'Firearm Legislation and Firearm-
Related Fatalities in the United States,'" *JAMA Internal Medicine* 173,
no. 9 (2013): 740. https://doi:10.1001/jamainternmed.2013.1292.

Chapter 39

Public Health Research Reduced Smoking Deaths—It Could Do the Same for Gun Violence

SANDRO GALEA and MICHAEL SIEGEL

IT HAS BECOME COMMONPLACE for US politicians to offer their "thoughts and prayers" to victims and their families after mass shootings. But prayers are not going to fix the fact that, each year, 45,000 deaths and many more injuries are caused by firearm violence.[1] Recognizing gun violence for the public health problem it is, however, might move the country in the right direction.

So what does it mean to view firearm violence as a public health problem? And how does that change the debate Americans are having about gun violence?

A Public Health Perspective on Firearms

First, and most importantly, viewing firearms violence as a public health problem means declaring that the current situation is unacceptable and preventable. We did not successfully tackle the AIDS epidemic until we made it a national health priority, a decision marked by the passage of the Ryan White Care Act in 1990. Today, this priority is reflected in the federal government's commitment to ensuring that at least 90% of HIV-infected individuals in the United States are properly treated by 2020. Federal funding has increased over the course of the AIDS epidemic, and the government is spending US$28 billion on domestic HIV prevention and treatment programs during fiscal year 2016.[2]

Second, treating firearm violence as a public health problem means conducting research to identify the underlying causes of the problem and to evaluate potential strategies to address it. For instance, research may reveal commonsense structural changes, such as firearm safety features, that limit the potential damage people can do with guns.

The Centers for Disease Control and Prevention has avoided conducting research on firearm violence since 1996, when Congress passed an appropriations bill barring the CDC from using funds to advocate or promote gun control. In 2012 President Obama ordered the CDC and other federal bodies to resume research on firearms violence in the wake of the Sandy Hook shooting. But allocation for research by Congress has been slow in coming. While the National Institutes of Health is undertaking firearms research, little funding is allocated for it.

Third, a public health perspective on firearm violence means moving beyond blaming individuals and toward designing societal programs and policies to curb the epidemic. Just as individual smokers are not to blame for the tobacco epidemic, individual gun owners are not to blame for what is a societal problem.

Taking a broad societal approach is exactly what we have done with other public health problems, such as smoking. Public health research helped identify a proven set of programs and policies that denormalized smoking, such as limitations on smoking in public places and anti-smoking media campaigns.[3] Thanks in large part to these societal-level public health interventions, the prevalence of cigarette smoking dropped to its lowest level in history last year.

And fourth, a public health approach means that the public is included in the discussion. We need to listen to concerns across sectors, including gun owners, gun dealers, law enforcement officials, and public health advocates. With a public health problem of this magnitude, everyone should be at the table. That might seem impossible now, given the polarization on both sides of the gun control debate. A lack of willingness even to discuss potential solutions to the problem, however, is simply unacceptable.

A collaboration between the public health community and gun dealers to reduce firearms-related suicide in New Hampshire offers an example of what this might look like.[4]

So What Does Public Health Research on Guns Look Like?

In 2013, some of us at Boston University's School of Public Health started to conduct research aimed at understanding social norms about firearms and gun culture. We have also created a dedicated Violence Prevention Research Unit. So what have we found so far?

In a 2013 study, we linked state homicide data from the CDC with data on gun ownership, which revealed a strong relationship between levels of household gun ownership and the rate of firearm-related homicide at the state level.[5] We found that this relationship is specific to homicides committed by offenders who are known to the victim.[6] In 2016, we published a study that documented a strong link between gun ownership levels and firearm-related suicide rates.[7]

These findings suggest that responding to mass shootings by arming teachers and ordinary civilians is not only unlikely to reduce homicide rates, but the resulting increase in the prevalence of firearms might actually *increase* deaths from both homicide and suicide.

We have also found a strong relationship between the implementation of state laws that require universal background checks for all gun sales and lower rates of firearm-related homicide.[8]

These findings suggest that the loophole in federal law allowing unlicensed dealers to sell guns to any individual without conducting a background check may be contributing to higher rates of firearm violence.

Where Research Is Headed

Our future work will explore the impact of various state firearm policies to identify policies that are effective specifically in reducing urban violence, which disproportionately impacts the African American community.

Even though much of this work has been done without external funding, it is essential that Congress allow the CDC to do its job and conduct research on gun violence and that other federal agencies like the NIH increase allocations for research in this area. Having limited funding available for research on a problem that results in about 45,000 deaths each year is not how we handle a public health issue.

Notes

1. Katherine A. Fowler, Linda L. Dahlberg, Tadesse Haileyesus, and Joseph L. Annest, "Firearm Injuries in the United States," *Preventive Medicine* 79 (October 2015): 5–14. https://doi.org/10.1016/j.ypmed .2015.06.002.
2. "U.S. Federal Funding for HIV/AIDS: Trends over Time," KFF, March 5, 2019. https://www.kff.org/global-health-policy/fact-sheet/u-s -federal-funding-for-hivaids-trends-over-time/.
3. Tim McAfee, Kevin C. Davis, Robert L. Alexander, Terry F. Pechacek, and Rebecca Bunnell, "Effect of the First Federally Funded US Antismoking National Media Campaign," *Lancet* 382, no. 9909 (September 9, 2013): 2003–11. https://doi.org/10.1016/s0140 -6736(13)61686-4.
4. Melissa Dahl, "Health Officials' Unlikely Partner in Preventing Gun Suicides: Gun-Shop Owners," The Cut, May 26, 2016. https://www .thecut.com/2016/05/health-officials-unlikely-partner-in-preventing -gun-suicides-gun-shop-owners.html.
5. Michael Siegel, Craig S. Ross, and Charles King, "The Relationship between Gun Ownership and Firearm Homicide Rates in the United States, 1981–2010," *American Journal of Public Health* 103, no. 11 (October 9, 2013): 2098–105. https://doi.org/10.2105/ajph.2013 .301409.
6. Michael Siegel, Yamrot Negussie, Sarah Vanture, Jane Pleskunas, Craig S. Ross, and Charles King, "The Relationship between Gun

Ownership and Stranger and Nonstranger Firearm Homicide Rates in the United States, 1981–2010," *American Journal of Public Health* 104, no. 10 (September 10, 2014): 1912–19. https://doi.org/10.2105/ajph.2014.302042.

7. Michael Siegel and Emily F. Rothman, "Firearm Ownership and Suicide Rates among US Men and Women, 1981–2013," *American Journal of Public Health* 106, no. 7 (June 10, 2016): 1316–22. https://doi.org/10.2105/ajph.2016.303182.

8. Bindu Kalesan, Matthew E. Mobily, Olivia Keiser, Jeffrey A. Fagan, and Sandro Galea, "Firearm Legislation and Firearm Mortality in the USA: A Cross-Sectional, State-Level Study," *Lancet* 387, no. 10030 (March 10, 2016): 1847–55. https://doi.org/10.1016/s0140-6736(15)01026-0.

Chapter 40

Indianapolis Is Trying Programs Ranging from Job Skills to Therapy to Reduce Gun Violence

THOMAS D. STUCKY

INDIANAPOLIS IS NO STRANGER to gun violence. The city is trying many promising approaches to reducing the violence, which, if proven successful, could benefit other urban areas across the United States.

The city's 2020 homicide rate of 24.4 per 100,000 residents was roughly triple the national average and the city's highest on record. Approximately 80% of those homicides were perpetrated using firearms. Gun homicides ended about 240 lives in a recent two-year period, according

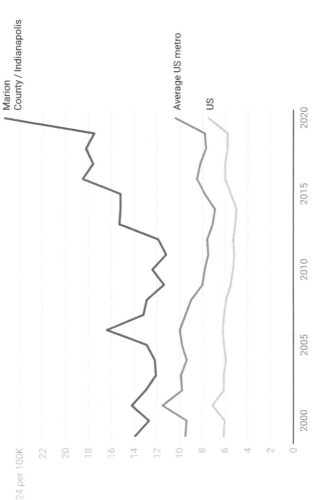

Indianapolis's homicide rate is far higher than the US metro-area average. More than 90% of Marion County's 977,000 residents live in Indianapolis. The Marion County homicide rate has, since 2013, been more than twice as high as the average for metropolitan regions across the nation. In 2020, at about 25 per 100,000 residents, it was more than triple the US rate overall. The average US metro rate includes many counties that encompass relatively small cities. The homicide rate in Marion County is comparable with levels seen in many cities with more than 500,000 residents. Guns are used in about 80% of US homicides. *The Conversation, CC BY-ND. Data from the Centers for Disease Control and Prevention*

to a study on gun violence in this city of 900,000 people.[1]
The number of people who were shot but survived was far
higher, and firearms account for a significant number of
suicide deaths.

I'm a former police officer who has studied policies and
programs seeking to prevent gun violence since the late
1990s. I have periodically partnered with Indianapolis officials
and community agencies on anti-violence initiatives coordi-
nated by the local government with many private- and
nonprofit-sector partners since 2004.

Though some approaches developed in other places have
worked here, and Indianapolis has implemented many
programs that have been shown to make a difference else-
where, there's still not enough data to pinpoint which specific
programs are the most effective. But given the urgency of the
problem, I believe it's important to keep test-driving promising methods based on the information available so far.
Because Indianapolis experiences many of the same gun
violence issues that other medium and large cities face,
what's learned here can apply in many other places.

Stepping Up Efforts to Reduce Gun Violence

Indianapolis intensified its efforts to reduce gun violence in
2006, when 144 people died by homicide—up 27% from a
year earlier. That year Bart Peterson, then serving as the city's
mayor, created the Community Crime Prevention Task Force,
in which I played a role. Its mission was to seek evidence-
based recommendations to reduce violence. After reviewing
the relevant academic research, I identified best practices
and the most promising violence-prevention strategies. The

task force, in turn, made recommendations to the Indianapolis City-County Council.

The city subsequently began to increase funding for efforts to reduce gun violence in coordination with the Indianapolis Foundation, a local charity. This private-public partnership has been supporting nonprofits engaged in several approaches to reducing gun violence ever since.

The overarching purpose of all these programs is to help people obtain services who are most likely to be wounded or killed by a gun, services such as job training and health care in their communities, and to shift norms away from gun violence to reduce that risk.

Because people killed by guns in Indianapolis are likely to be young, male, and Black, young Black men are a major focus of all the programs. Researchers also determined that three in four gun homicide victims and suspects in the city were known to law enforcement from prior investigation, arrest, or conviction. So that is another factor in determining who gets these services.

Employing Formerly Incarcerated People

Other grants from the private-public partnership in Indianapolis have funded cognitive behavioral therapy for people at risk of engaging in or being victims of gun violence. This is a therapy in which people get help identifying and pushing back on their negative thoughts and behaviors, making it easier to resolve disputes without resorting to violence.

The city has also partnered with several community organizations to prevent gun violence. One such group is RecycleForce, which hires formerly incarcerated people to recycle old electronic goods. It's among several enhanced transitional job programs that provide services and training to the recently incarcerated.

One study showed that RecycleForce participants were 5.8% less likely to be arrested and 4.8% less likely to be convicted of a crime in the first six months of the period reviewed.[2] In the second six months, however, the benefits were no longer statistically significant. A second study used in-depth interviews to assess the program; its findings suggested that the peer-mentor model RecycleForce follows works well.[3]

Preventing Future Gunshot Wounds

A large Indianapolis hospital, Eskenazi, runs several important antiviolence programs. One, called Prescription for Hope, assists people treated there for gunshot wounds. Like similar hospital-based programs around the country, the one at Eskenazi helps participants develop effective life skills and connects them with community resources to reduce criminal and risky behaviors.

An initial study of the program showed that only about 3% of participants returned to the emergency department with a repeat violent injury within the first year, compared with an 8.7% rate when the program wasn't in operation.[4] This translates into a two-thirds reduction in the likelihood that someone with a violent injury will need similar emergency medical assistance in the future.

Interrupting Violence

In 2021, Indianapolis began to hire "violence interrupters" to calm contentious situations and reduce the risk of violent retaliation. The violence interruption method connects people with personal ties to those most at risk of becoming involved in gun violence as victims or perpetrators. Violence interrupters try to mediate disputes and calm things down on the streets, at parties, and during funerals before any shooting starts. They have credibility with violence-prone people because of their past experiences. The interrupters also help at-risk people obtain services and work to change gun violence norms in their communities.

Violence interruption, part of a growing public health approach to reining in violence, originated in Chicago in 2000. Now called the "cure violence model," it has spread quickly amid generally positive research results.[5] Indianapolis is employing about 50 violence interrupters as of mid-2022.

Increasing Federal Funding

Most of the city's violence-prevention grants that fund these efforts have been relatively small, ranging from $5,000 to $325,000.

But US cities, including Indianapolis, now have until 2024 to tap into a comparatively large stream of federal funding for community-based violence intervention. That money was included in the $1.9 trillion stimulus package enacted in 2021. Using these federal funds, the city is partnering with the Indianapolis Foundation to award grants totaling $45 million from 2022 through 2024 for local efforts to reduce gun violence.

Fortunately, homicides in Indianapolis appeared to be declining in 2022 compared with a year earlier. As a local resident, I certainly welcome this news. But as a researcher, I consider it too soon to tell whether this trend will continue and too soon to say what the many public and private efforts to reduce gun violence now under way will accomplish.

Notes

1. *Indianapolis Gun Violence Problem Analysis: Summary Report*, National Institute for Criminal Justice Reform, https://www.wishtv.com/wp-content/uploads/2021/08/Indianapolis-Gun-Violence-Problem-Analysis-Summary-Narrative.pdf.
2. Cindy Redcross, Bret Barden, and Dan Bloom, *The Enhanced Transitional Jobs Demonstration: Implementation and Early Impacts of the Next Generation of Subsidized Employment Programs* (Washington, DC: Employment and Training Administration, United States Department of Labor, November 2016).
3. Chad Harrod, "The Peer Mentor Model at RecycleForce: An Enhancement to Transitional Jobs Programs," *Journal of Offender Rehabilitation* 58, no. 4 (May 13, 2019): 327–51. https://doi.org/10.1080/10509674.2019.1596190.
4. Gerardo Gomez, Clark Simons, Wendy St. John, Diana Creasser, Jodi Hackworth, Pari Gupta, Theresa Joy, and Heather Kemp, "Project Prescription for Hope (RxH): Trauma Surgeons and Community Aligned to Reduce Injury Recidivism Caused by Violence," *American Surgeon* 78, no. 9 (2012): 1000–1004. https://doi.org/10.1177/000313481207800942.
5. Jeffrey A. Butts, Caterina Gouvis Roman, Lindsay Bostwick, and Jeremy R. Porter, "Cure Violence: A Public Health Model to Reduce Gun Violence," *Annual Review of Public Health* 36, no. 1 (2015): 39–53. https://doi.org/10.1146/annurev-publhealth-031914-122509.

Part VI

Technology and the Future of Gun Ownership

The history of firearms is a history of technical innovation that started with the discovery of gunpowder by Chinese alchemists over 1,000 years ago.[1] Whether or not you approve of their work, there is no denying that firearms inventors and their inventions—Christian Sharps (breech-loading rifle and pistol), Samuel Colt (revolver), Richard Gatling (Gatling gun), Hiram Maxim (automatic machine gun), John Browning (modern repeating, semiautomatic, and automatic firearms), Hugo Schmeisser ("Sturmgewehr," literally "assault rifle"), John Thompson (Thompson submachinegun, or as the gangsters called it, "Tommy gun"), Mikhail Kalashnikov (AK-47), Eugene Stoner (AR-15), and others like them—have left their mark on the world. These innovations have won wars, toppled governments, and catalyzed social change. They have claimed or changed countless lives, bringing great joy but also great pain and sadness to millions of people.

Almost any gun operates by the same mechanism: apply explosive pressure behind a projectile to launch it down a barrel. The earliest, and simplest, application of this mechanism was the cannon, and the first handheld guns, like the famed muskets of the Revolutionary War, were essentially miniature cannons: pack some gunpowder down into the shaft with a steel ball, then light the fuse.

Eventually, this technology gave way to trigger-activated weapons, such as flintlock guns that ignited gunpowder by producing a tiny spark, and percussion cap guns that used an explosive compound that ignited when hit hard enough.[2] Next came the enclosed metallic cartridge, which combined the projectile (the bullet), the propellant (gunpowder), and the primer (the explosive cap) inside one brass casing. Then there were innovations in locking and loading mechanisms, such as Colt's famous revolving ammunition cylinder, ejection systems for spent shells, and magazines for multiple cartridges. Finally, there were recoil systems, blowback systems, and gas mechanisms that lay the foundation for modern semiautomatic weapons, which fire one shot with one pull of the trigger, and automatic weapons, which continue to fire as long as the trigger remains depressed.[3]

Most popular firearms throughout history, from the Henry repeating rifle to the AR-15, which is affectionately known as "America's rifle,"[4] were originally designed to be weapons of war; they are lethally efficient. Gun rights advocates argue that civilian-owned modern sporting rifles based on the design of the Colt AR-15 do not meet the US Army's standard for "assault weapons" or "assault rifles" because they lack a setting for fully automatic fire. But any gun like the AR-15 that can accept a detachable ammunition magazine, and includes one or more additional features such as a folding, telescoping, or thumbhole rifle stock, would still be illegal under the 1994 Federal Assault Weapons Ban, which expired in 2004.

Technically, there is no difference between a *defensive* firearm you keep at home for protection and an *offensive* firearm you take out to kill—they are one and the same.[5] Mass shootings are increasingly perpetrated by gunmen using high-powered assault rifles. Twenty-two of 66 mass shooters who killed four or more people in a public place from 2012 through 2022 used AR-15s, according to The Violence Project mass shooter database.[6] The rifle had been used just five times by the prior 123 attackers going back to 1966. What is especially appealing about the AR-15 and guns like it is its incredible accuracy combined with its adaptability; it can be modified and customized for a range of applications. And with the advent of the internet and 3D printing, it is easier than ever for regular civilians to override a semiautomatic weapon's trigger bar with a bespoke auto sear, or "switch," and convert it into an automatic weapon.

Modification is the theme of this next and final set of chapters, which look at the evolution of firearm technology and the future of gun ownership. They focus specifically on "smart guns," which use biometrics to prevent unauthorized use, and on unserialized and untraceable "ghost guns," which can be bought online and assembled at home. They provide both a glimpse of where firearm technology could go and explain the role technology can have in improving gun safety.

Recommended Further Reading

- *The Gun* by C. J. Chivers
- *Glock: The Rise of America's Gun* by Paul Barrett
- *Guns, Germs, and Steel* by Jared Diamond
- *American Gun: The Story of the AR-15, the Rifle That Divided a Nation* by Cameron McWhirter and Zusha Elinson

Notes

1. "Firearms," History.com, August 21, 2018. https://www.history.com/topics/inventions/firearms.
2. Matthew Connor, "Firearms History and the Technology of Gun Violence," online exhibit, UC Davis Library, 2019. https://www.library.ucdavis.edu/exhibit/firearms-history-and-the-technology-of-gun-violence/.
3. Connor, "Firearms History and the Technology of Gun Violence."
4. Ali Watkins, John Ismay, and Thomas Gibbons-Neff, "Once Banned, Now Loved and Loathed: How the AR-15 Became 'America's Rifle,'" *New York Times*, March 3, 2018. https://www.nytimes.com/2018/03/03/us/politics/ar-15-americas-rifle.html.
5. Jon Stokes, "Why Millions of Americans—Including Me—Own the AR-15," Vox, June 20, 2016. https://www.vox.com/2016/6/20/11975850/ar-15-owner-orlando.
6. The Violence Project. https://www.theviolenceproject.org.

Chapter 41

Why Do Gun-Makers Get Special Economic Protection?

ALLEN ROSTRON

THE GUN INDUSTRY IS one of very few industries to have congressionally backed immunity from liability. As a result, it's been largely shielded from responsibility for the deaths and injuries its products cause, with few exceptions.

How did this happen? And with America experiencing one tragic mass shooting after another, could this protection ever be overturned? As an expert in constitutional law and product liability, I believe the answer to these questions lies in examining the economic and political clout of the gun industry.

Gun Industry Gets a Protector

The gun industry acquired its protective shield in 2005 after a wave of lawsuits by cities threatened gun companies' survival.[1] The City of New Orleans became the first government to file a lawsuit against gun manufacturers in 1998. More than 30 other American cities and counties soon followed.

The suits, prompted by the growing epidemic of urban gun violence and patterned after claims brought by states against tobacco companies, initially succeeded by shining a spotlight on the industry. I was one of the lawyers at the Brady Center to Prevent Gun Violence who helped put these cases together. The litigation uncovered evidence about how gun manufacturers could reduce risks by making changes to the way they design and distribute their products.[2]

But then came the Protection of Lawful Commerce in Arms Act, which gave gun-makers a special immunity from legal responsibilities and blocked most of the claims. While Congress has occasionally limited the liability of companies making other products, such as medical devices and small aircraft, the degree of protection given to the gun industry was unusual and didn't create alternative ways to regulate the industry and compensate those injured, as Congress did with the makers of childhood vaccines.

Good Times for Gun-Makers

A string of mass shootings, from Orlando to Las Vegas to Parkland and Uvalde, has brought scrutiny to the gun industry's products and practices. At the same time, the firearms industry has enjoyed remarkable growth. In an unintended and sadly ironic way, mass shootings contribute to the industry's financial success.

Gun sales are strongly correlated with prospects for legislating gun control and surge whenever it seems that new legal restrictions on guns may be imposed. This was the case in 2008, when the election of Barack Obama rejuvenated the then-stagnant industry. Fearful that President Obama would take away their guns, many Americans rushed to stock up on new weaponry. Production of firearms rose steadily throughout Obama's first term, even though he did virtually nothing at that time to advance a gun control agenda.

The massacre at Sandy Hook Elementary School shortly after Obama won reelection in 2012 drove up gun sales to unprecedented levels, with production reaching a high of nearly 11 million firearms in 2013, yielding more economic clout for the industry than ever before. That record would be broken just a few years later in 2016, when gun manufacturers produced nearly 11.5 million guns amid speculation that a victory for Hillary Clinton in the presidential election would lead to new legal restrictions on firearms. Gun sales surged again in 2020 amid worries and uncertainty related to the coronavirus pandemic, social justice protests, and a bitterly contested presidential election.

The industry's economic impact rose from $19 billion in 2008 to over $70 billion in 2021, according to the National Shooting Sports Foundation, the firearms industry's trade association. And its impact is felt across the country in both red and blue states and politically important ones, from Texas and California to Florida and Ohio. Some of the nation's oldest and largest gun companies are still based in the legendary

"Gun Valley" region of New England, but there are other manufacturers scattered around the nation. Wholesale distributors and retail dealers operate virtually everywhere.

The number of jobs supported by the industry more than doubled to about 375,000 in that period, with the largest numbers in Texas and California. The taxes paid by the industry have increased even more dramatically.

The Gun Lobby's Power

Gun companies have made it clear they are willing to relocate their operations if the price is right. State and local governments have thrown millions of dollars in subsidies and tax breaks at them. Political considerations have also played a role in relocations, with some gun-makers opting to move to states perceived to be friendlier to guns. For example, Remington Arms relocated much of its manufacturing from New York to Alabama in 2014, drawn by $68.9 million in government handouts, as well as displeasure with New York's enactment of tougher gun laws. The governments that provided the incentives wound up scrambling to recoup the money a few years later after Remington went bankrupt and was dissolved.

The relocation trend continued in 2020, when Smith & Wesson announced that it was moving its headquarters from Massachusetts to Tennessee, Kimber Manufacturing relocated from New York to Alabama, and Stag Arms shifted its operations from Connecticut to Wyoming.

The industry has used the growth in wealth, employment, and taxes to exercise its political muscle at the state and national levels. The trade association's annual lobbying expenditures, negligible prior to Obama's election, tripled in

2013, the year after Sandy Hook, and continued to climb, reaching $5 million in 2021.

The industry's biggest political influence comes through its customers, who are a uniquely potent force. The National Rifle Association, which purports to represent the interests of gun owners, has long been one of the nation's most powerful and feared lobbying groups.

In 2019, serious problems within the organization became apparent, as allegations of financial mismanagement and lavish spending by the group's leaders sparked an unsuccessful effort to oust CEO Wayne LaPierre. New York's attorney general launched an investigation into fraud and other misconduct, a probe that the NRA unsuccessfully tried to dodge by declaring bankruptcy. Although the group's severe financial and legal struggles forced it to cut back on lobbying and political spending in 2020, it remains a powerful entity that can outspend gun-control organizations.

The industry's interests are usually aligned with those of the NRA, but when a gun-maker wants to take a softer position on gun policy, it's extremely risky to do so. A case in point came in 2000, when Smith & Wesson tried to ease the burden of the lawsuits against it by agreeing to be more careful in how it designed and distributed its products as part of a settlement agreement. Its modest steps prompted boycotts by gun owners that nearly destroyed the company in a few short months.

Turning the Tables

Can the increasing frequency of tragedies like the Parkland school shooting and the resulting outrage ever turn the tables on the gun industry?

Applying financial pressure is one way to get the industry's attention. In 2014, a coalition of organizations began a divestment campaign, encouraging people to move their savings out of mutual funds that invest in gun companies. Fund managers said the campaign had its intended effect, with more investors demanding that funds dump gun stocks. According to one study, the amount of assets precluded from investment in companies that make weaponry for military or civilian use increased 1,042% in four years after the Sandy Hook shooting.[3] This campaign was cited as a factor that led to the bankruptcy of Remington, the maker of the AR-15 rifle used in that shooting.

The idea gained some attention. Legislators in New Jersey and teachers in Florida called for public employee pension funds to sell their shares of firearms companies. Connecticut's treasurer announced in 2019 that the state's public pension funds would no longer invest in gun manufacturers. Other socially conscious investors kept their shares but used them as a channel to express concerns. Shareholders of companies that make or sell firearms, like Sturm, Ruger & Co. and Dick's Sporting Goods, called for gun-makers to explain what they are doing to reduce the risks posed by their products.

Americans fed up with the NRA's intransigence also began putting pressure on a range of businesses to cut ties with the gun rights group.

What the Future Holds

Preventing some NRA members from getting a discount on a car rental or airline flight is obviously not going to bring the gun lobby to its knees or lead to a repeal of the industry's immunity. But every small step brings attention to the issue and builds the pressure that will eventually change the political calculus for legislators.

A large majority of Americans support the enactment of stricter gun laws, but the crucial question will be whether the intensity of their feelings about the issue ever match the passion of those who fiercely favor gun rights. Change will happen if enough people make it clear that their preference for stronger regulation of firearms is something that affects how they spend their money and how they cast their votes.

Notes

1. Allen K. Rostron, "Lawyers, Guns & Money: The Rise and Fall of Tort Litigation against the Firearms Industry," review of *Suing the Gun Industry: A Battle at the Crossroads of Gun Control and Mass Torts*, by Timothy Lytton, ed., *Santa Clara Law Review* 46, no. 2 (2006): 481–512.
2. Allen K. Rostron, *Smoking Guns: Exposing the Gun Industry's Complicity in the Illegal Gun Market* (Washington, DC: Legal Action Project, Brady Center to Prevent Gun Violence, 2003).
3. Alexia Fernández Campbell, "Mass Shootings Have Made Gun Stocks Toxic Assets on Wall Street," Vox, February 28, 2018. https://www.vox.com/2018/2/28/17058342/wall-street-gun-stocks-divestment.

Chapter 42

World's Deadliest Inventor
Mikhail Kalashnikov and His AK-47

RICHARD GUNDERMAN

WHAT IS THE DEADLIEST WEAPON of the 20th century? Perhaps you think first of the atomic bomb, estimated to have killed as many as 200,000 people when the United States dropped two on the Japanese cities of Hiroshima and Nagasaki in 1945. But another weapon is responsible for far more deaths, numbering up into the millions. It's the Kalashnikov assault rifle, commonly known as the AK-47.

Originally developed in secrecy for the Soviet military, an estimated 100 million AK-47s and its variants have been produced to date. This gun is now found throughout the world, including in the hands of many American civilians, who in 2012 bought as many AK-47s as the Russian police and military. As a physician, I have witnessed the destruction this weapon can wreak on human flesh.

Kalashnikov's Invention

Russian Mikhail Kalashnikov invented the weapon that bears his name in the middle of the 20th century. Born on November 10, 1919, Kalashnikov was a tank mechanic in the Soviet military during the Second World War. He was wounded during the German invasion of the USSR in 1941.

Having seen firsthand the combat advantage conferred by Germany's superior firearms, Kalashnikov resolved to develop a better weapon. While still in the military, he produced several designs that lost out to competitors before eventually producing the first AK-47. The name of Kalashnikov's greatest invention stands for Automat Kalashnikova 1947, the year it was first produced.

In 1949, the AK-47 became the assault rifle of the Soviet Army. Later adopted by other nations in the Warsaw Pact, the weapon quickly spread around the world, becoming a symbol of revolution in such far-flung lands as Vietnam, Afghanistan, Colombia, and Mozambique, on whose flag it figures prominently.

Over the course of his long life, Kalashnikov continued to tweak his classic design. In 1959, production began on his AKM, which replaced the AK-47's milled receiver with one made of stamped metal, making it both lighter and less expensive to produce. He also developed the cartridge-fed PK machine gun. Modified AK-47s are still in production in countries around the world.

The inventor with his eponymous weapon.
AP Photo / Vladimir Vyatkin

The AK-47's Advantages and Abundance

Why was the AK-47 such a revolutionary rifle?[1]

It is relatively inexpensive to produce, short and light to carry, and easy to use, with little recoil. It also boasts legendary reliability under harsh conditions ranging from waterlogged jungles to Middle Eastern sandstorms, in both extreme cold and heat. It also requires relatively little maintenance. This stems from its large gas piston and wide clearances between moving parts, which help to prevent it from jamming.

Kalashnikov liked to boast about the rifle's superiority to the American military's M-16 rifle. "During the Vietnam War," he said in a 2007 interview, "American soldiers would throw away their M-16s to grab AK-47s and bullets for it from dead

Vietnamese soldiers. And I hear American soldiers in Iraq use it quite often."[2]

The world's most abundant firearm is also well suited to crime and terrorism. The hostage-takers who stormed the Olympic Village in Munich in 1972 were armed with Kalashnikovas, and mass shooters in the United States have used semiautomatic versions of the weapon in killings in Stockton, California, and in Dallas.

The US military has acted as a distributor of the weapon in conflicts in Afghanistan and Iraq. With a service life of 20 to 40 years, AK-47s are easily relocated and repurposed.

Today, global prices for the weapon often run in the hundreds of dollars, but some AK-47s can be had for as little as US$50. The huge worldwide production of the weapon, particularly in countries with low labor costs, has driven prices downward.

Kalashnikov's Legacy

For his labors, the Soviet Union awarded Kalashnikov the Stalin Prize, the Red Star, and the Order of Lenin. In 2007, President Vladimir Putin singled out the Kalashnikov rifle as "a symbol of the creative genius of our people." Kalashnikov died a national hero in 2013 at the age of 94.

Throughout most of his life, Kalashnikov rebuffed attempts to saddle him with guilt over the vast number of killings and injuries inflicted with his invention. He insisted that he had developed it for defense, not offense. When a reporter asked in 2007 how he could sleep at night, he replied, "I sleep well. It is the politicians who are to blame for failing to come to an agreement and resorting to violence."[3]

Yet in the final year of his life, Kalashnikov may have experienced a change of heart. He wrote a letter to the head of the Russian Orthodox Church, saying, "The pain in my soul is unbearable. I keep asking myself the same unsolvable question: If my assault rifle took people's lives, that means that I am responsible for their deaths." It's a perennial debate: What kills? Guns or those who carry them? At the bottom of the letter, he signed it, "a slave of God, the designer Mikhail Kalashnikov."[4]

Notes

1. Stephan Wilkinson, "How the AK-47 Became the 'Weapon of the Century.'" *Military Times*, December 12, 2017. https://www.military times.com/off-duty/gearscout/2017/12/12/how-the-ak-47-became -the-weapon-of-the-century/.
2. "AK-47 Inventor Says Conscience Is Clear," CBS News, July 6, 2007. https://www.cbsnews.com/news/ak-47-inventor-says-conscience-is -clear/.
3. "AK-47 Inventor Says Conscience Is Clear," CBS News.
4. Sarah Wolfe, "Weapons Designer Kalashnikov Repented AK-47 Killings in a Letter before His Death," GlobalPost, January 13, 2014. https:// theworld.org/stories/2014-01-13/weapons-designer-kalashnikov -repented-ak-47-killings-letter-his-death.

Chapter 43

What Are "Ghost Guns"?

GAREN WINTEMUTE

IT'S NOT EXPENSIVE or difficult to produce large numbers of untraceable firearms in the United States. Whether for private use, sale on the criminal market, or arming violent extremists, mass-producing firearms that police can't track is actually startlingly cheap and easy to do. These weapons are often called "ghost guns."

For just over US$2,000, I can buy a machine—not much bigger than a desktop laser printer—that will do the trick. If I'm feeling handy, I can get it done instead with just some simple power tools. As I discuss in my 2021 journal article about

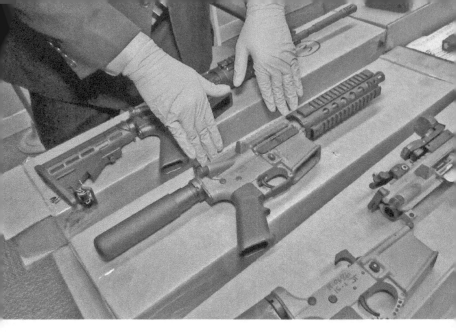

A San Francisco police officer displays several "ghost guns"—untraceable firearms with no serial numbers or manufacturing marks.
AP Photo / Haven Daley

ghost guns,[1] it's perfectly legal to manufacture firearms privately without a license in the United States. But it's illegal to sell or give away privately manufactured firearms without a license.

A person producing a single ghost gun for their own personal use may not rise to the level of official concern, but the undetected production of untraceable weapons makes it difficult to map and disrupt illicit markets that supply such guns for use in crime. Federal law does not require privately made firearms to have serial numbers or other identifiers, which makes it impossible to trace transfers of ownership—to "follow the guns"—when they have been used in crimes. They have no history and come from nowhere.

An Almost-Gun

Federal firearms laws and regulations have, over time, developed a loophole through which these ghost guns can easily fit. Every firearm has a component, sometimes called a "frame" but also called a "receiver," which is the keystone element to which other parts are attached.

Finished frames and receivers are considered to be firearms under federal law. To be sold, they must have identifying marks and serial numbers, and sellers must keep records of who bought which weapons. If the firearm is used in a crime, police can investigate current and previous owners to see if they might be involved.

But nearly finished receivers are considered nothing more than pieces of metal or plastic. These items are often called "80 percenters" because most, but not all, of the work has been done to make the piece of metal or plastic into a working receiver. They are available for purchase without a license, background check, or other protections put in place for firearms purchases, and they cost as little as $50 to $75 apiece, with volume discounts available.

The work needed to turn an 80 percenter into a fully functional frame or receiver takes about half an hour. All the other parts, such as a stock to support the firearm and a barrel through which bullets are fired, are freely available without regulation and are easily attached to the receiver during manufacture of a weapon.

An Uncountable Number

There is no estimate of the number of fully functional ghost guns in circulation—indeed, how could there be?—but the

Bureau of Alcohol, Tobacco, Firearms and Explosives disclosed in May 2021 that nearly 24,000 had been recovered by law enforcement agencies in the previous five years.[2] That's a small but meaningful proportion of total firearms recoveries. The ATF has said, in a series of data reports, that in 2019 it "traced and recovered" between 250,000 and 350,000 firearms. CBS's *60 Minutes* reported in May 2020 that 38 states had identified criminal cases involving ghost guns; they had been used in at least four mass shootings.[3] A Florida man was convicted of making more than 200 ghost guns, mostly AR–15–type rifles.

Some crimes committed with ghost guns involve domestic terrorism. In mid-2020, an adherent of the violent, extremist "boogaloo movement"—an active-duty US Air Force sergeant—was charged with the murder of two law enforcement officers and the attempted murder of a third. At least one of the killings, and possibly all three shootings, involved a ghost machine gun. In October 2020, more than a dozen men were arrested for plotting to kidnap Michigan governor Gretchen Whitmer. They were allegedly participants in the boogaloo and militia movements, and police said they had ghost guns.

Fixes are being put into place. As of this writing 10 states and the District of Columbia regulate or prohibit ghost guns.[4] In April 2022, the Department of Justice issued new rules and regulations that should make it much more difficult to manufacture and distribute firearms clandestinely.

Notes

1. Garen J. Wintemute, "Ghost Guns: Spookier Than You Think They Are," *Injury Epidemiology* 8, no. 1 (April 5, 2021). https://doi.org/10.1186/s40621-021-00306-0.

2. US Bureau of Alcohol, Tobacco, Firearms and Explosives, "Definition of 'Frame or Receiver' and Identification of Firearms," *Federal Register*, May 21, 2021. https://www.federalregister.gov/documents /2021/05/21/2021-10058/definition-of-frame-or-receiver-and -identification-of-firearms.

3. Bill Whitaker, "Ghost Guns: The Build-It-Yourself Firearms That Skirt Most Federal Gun Laws and Are Virtually Untraceable," *60 Minutes*, May 10, 2020. https://www.cbsnews.com/news/ghost-guns -untraceable-weapons-criminal-cases-60-minutes-2020-05-10/.

4. "Ghost Guns," Giffords Law Center. https://giffords.org/lawcenter/gun -laws/policy-areas/hardware-ammunition/ghost-guns/.

Chapter 44

3D-Printed Guns May Be More Dangerous to Their Users Than to Targets

JEREMY STRAUB

DESPITE FEARS THAT GUNS made with 3D printers will let criminals and terrorists easily make untraceable, undetectable plastic weapons at home, my own experience with quality control in 3D manufacturing suggests that, at least for now, 3D-printed firearms may pose as much, or maybe even more, of a threat to the people who try to make and use them than to others. One firearms expert suggested that even the best 3D-printed guns might fire only "five shots [before] blowing up in your hand."[1] A weapon with a design or printing defect

A company called Defense Distributed developed a 3D-printed gun called the Liberator, which many fear could pass through security checkpoints undetected.
AP Photo / Eric Gay

might blow up or come apart in its user's hand before firing even a single bullet.

As someone who uses 3D printing in his work,[2] and who researches quality assurance technologies,[3] I've had the opportunity to see numerous printing defects and analyze what causes them. The problem is not with the concept of 3D printing but with the process followed to create a specific item. Consumer 3D printers don't always create high-quality items, and regular people aren't likely to engage in rigorous quality-assurance testing before using a 3D-printed firearm.

Problems with 3D Printing Are Common at Home

Many consumer 3D printers are liable to a variety of glitches, causing defects in the items they make. At times, an object detaches from the platform it's on while being made, ending up lopsided, broken, or otherwise damaged. Flaws can be much harder to detect when the filament—the melted plastic material the item is being made from—is too hot or cold or flows too fast or slow, or stops when it shouldn't. Even with all of the settings right, sometimes 3D-printed objects still have defects.

When a poorly made toy or trinket breaks, it can be hazardous. A child might be left with a part that he or she could choke on, for example. When a firearm breaks, however, the result could be even more serious, even fatal. In 2013, agents from the US Bureau of Alcohol, Tobacco, Firearms and Explosives tested 3D-printed guns and found that the quality of materials and manufacturing determined whether a gun would fire multiple rounds successfully or break apart during or after the first shot.

With home printing, nefarious people might tamper with the design files on a website, publish intentionally defective designs, or even create a virus that interferes with the operation of a 3D printer.[4] Hackers may deliberately target 3D-printed guns, for ideological or other reasons, or inadvertently cause defects with general attacks against 3D-printing systems.

Not Up to Commercial Standards

Commercial manufacturers of guns double-check their designs, test models, and perform rigorous examinations to ensure their firearms work properly. Defects still happen, but they're much less likely than with home-printed weapons. Home printers are not designed to produce the level of consistent quality required for weapon production. They also don't have systems to detect all of the things that could go wrong and thus make printed weapons potentially dangerous.

This is not to say that 3D printing itself is unsafe. Many companies, in fact, use 3D printing to manufacture parts where safety is critical. Printed parts are used in airplanes and for medical devices, patient-specific surgical instruments, customized time-release drugs, prosthetics, and hearing aids. Scientists have even proposed printing scaffolding to grow or repair human body parts.[5]

Solutions to Defects Yet to Come

In time, improvements to 3D printers available on the consumer market may allow for safe production of reliable parts. For instance, emerging technologies could monitor the process of printing and the filament used.[6] The group I work with and others have developed ways to assess parts, both during printing and afterward. Other researchers are developing ways to prevent malicious defects from being added to existing printing instructions and to secure printing generally.[7]

The quality of most consumer-grade 3D printers is not at a point where they should be used to produce parts for which safety is critical, such as parts for a weapon. For the moment, most quality control for 3D-printed parts is left to the person operating the printer or to whoever is using the item. Most consumers don't have the technical skills needed to perform tests and likely won't learn them. Until printers are more sophisticated, whatever is made with them—whether firearms or other items—isn't guaranteed to be reliable enough to use safely.

Notes

1. Quoted in Mark Gollom, "Any 3D-Printed Guns Created Here Would Be Subject to Canada's Gun Laws, Officials Say, CBC News, August 1,

2018. https://www.cbc.ca/news/politics/3d-guns-printers-plastic
-canada-1.4768714.

2. Michael Hirsch, Thomas McGuire, Michael Parsons, Skye Leake, and
    Jeremy Straub, "Enablement of Scientific Remote Sensing Missions
    with In-Space 3D Printing," *SPIE Proceedings* 9854 (May 26, 2016).
    https://doi.org/10.1117/12.2223467; Michael Hirsch, Thomas McGuire,
    Michael Parsons, Skye Leake, and Jeremy Straub, "An Aerial 3D
    Printing Test Mission," *SPIE Proceedings* 9828 (May 17, 2016).
    https://doi.org/10.1117/12.2223469.

3. Jeremy Straub, "Initial Work on the Characterization of Additive
    Manufacturing (3D Printing) Using Software Image Analysis,"
    Machines 3, no. 2 (2015): 55–71. https://doi.org/10.3390
    /machines3020055.

4. Jeremy Straub, "An Approach to Detecting Deliberately Introduced
    Defects and Micro-defects in 3D Printed Objects," *SPIE Proceedings*
    10203 (June 6, 2017). https://doi.org/10.1117/12.2264588.

5. Nick Tovar, Lukasz Witek, Pablo Atria, Michael Sobieraj, Michelle
    Bowers, Christopher D. Lopez, Bruce N. Cronstein, and Paulo G.
    Coelho, "Form and Functional Repair of Long Bone Using 3D-Printed
    Bioactive Scaffolds," *Journal of Tissue Engineering and Regenerative
    Medicine* 12, no. 9 (July 25, 2018): 1986–99. https://doi.org/10.1002
    /term.2733.

6. T. Fang, M. A. Jafari, I. Bakhadyrov, A. Safari, S. Danforth, and
    N. Langrana, "Online Defect Detection in Layered Manufacturing
    Using Process Signature," *SMC'98 Conference Proceedings*
    (conference paper, IEEE International Conference on Systems, Man,
    and Cybernetics, San Diego, CA, October 14, 1998). https://doi.org/10
    .1109/icsmc.1998.727536.

7. Yang Gao, Borui Li, Wei Wang, Wenyao Xu, Chi Zhou, and Zhanpeng
    Jin, "Watching and Safeguarding Your 3D Printer," *Proceedings of the
    ACM on Interactive, Mobile, Wearable and Ubiquitous Technologies* 2,
    no. 3 (September 18, 2018): 1–27. https://doi.org/10.1145/3264918.

Chapter 45

What Makes a "Smart Gun" Smart?

DONALD H. SEBASTIAN

EVERY TIME A TODDLER accidentally shoots a friend or family member, a teen kills himself by gunshot, or a shooter perpetrates an act of mass violence, public discussion circles back to "smart gun" technology. The concept has roots in a 1995 National Institute of Justice (NIJ) study that recommended a technology-based approach to reducing the incidence of police officers killed in gun-grabs by assailants. President Barack Obama's 2016 memorandum on gun violence included recommendations on federal actions designed to promote the development and commercialization of electronic gun-safety systems.

The term *smart gun* has been embraced by the popular press as a catchall term for all forms of electronic personalized safety technology. The idea is to make sure a gun can be fired only by its authorized user. But the various scenarios in which a gun could be inappropriately discharged call for fundamentally different safety systems.

The metaphor of a common door lock is a useful way to think about the various technological approaches. The key serves as the personal identifier. The pin tumblers that recognize the key inside the lock serve as the authenticator. And the latch serves as the block. All electronic gun–safety systems must accomplish all three of these basic functions: identify authorized operators, authenticate their credentials, and release the block to the firing mechanism.

How one satisfies those requirements is subject to the performance constraints of the application environment and the physical constraints of the weapon. These differences create distinct branches on the family tree of personalized-weapons technology.

Proximity Sensors: Can You Hear Me Now?

One group of solutions owes its heritage to the NIJ study focused on protecting police weapons from being taken away during a close-quarters struggle. It suggested a token-based proximity sensor using radio frequency identification (RFID). A number of working RFID prototype guns have been demonstrated, beginning with Colt's 1996 handgun and including TriggerSmart, iGun M-2000, and the Armatix iP1.

In a badge, wristband, or ring, a user wears a passive RFID tag, like those embedded in products to prevent shoplifting. It's the "token" and serves as the key in the front door metaphor. Like a physical key, it can be duplicated or shared. What matters is possession of the token, not the identity of the token holder.

A wireless RFID reader is built into the gun and serves the role of authenticator. It generates a signal that activates the RFID tag to respond with an embedded code. If there's a match, then the electromechanical components unblock the weapon's firing system and the gun functions normally. The response time of these systems is generally dependent on the choice of electromechanical components used in the blocking system (for example, servomotors, solenoids, shape memory metals) but is generally less than half a second. By design, the gun can remain active as long as there is a signal link or, in some configurations, as long as pressure sensors detect the gun is being held.

If the tag is too far away from the transmitter to self-activate and respond, then the gun remains locked down. The Armatix iP1, for example, specifies a range of 15 inches. If you try to spoof the transponder with a signal that does not contain the individual code, it's like using the wrong key in a door: it may fit the slot but cannot be turned because it does not match the tumblers, so the gun remains locked down.

Various designs interfere with the firing mechanism in different places—from trigger bar to firing pin. There are also different technologies including solenoid actuators, shape memory alloy-based components, and even electronic firing systems that serve as the deadbolt to be released upon receiving a signal from an authentication system. The details are proprietary to the individual products on the market and reflect design trade-offs in power consumption, free space to accommodate components, and response time.

The proximity of gun to token is not an absolute determinant of rightful possession during a close-quarters struggle. But the technology does offer simplicity of operation and easy weapons exchange across permitted users, and it reliably disables a weapon from use if a police officer, say, has been overpowered and the duty weapon taken.

Biometrics: Do I Know You?

The benefits of a token-based system in a street encounter become a liability in the home. The viability of the approach is wholly dependent on the owner securing the token where it cannot be accessed by denied users. But guns used for home protection are more likely to have the token and weapon stored together to prevent any delay in the event of an intrusion. And anyone who has both the token and the weapon can fire it.

A second group of technologies evolved in response to child-safe handgun legislation adopted in New Jersey and Maryland in the early 2000s, designed to prevent unauthorized use of personal firearms stored in the home. Biometric authentication systems eliminate the physical token. Instead, a measurable physical characteristic of any authorized user becomes the key. It can't be taken without permission, counterfeited, or otherwise transferred.

To date, fingerprints have been the primary attribute used in biometric systems. Kodiak Arms Intelligun and Safe Gun Technology's retrofit for rifles use fingerprint detection as a primary mode of security. If the fingerprint is the key, then the sensor and pattern-matching software are the pin tumblers that perform the authentication function in these guns.

A widely used sensor technology relies on capacitance imaging of the fingerprint. The variation in distance between the ridges and grooves of the finger and the sensor plate creates a distribution of electrical charge storage (capacitance) that can be measured in an array of conductor plates in the sensor. Other fingerprint sensors rely on infrared (thermal) imaging, and some use pressure detection to create a digital pattern that is a unique representation of the print.

The sensor software needs to be trained to store acceptable patterns that may represent different fingers of a single user or various fingers from multiple authorized users. After that, any pattern that doesn't match within some specified tolerance is rejected. The reliability of the authentication process is influenced by the resolution of the sensor, the extent and orientation of the exposed finger, and physical factors that can interfere with the mapping. For example, moisture on the finger can defeat a capacitive detector, cold fingers can reduce the reliability of thermal imaging, and dirt, paint, or gloves can obscure the fingerprint beyond recognition.

There are other types of biometric security being explored. One prototype sponsored by NIJ adopted vascular biometrics that detect the blood vessel structure below the skin surface. An emerging class of biometrics is dynamic or behavioral and combine some element of individualized physicality amplified by learned patterns of behavior.[1] For instance, voice identification combines the structure of one's vocal cords with the breath patterns of speech learned in infancy. Electronic signature authentication captures the speed and pressure of a pen on an LCD (liquid-crystal display) pad, not the image of the signature, as the signer executes handwriting in a pattern ingrained early in life.

Our research team at the New Jersey Institute of Technology has developed a gun safety system based on a novel behavioral biometric called Dynamic Grip Recognition™ (DGR). The team demonstrated that changes over time to the pressure pattern created on the grip of a handgun as one counter-braces the force of trigger pull were particular to the user, reproducible, and measurable.[2] Our prototype detects grip patterns in a 10th of a second when the trigger is pulled and unlocks the weapon with no apparent lag to the shooter. Because DGR works during trigger pull of a properly held weapon, the approach can also reduce accidental firings from mishandling a loaded weapon.

Reliability: Can I Trust You?

Reliability is always a concern raised in discussions of electronic gun safety systems.

The interior of a firing weapon is not a friendly environment for electronics, but there is now a sufficient history of ruggedized circuitry such that failure rates of the underlying electronic hardware are orders of magnitude less than the predicted failure rates of the mechanical weapon (somewhere between 1 in 1,000 and 1 in 10,000, depending on the precision and quality of the weapon).

Power is clearly a concern here too. Advances in microprocessor technology and battery storage driven by smartphones and portable electronics remove this issue as a hindrance. Motion detection and wake-up software can reduce battery drain during storage. Integrating the power supply with the ammunition clip and even charging by mechanical cycling are ways to address power loss as a mode of failure.

In biometric systems, there is another element to consider: failure of the identification algorithm. Those are either false negatives, in which a rightful user is not recognized, or false positives, in which an impostor is wrongly authenticated. The recognition rates for fingerprint detectors have been claimed to be as high as 99.99% (a 1 in 10,000 failure rate).

As the array of sensor technologies grows, one might expect a multisensor or multispectral approach to be the ultimate choice for a biometric systems. These have the advantage of multiplying reliability rates when independent measures are used. For example, a fingerprint sensor with a 1-in-10,000 failure rate, coupled with a dynamic grip recognition with a failure rate of 1 in 1,000, would produce a combined reliability of 1 in 10,000×1,000 or 1 in 10,000,000.

Will We Ever Be Able to Buy One?

Throughout the 20-year-long discussion of "smart guns," the topic has been a lightning rod for debate between pro- and anti-gun lobbies. Too often there isn't substantive knowledge of the underlying technologies, their appropriate use, and their design limitations. Personalized weapons technology can contribute to reducing death and injury from accidental or unauthorized use of weapons. It is not a panacea; the technology can't stop shootings like what happened at Virginia Tech, Aurora, or Sandy Hook, or the more recent Parkland, Buffalo, Uvalde, and Highland Park, where lawfully purchased weapons were used. But it can be an option for gun buyers to ensure their weapons don't fall into the wrong hands.

The existing platforms show that smart guns are not science fiction and could be a commercial reality much sooner than later. A 2013 survey conducted by the National Institute of Justice identified 13 different personalized weapon systems, at least three of which were deemed to be in commercial preproduction.[3] President Obama's initiative was thought to be an important step toward accelerating development and prompting the private-sector investment necessary to mature these technologies to the point of attaining the reliability and affordability that will spur consumer adoption. This did not come to pass, and there is still no viable domestic market for personalized weapons as of this writing.

Notes

1. Roman V. Yampolskiy and Venu Govindaraju, "Behavioural Biometrics: A Survey and Classification," *International Journal of Biometrics* 1, no. 1 (2008): 81–113.
2. T. Chang, Z. Chen, B. Cheng, M. Cody, M. Liska, W. Marshall, M. Recce, D. Sebastian, and D. Shishkin, "Enhancing Handgun Safety with Embedded Signal Processing and Dynamic Grip Recognition" (conference paper, 31st Annual Conference of IEEE Industrial Electronics Society, Raleigh, NC, November 6–11, 2005). https://doi.org/10.1109/iecon.2005.1569229.
3. Mark Greene, *A Review of Gun Safety Technologies* (Washington, DC: US Department of Justice Office of Justice Programs, National Institute of Justice, June 2013).

Contributors

PIERRE M. ATLAS is a Senior Lecturer in the Paul H. O'Neill School of Public and Environmental Affairs at Indiana University Indianapolis and teaches courses on gun culture and policy and terrorism and public policy. Prior to joining the O'Neill School in fall 2021, he was a Professor of Political Science at Marian University in Indianapolis. Atlas is a comparative political scientist by training, and his research and publications examine how the legacy of the North American frontier helps to explain contemporary political differences between the United States and Canada on issues such as Indigenous policy and gun laws and gun culture.

DEBORAH AZRAEL, Director of Research at the Harvard Injury Control Research Center, has over 25 years' experience conducting and leading grant-funded research on firearm violence, injury surveillance, and suicide prevention. Dr. Azrael was the Codirector of the pilot for what became the National Violent Death Reporting System, a 50-state surveillance system that collects data on all homicides, suicides, and unintentional firearm deaths. Much of Dr. Azrael's scholarship, especially over the past decade, has focused on studies designed to inform interventions to reduce suicide. Azrael received her PhD in Health Policy (concentration in Statistics and Evaluative Sciences) from Harvard University. In 2015, Dr. Azrael was named one of the 10 Americans who shaped the gun debate by The Trace.

MICHELLE BARNHART, PhD, is an Associate Professor of Marketing at Oregon State University. Her research focuses on the ways that cultural norms, social groups, identity, and consumer well-being relate to consumption and markets. Her current research investigates firearm consumption and policy. Her research has been published in the *Journal of Consumer Research*, the *Journal of Business Research*, the *Journal of Marketing Management*, and the *Journal of Macromarketing*.

PAUL BOXER is a Professor in the Psychology Department at Rutgers University–Newark, as well as the Director of the Rutgers Social Development Research Program. Dr. Boxer studies the development, prevention, and treatment of violent and nonviolent antisocial behavior, particularly among youths in the juvenile justice system. Currently Boxer's scholarly agenda centers on evidence-based practices in the juvenile justice system, the impact of violence and crime in communities on youth development, and the role of youth gangs in the development and persistence of antisocial behavior.

BRAD J. BUSHMAN earned a PhD in Psychology in 1989 from the University of Missouri. Bushman is a Professor of Communication at The Ohio State University, where he holds the Rinehart Chair of Mass Communication. Previously he was a Professor at Iowa State University (1990–2003) and the University of Michigan (2003–2010). He was a member of President Obama's committee on gun violence. Following the Sandy Hook school shooting, he was a cochair for a National Science Foundation subcommittee report on youth violence, and he testified before the US Congress on that report. He has published more than 250 peer-reviewed journal articles that have been cited over 60,000 times.

MARIKA CABRAL is an Associate Professor of Economics at the University of Texas at Austin and a Research Associate at the National Bureau of Economic Research. Professor Cabral's research covers a range of topics in health economics and public finance. Much of her research focuses on understanding the role of market failures, the impacts of incentive design, and the consequences of government intervention in health-related insurance markets. In 2019, she was awarded a National Science Foundation CAREER award.

PATRICK CARTER is the Codirector of the University of Michigan Institute for Firearm Injury Prevention; the Director of the University of Michigan Injury Prevention Center, funded by the Centers for Disease Control and Prevention; and a member of the leadership team for the Firearm Safety Among Children and Teens consortium, funded by the Eunice Kennedy Shriver National Institute of Child Health and Human Development. He is an Associate Professor of Emergency Medicine (School of Medicine) and Health Behavior and Health Education (School of Public Health) at the University of Michigan. Dr. Carter's research is in the field of firearm injury prevention, specifically the development, testing, and implementation of emergency department–based interventions to decrease firearm violence, youth violence, and associated risk behaviors such as substance use among high-risk urban youth populations.

PHILIP J. COOK is ITT/Sanford Professor Emeritus of Public Policy and Professor Emeritus of Economics at Duke University. He served as the Director and Chair of Duke's Sanford Institute of Public Policy from 1985 to 1989 and again from 1997 to 1999. Cook is an honorary Fellow in the American Society of Criminology and an elected member of the National Academy of Medicine. In 2020 he was awarded the Stockholm Prize in Criminology for his research on gun violence prevention. He has researched and written about gun violence for four decades and is the coauthor with Kristin A. Goss of *The Gun Debate* (Oxford University Press, 2020), which is in its second edition.

SAUL CORNELL, the Paul and Diane Guenther Chair in American History at Fordham University, is the author of two prize-winning works in American legal history. He is one of the nation's leading authorities on early American constitutional thought. His work has been widely referenced by legal scholars and historians and has been cited by the US Supreme Court and many state supreme courts. He authored the chapter on the right to bear arms in *The Oxford Handbook of the U.S. Constitution* and coauthored the section in *The Cambridge History of Law in America* on the Bill of Rights and early years of the Marshall Court.

REBECCA CUNNINGHAM is the former Director of the University of Michigan Injury Prevention Center, 1 of 10 US injury control research centers funded by the Centers for Disease Control and Prevention to address urgent injury issues through research, education, and outreach. She led a consortium of 25 researchers across 12 universities and health systems that aimed to improve firearms safety through an injury prevention approach. The Firearm Safety Among Children and Teens consortium was a historic funding commitment from the National Institutes of Health to reduce firearm injury. In 2019, Cunningham was elected to the National Academy of Medicine. She currently serves as the Vice President of Research at the University of Michigan.

JAMES DENSLEY is a Professor of Criminal Justice and the Department Chair of the School of Law Enforcement and Criminal Justice at Metro State University, part of the Minnesota State system. He is the cofounder and copresident of The Violence Project research center, best known for its database of mass shooters. Densley has received global media attention for his work on street gangs, criminal networks, violence, and policing. He is the author or coauthor of eight books including *The Violence Project: How to Stop a Mass Shooting Epidemic*, winner of the 2022 Minnesota Book Award; 50 peer-reviewed articles in leading social science journals; and more than 100 book chapters, essays, and other works in outlets such as CNN, the *Guardian*, the *Los Angeles Times*, *TIME*, *USA Today*, the *Wall Street Journal*, and the *Washington Post*.

GREG DICKINSON is the Chair of the Department of Communication Studies at Colorado State University. He received the College of Liberal Arts Excellence in Teaching Award and the CSU Alumni Best Teacher Award. He also received the National Communication Association's Gerald R. Miller Dissertation Award and, with his coauthors Brian L. Ott and Eric Aoki, the National Communication Association's Golden Anniversary Monograph Award. He writes about ways that buildings and human landscapes engage viewers and users on questions of values, beliefs, and actions. His work advances critical and theoretical understanding of memory, place, and everyday life.

JOHN J. DONOHUE III, the C. Wendell and Edith M. Carlsmith Professor of Law at Stanford Law School and Research Associate of the National Bureau of Economic Research, has been a leading empirical researcher in the legal academy over the past 25 years. Professor Donohue is an economist and a lawyer and is well known for using empirical analysis to determine the impact of law and public policy in a wide range of areas, including civil rights and antidiscrimination law, employment discrimination, crime and criminal justice, and school funding.

FRANK EDWARDS is an Assistant Professor in the School of Criminal Justice at Rutgers University–Newark and a fellow at the Bronfenbrenner Center for Translational Research at Cornell University, which is affiliated with the National Data Archive on Child Abuse and Neglect. He received a PhD in Sociology from the University of Washington in 2017. His work has appeared in *Proceedings of the National Academy of Sciences*, *American Sociological Review*, the *American Journal of Public Health*, *Children and Youth Services Review*, the *Annual Review of Criminology*, the *Russell Sage Foundation Journal of the Social Sciences*, and other outlets.

SANDRO GALEA, a Physician and an Epidemiologist, is the Dean and Robert A. Knox Professor at Boston University's School of Public

Health. He previously held academic and leadership positions at Columbia University, the University of Michigan, and the New York Academy of Medicine. Dr. Galea's scholarship has been at the intersection of social and psychiatric epidemiology, with a focus on the behavioral health consequences of trauma, including firearm violence.

RICHARD GUNDERMAN is a Chancellor's Professor of Radiology, Pediatrics, Medical Education, Philosophy, Liberal Arts, Philanthropy, and Medical Humanities and Health Studies at Indiana University, where he also serves as the John A. Campbell Professor of Radiology and a Bicentennial Professor. He received his AB summa cum laude from Wabash College, his MD and PhD (Committee on Social Thought) with honors from the University of Chicago, and his MPH from Indiana University. He is a 10-time recipient of the Indiana University Trustees Teaching Award and received the 2012 Robert Glaser Award, the highest teaching award of the Association of American Medical Colleges. He has authored more than 900 articles and has published 15 books. More importantly, his students are widely published and have gone on to win many awards and achieve professional distinction in service to others.

CONNIE HASSETT-WALKER is an Assistant Professor in the School of Criminology and Criminal Justice at Norwich University in Vermont. She is the author of two books, including *Guns on the Internet: Online Gun Communities, First Amendment Protections, and the Search for Common Ground on Gun Control* (Routledge, 2018). Her research has been published in a variety of scholarly journals including the *Journal of Developmental and Life-Course Criminology, Journal of Interpersonal Violence*, and *Journal of Ethnicity in Criminal Justice*.

PAUL HIRSCHFIELD is an Associate Professor of Sociology and the Director of the Program in Criminal Justice at Rutgers University. He earned his PhD in Sociology from Northwestern University in 2003. His theoretical and empirical work has focused on expanded criminalization and surveillance, especially in schools, and the subsequent rise of alternatives to criminalization. He also studies variations in deadly force and related policies within the United States and internationally.

AIMEE DINNIN HUFF is an Associate Professor of Marketing in the College of Business at Oregon State University. Her research explores market dynamics, consumer culture, and experience in contested contexts, including recreational cannabis markets and American gun culture. Her work has been published in the *Journal of Consumer Research, Journal of Business Research, Journal of the Association for Consumer Research, Journal of Marketing Management, European Journal of Marketing, Journal of Consumer Affairs, Journal of*

Macromarketing, *Academy of Management Learning & Education*, and *Journal of Business Ethics*.

ARASH JAVANBAKHT, MD, is the Director of the Stress, Trauma, and Anxiety Research Clinic (STARC) at Wayne State University. He is known for his clinical and research work on anxiety, trauma, and PTSD. He is heavily involved in the treatment of civilians, refugees, and first responders with PTSD. Dr Javanbakht's research examines the impact of exposure to war trauma in adult and child Syrian and Iraqi refugees, and biological and psychological factors of risk and resilience. STARC also uses art, dance, and movement therapies in helping refugee families.

BOKYUNG KIM is an economics PhD student at the University of Texas at Austin. Her research interests are health economics, public economics, and labor economics.

MICHAEL J. KLEIN is an Assistant Professor of Surgery at the New York University Grossman School of Medicine and a trauma surgeon at NYC Health + Hospitals / Bellevue, the highest-volume level 1 trauma center in Manhattan. His priorities are to deliver high-quality, timely, and cost-effective care to the sick and injured. As Director of the Advanced Surgery Clerkship for the School of Medicine, he is heavily involved in educating medical students and training surgery residents. His research interests include device development for the early detection of traumatic injuries and the use of high-fidelity operative simulation to enhance surgeons' readiness to manage devastating injuries.

ANITA KNOPOV is an Emergency Medicine Physician interested in the relationship between policy and medicine. She was previously a Predoctoral Research Fellow at the Boston University School of Public Health. She has researched the racial disparity in firearm violence.

SUSANNA LEE is a Professor in the Department of French and Franco-phone Studies at Georgetown University. Her research interests include the 19th-century French novel, 20th-century crime fiction, popular culture, and literary theory. She is the author of *Detectives in the Shadows* (Johns Hopkins University Press, 2020), *Hard-Boiled Crime Fiction and the Decline of Moral Authority* (Ohio State University Press, 2016), and *A World Abandoned by God: Narrative and Secularism* (Bucknell University Press, 2006). She edited Norton Critical Editions of Proust's *Swann's Way* (2013) and Stendhal's *The Red and the Black* (2007) and has also published in the field of law and humanities.

MORGAN MARIETTA studies the political consequences of belief. He is the author of four books, *The Politics of Sacred Rhetoric: Absolutist Appeals and Political Influence, A Citizen's Guide to American Ideology,*

A Citizen's Guide to the Constitution and the Supreme Court, and most recently *One Nation, Two Realities: Dueling Facts in American Democracy*, published by Oxford University Press. He teaches at the University of Massachusetts Lowell and is the Editor of the annual SCOTUS book series from Palgrave Macmillan on major decisions of the US Supreme Court.

FRANK T. MCANDREW is the Cornelia H. Dudley Professor of Psychology at Knox College, a blogger for *Psychology Today* magazine, and an elected Fellow of the Association for Psychological Science and several other scholarly societies. He is an evolutionary social psychologist who studies gossip, aggression, and creepiness. Consistent with his long tenure at a liberal arts college, McAndrew is an award-winning teacher who is particularly proud of the fact that more than 110 of his former students have gone on to complete a doctoral degree in psychology or a closely related field.

JONATHAN M. METZL, MD, PhD, is the Frederick B. Rentschler II Professor of Sociology and Psychiatry, and the Director of the Department of Medicine, Health, and Society at Vanderbilt University in Nashville, Tennessee. Winner of the 2020 Robert F. Kennedy Human Rights Book Award, Dr. Metzl has written extensively for medical, psychiatric, and popular publications. His books include *The Protest Psychosis*, *Prozac on the Couch*, *Against Health: How Health Became the New Morality*, and *Dying of Whiteness: How the Politics of Racial Resentment is Killing America's Heartland*.

MATTHEW MILLER is a Professor of Health Sciences and Epidemiology at Northeastern University, Adjunct Professor of Epidemiology at the Harvard T.H. Chan School of Public Health, and Codirector of the Harvard Injury Control Research Center. Dr. Miller is an expert in injury and violence prevention. His research encompasses intentional and unintentional injury, with an emphasis on firearm-related violence and suicide prevention. In addition to research in injury and violence prevention, Dr. Miller's scholarship includes observational studies in pharmacoepidemiology and commentaries about the fundamental and often unrecognized tension between research and therapy in clinical trials.

BRIAN L. OTT, PhD, The Pennsylvania State University, is a scholar and public intellectual who has been studying rhetoric, media, and their intersection for more than 20 years. He is currently a Professor of Communication at Missouri State University. His op-eds have appeared in outlets such as *USA Today*, *Newsweek*, Salon, Business Insider, and The Hill. Ott is the former Department Head of Communication at Missouri State University, former Director of Texas Tech University Press, former Editor-in-Chief of the *Western Journal of Communication*, and a former President of the Western States Communication Association.

MOLLY PAHN completed her Master's in Public Health at Boston University, where she studied in the Department of Community Health Science and focused on health policy and advocacy. She conducted research on the impact of firearm-related laws on health outcomes from 2015 to 2017, including compiling a database of firearm laws in all 50 states over the years 1991–2017. Pahn has worked at the Tennessee General Assembly on several political campaigns as a political researcher and in a domestic violence assessment center. She has also conducted research on state education policies regarding bullying laws for schools. Following her work on gun violence, Pahn obtained a Master's and Licensure in Social Work. She has worked at an organization providing care and therapy to children in foster care and in inpatient mental health care. She is now a Medical Social Worker.

JILLIAN PETERSON is a Forensic Psychologist, Associate Professor of Criminology and Criminal Justice at Hamline University, and Copresident of The Violence Project. She earned her PhD in Psychology and Social Behavior from the University of California, Irvine. Dr. Peterson's areas of interest and expertise are forensic psychology, mental illness in the criminal justice system, cyber-violence, school violence, and mass shootings. She recently directed a large-scale research project funded by the National Institute of Justice that examined the life histories of more than 170 mass shooters.

DAN ROMER is the Research Director of the University of Pennsylvania's Annenberg Public Policy Center. He has conducted research at the Annenberg School and the Annenberg Public Policy Center since 1990, focusing on media and social influences on adolescent health, with particular attention paid to the social transmission of risky behavior. Most of his work has concerned the social and personal factors that influence healthy decision-making during adolescence. He is currently interested in gun violence as a risk for adolescents, especially fictional screen media as a source of approval for gun use.

MAYA ROSSIN-SLATER is an Associate Professor of Health Policy at Stanford University School of Medicine. She is also a Senior Fellow at the Stanford Institute for Economic and Policy Research, a Research Associate at the National Bureau of Economic Research, and a Research Affiliate at the Institute of Labor Economics. She received her PhD in Economics from Columbia University and her BA in Economics and Statistics from the University of California at Berkeley. Rossin-Slater's research includes work in health, public, and labor economics. She focuses on issues in maternal and child well-being, family structure and behavior, health disparities, and public policies affecting disadvantaged populations in the United States and other developed countries.

ALLEN ROSTRON joined the faculty in the University of Missouri–Kansas City's School of Law in 2003. He teaches and writes in the areas of constitutional law, tort law, products liability, and conflict of laws. Rostron previously worked in Washington, DC, as a Senior Staff Attorney at the Brady Center to Prevent Gun Violence, where he was part of a nationwide litigation effort that included lawsuits brought against gun manufacturers by several dozen major cities and counties.

MOLLY SCHNELL is an Assistant Professor in the Department of Economics at Northwestern University. Her research examines how incentives and constraints facing both providers and consumers influence health care access, health behaviors, and health outcomes. Much of her work considers the provision of pharmaceuticals in markets across the United States. Schnell spent 2018–19 as a Postdoctoral Fellow at Stanford after receiving her PhD in Economics from Princeton.

HANNES SCHWANDT is an Associate Professor of Education and Social Policy at Northwestern University. He is also an Associate Director at the Buehler Center for Health Policy and Economics at the Northwestern Feinberg School of Medicine, a Research Associate at the National Bureau of Economic Research, and a Research Affiliate at the Institute of Labor Economics. He received his PhD in Economics from Universitat Pompeu Fabra in Barcelona, Spain. His research agenda lies at the intersection of health economics, labor economics, and economic demography, with a particular focus on the role of health in determining economic inequality.

DONALD H. SEBASTIAN is a Professor of Chemical and Materials Engineering at the New Jersey Institute of Technology. He was the founding President and CEO of the New Jersey Innovation Institute from 2014 to 2020. Previously, as NJIT's Vice President for Research and Development in 1999, he launched and managed programs of national prominence, including manufacturing extension, digital health care, biopharmaceuticals, and the personalized weapons program initiated with a state challenge grant in 1999. Until 1995 he was a Professor of Chemical Engineering at Stevens Institute of Technology, founding Codirector of the Design & Manufacturing Institute, Cofounder of the Polymer Processing Institute, and a Henry Morton Distinguished Teaching Professor.

MICHAEL SIEGEL is a faculty member in the Department of Public Health and Community Medicine at the Tufts University School of Medicine. Previously, he spent 26 years as a faculty member in the Department of

Community Health Sciences at the Boston University School of Public Health. His research has focused in the areas of alcohol, tobacco, and firearms. Tying this work together is the study of corporate influences on health—especially advertising and marketing—and strategies to counteract them. More recently, his research has focused on racial inequities in health and the role of structural racism in causing these inequities.

REBECCAH SOKOL, PhD, MSPH, is an Assistant Professor in the School of Social Work at the University of Michigan and an affiliated faculty member of the University of Michigan Institute for Firearm Injury Prevention. Dr. Sokol is a behavioral scientist who studies youth exposure to adversity. Her overarching research agenda seeks to ease the burden of adversity experienced in childhood and adolescence, with a central focus on reducing youth violence exposure and involvement. Sokol uses a developmental lens, public health framework, quasi-experimental methods, and data science techniques to inform strategies that prevent youth trauma. A common thread of Sokol's research involves describing risk and identifying etiological factors for youth firearm violence exposure in different populations, with the ultimate goal of improving firearm injury and violence prevention interventions and policies.

ROBERT SPITZER is the author of 16 books, including 4 on the presidency and 6 on gun policy, and more than 700 scholarly articles, book chapters, reviews, papers, and essays. He is a Distinguished Service Professor Emeritus in the Political Science Department at SUNY Cortland. He is the Series Editor for the book series American Constitutionalism published by SUNY Press and for the book series Presidential Briefings published by Routledge. He has testified before Congress, participated in meetings at the White House, and has had his work cited by federal courts. In the 1980s, he served as a member of the New York State Commission on the Bicentennial of the U.S. Constitution.

PETER SQUIRES began working at the University of Brighton in 1986. He graduated with a degree in Sociology and Social Policy from the University of Bristol and completed a PhD thesis there, titled "Studies in the Criminalisation of Poverty," in 1985. After his experience as a member of the Management Committee of the Brighton Community Law Centre and the Community Health Council, he was elected a Brighton Borough Councillor for Regency Ward (1990–1994). Since the early 1990s he has helped develop the new teaching and research specialism in criminology and criminal justice in the School of Applied Social Science.

JEREMY STRAUB is an Assistant Professor in the Department of Computer Science at North Dakota State University. He holds a PhD in

Scientific Computing, along with an MS, an MBA, and two BS degrees. He has published over 40 journal articles and more than 120 full conference papers, in addition to making numerous other conference presentations. Straub's research spans the gamut from technology to commercialization to technology policy. His research has recently focused on robotic command and control, aerospace command, and 3D-printing quality assurance.

THOMAS D. STUCKY joined the criminal justice faculty at Indiana University Indianapolis in 2004 after spending three years on the criminal justice faculty at Indiana University–Purdue University at Fort Wayne. Dr. Stucky recently completed research on factors associated with incarceration for a cohort of low-level offenders entering the Indiana Department of Correction and was the Principal Investigator for the Indianapolis Comprehensive Anti-Gang Initiative research partnership, which had a $2.5 million grant to reduce gang crime in Indianapolis. He also provided research consultation to the Indianapolis mayor's Task Force on Violent Crime, working with Gerald Bepko, former chancellor of Indiana University–Purdue University Indianapolis. Prior to his graduate studies, Dr. Stucky served as an Undercover Enforcement Agent in the Ohio Department of Liquor Control.

ASHWINI TAMBE is a Professor and the Director of Women's, Gender, and Sexuality Studies and a Professor of History at George Washington University in Washington, DC. She is also the Editorial Director of *Feminist Studies*, the oldest journal of interdisciplinary feminist scholarship in the United States. She previously taught at the University of Maryland and the University of Toronto. Dr. Tambe is a scholar of transnational South Asian history who focuses on the regulation of sexual practices.

JENNIFER TUCKER is a scholar of modern British history who specializes in the study of 19th-century technology, industry, and visual studies. The author of *Nature Exposed: Photography as Eyewitness in Victorian Science* and coeditor of *A Right to Bear Arms? The Contested Role of History in Contemporary Debates on the Second Amendment* (2019), she is the founding Director of the research-oriented Center for the Study of Guns and Society at Wesleyan University in Middletown, Connecticut.

JOHN A. TURES is a Professor of Political Science at LaGrange College. He has written for academic journals on international and domestic politics, as well as for Yahoo News, Huffington Post, The Observer, MSN, the *Savannah Morning News*, and The Conversation. He has been interviewed for television, radio, and magazines in other countries and the United States by NPR, Vice News, and WGN.

LACEY WALLACE is a Research Analyst at the National Association of College Stores. Her previous research concerned (1) the influence of siblings and peers on delinquency and substance use through social networks; (2) weapon carrying, gun ownership, and gun acquisition behavior; and (3) the effects of intervention and policy on these processes.

ANDREW P. WHEELER is a Principal Data Scientist at Gainwell Technologies and an affiliated faculty member at Georgia State University in the Department of Criminal Justice and Criminology. He received his Doctorate in Criminal Justice from the University at Albany SUNY. His research focuses on the applications of predictive policing and operations research within the criminal justice field.

GAREN WINTEMUTE is a longtime researcher in injury epidemiology and firearm violence. His work helped create the public health approach to violence prevention. Dr. Wintemute directs the California Firearm Violence Research Center and the Violence Prevention Research Program, both at the University of California at Davis. He is a practicing Emergency Medicine Physician.

CARY WU is an Assistant Professor of Sociology at York University, Canada. He conducts research focused on political sociology and inequality. He often shares his research with the public via national and international TV, radio, and newspapers including NPR, CBC, CTV, the *Washington Post, Toronto Star, Maclean's*, the *Financial Times*, and the *Economist*.

APRIL M. ZEOLI, PhD, MPH, is an Associate Professor in the School of Public Health and Policy and the Core Director for the Institute for Firearm Injury Prevention at the University of Michigan. She is a leading expert on the intersection of intimate partner violence and gun violence and on gun policy. Her interdisciplinary research—which aims to bring together the fields of public health, criminology, and criminal justice—is focused on the impact of state-level gun laws on homicide, particularly intimate partner homicide, and the implementation of those policies at the local level. She is primarily interested in firearm policies that restrict high-risk individuals from purchasing and possessing guns and those that facilitate the implementation of firearm restriction policies.

MARC A. ZIMMERMAN is the Marshall H. Becker Collegiate Professor at the University of Michigan. He studies adolescent health and resiliency and empowerment theory. His work on adolescent health examines how positive factors in adolescents' lives help them overcome risks they face. His research focuses on an analysis of adolescent resiliency for risks associated with violent behavior, school safety, and community engagement. Dr. Zimmerman's work on empowerment theory includes the measurement and analysis of psychological and community empowerment. Dr. Zimmerman is the Codirector of the University of Michigan Institute for Firearm Injury and Prevention and the Director of the Prevention Research Center of Michigan and the Youth Violence Prevention Center, funded by the Centers for Disease Control and Prevention.

Index

Abbott, Greg, 251
accidental shootings: correlated with looser gun controls, 201; data on, 76; gun ownership and risk of, 18; and rurality, 90; and weapon storage, 78, 91, 150, 159, 201, 214
active shooter drills, 136, 149
Adams, Eric, 27
age: and gun ownership, 37–38, 152, 199, 250–54; and gun violence reduction programs, 276; and mass shootings, 54–60; and police shootings, 117, 118; and school shootings, 149, 250–51
aggression: interventions for, 153–54; and media, 155; and testosterone, 57–60; and "weapons effect," 50–51, 78
AK-47, 134, 229, 282, 292–96
AKM rifle, 293
Alabama, xviii, 288

American gun culture: and evolutionary psychology, 54–60; and Founding Fathers, 7–11; and frontier mythology, 26–31, 50; and "good guy with a gun" trope, 20–24; and manufacturers, 3, 40–47; and media, 3, 4, 21–24, 29, 30, 48–52; and NRA, 17–18, 33–38; and police shootings, 110; and rugged individualism, 3, 17, 27, 111; and storytelling, 13–19; and videos by gun owners, 62–66
American Legislative Exchange Council (ALEC), 223
Americans for Responsible Solutions, 230–31
ammunition, 229, 230, 282
AR-15, 16, 256, 282, 283, 290
Arizona, 107, 148
Arkansas, 134
Armatix iP1, 308, 309
assassinations, 206, 226, 227, 228

Kalashnikov, Mikhail, 282, 292–96
Kalashnikov rifle. See AK-47
Kavanaugh, Brett, 238
Kelly, Mark, 231
Kennedy, John F., 227
Kennedy, Robert F., 227
Kimber Manufacturing, 41, 288
knives. See bladed weapons
Koch, Brandon, 234
Kodiak Arms Intelligun, 310

LaPierre, Wayne, 18, 21, 23, 31,
    289
Las Vegas shooting (2017), xvii, 63
laws. See gun control
leg shots and police shootings, 113
lethal means counseling, 96
locking devices, for gun storage,
    230
Louisiana, xviii
loyalty oaths, and right to bear
    arms, 11

M-16 rifle, 294–95
magazines, ammo, 229, 230, 282
Malcolm, Joyce, 70–71
manufacturers of firearms: and
    COVID-19, 194–95; and divest-
    ment in, 290; economic impact
    of, 287–88; growth of, 41–42,
    286–87; and gun culture, 3, 29,
    40–47; lawsuits and liability, 41,
    221–22, 285–91; lobbying by,
    288–89; marketing by, 3, 29,
    43–46; and mass shootings,
    286, 289–90; numbers of guns
    produced, 41; product place-
    ment by, 50
March For Our Lives, 231–32
Marjorie Stoneman Douglas High
    School shooting. See Parkland,
    FL, shooting (2018)
Martin, Trayvon, 45
Maryland, 234, 310
Marysville High School shooting,
    WA (2014), 135
Massachusetts, xix, 10, 234, 288
mass shootings: age of perpetrator,
    54–60; anxiety about, xvi, 171,
    185; and assault weapons, xvii,
    229, 250, 255–59, 283, 295;
    data on, xv–xvi, 127–29; and
    domestic violence, 247; and
    gender, 54–60; and "ghost
    guns," 300; and gun sales,
    286–87; increase in, xvii, 126–31,
    135, 229, 255–59; increase

in deaths, 129; international
    comparisons, xvi, 148, 216,
    217–18; and manufacturers of
    guns, 286, 289–90; and media,
    xv–xvi, xvi, 129, 171, 181, 185–86,
    252; as percentage of gun-
    related deaths, 126; political
    responses to, 26, 225–32, 247,
    251; public opinion on, 129–31;
    stopping of, by armed citizens,
    18, 20–24, 208; and trauma, xvi,
    170, 171, 175–79, 181–86
"may issue" laws, 234
media: and aggression, 155;
    coverage of mass shootings,
    xv–xvi, 129, 171, 181, 185–86,
    252; and data collection, 127,
    143; and "good guy with a gun"
    trope, 21–24; and gun culture,
    3, 4, 21–24, 29, 30, 48–52;
    and Old West tropes, 29, 30,
    50; police shooting data, 76;
    and product placement, 50.
    See also social media
mental health: and gun violence
    reduction programs, 276; and
    school shootings, 136, 176–77,
    179; and survivors, 182–84; and
    trust, 187–91; and violence risk
    assessments, 152–53. See also
    trauma
metal detectors, 154–55
Michigan, 135, 145, 146, 147, 149,
    157, 158
militias, 2, 8–9
Minnesota, 248
Mississippi, xviii
Missouri, xviii, 107, 113, 116, 166,
    197–203
Moms Demand Action, 201, 231
Montana, 111, 166
Mother Jones, 127
Munich Olympics shooting (1972),
    295

Nash, Robert, 234
National Coalition to Ban Handguns,
    228
National Crime Victimization Survey,
    213, 262–63
National Firearms Act of 1934, 34,
    206, 227
National Instant Criminal Back-
    ground Check System (NICS),
    192, 232
National Institutes of Health (NIH),
    91, 263, 269, 271